The Music of the *How to Train Your Dragon* Trilogy

The Music of the *How to Train Your Dragon* Trilogy

A Guide to the Scores of John Powell

ERIK HEINE

Foreword by Tim Greiving

McFarland & Company, Inc., Publishers
Jefferson, North Carolina

This book has undergone peer review.

Library of Congress Cataloguing-in-Publication Data

Names: Heine, Erik, 1976– author. | Greiving, Tim, writer of foreword.
Title: The music of the How to train your dragon trilogy : a guide to the scores of John Powell / Erik Heine ; foreword by Tim Greiving.
Description: Jefferson, North Carolina : McFarland & Company, Inc., Publishers, 2024. | Includes bibliographical references and index.
Identifiers: LCCN 2024017163 | ISBN 9781476693675 (paperback : acid free paper) ∞
ISBN 9781476652320 (ebook)
Subjects: LCSH: Powell, John, 1963- How to train your dragon. | Powell, John, 1963- How to train your dragon 2. | Powell, John, 1963- How to train your dragon, the hidden world. | Motion picture music—Analysis, appreciation. | How to train your dragon (Motion picture) | How to train your dragon 2 (Motion picture) | How to train your dragon, the hidden world (Motion picture)
Classification: LCC ML410.P7884 H45 2024 | DDC 781.5/42092—dc23/eng/20240426
LC record available at https://lccn.loc.gov/2024017163

British Library cataloguing data are available
ISBN (print) 978-1-4766-9367-5
ISBN (ebook) 978-1-4766-5232-0

© 2024 Erik Heine. All rights reserved

No part of this book may be reproduced or transmitted in any form or by any means, electronic or mechanical, including photocopying or recording, or by any information storage and retrieval system, without permission in writing from the publisher.

Front cover images: © Gabriel Lissoni/Shutterstock

Printed in the United States of America

*McFarland & Company, Inc., Publishers
Box 611, Jefferson, North Carolina 28640
www.mcfarlandpub.com*

To Stephen and Theodore:
There were dragons when you were boys….

Images of scores are reproduced under the following licenses:

HOW TO TRAIN YOUR DRAGON
Words and Music by Michael John Mollo and John Powell
Copyright © 2010 DWA SONGS
This arrangement Copyright © 2022 DWA SONGS
All Rights Administered by ALMO MUSIC CORP.
All Rights Reserved Used by Permission
This edition licensed for study use only. No portion may be reproduced for arrangement or performance purposes without securing permission from the copyright owner.
Reprinted by permission of Hal Leonard LLC

HOW TO TRAIN YOUR DRAGON 2
By John Powell
Copyright © 2014 DWA SONGS
This arrangement Copyright © 2022 DWA SONGS
All Rights Administered by ALMO MUSIC CORP.
All Rights Reserved Used by Permission
This edition licensed for study use only. No portion may be reproduced for arrangement or performance purposes without securing permission from the copyright owner.
Reprinted by permission of Hal Leonard LLC

HOW TO TRAIN YOUR DRAGON: THE HIDDEN WORLD
By John Powell
Copyright © 2019 DWA SONGS
This arrangement Copyright © 2022 DWA SONGS
All Rights Reserved Used by Permission
This edition licensed for study use only. No portion may be reproduced for arrangement or performance purposes without securing permission from the copyright owner.
Reprinted by permission of Hal Leonard LLC

Table of Contents

Acknowledgments	viii
Foreword by Tim Greiving	1
Preface	3
Introduction	5
1. Musical Influences on the *HTTYD* Music	15
2. Pitch Collections	24
3. The Themes of the *HTTYD* Trilogy	30
4. *How to Train Your Dragon* Cue Analysis	58
5. *How to Train Your Dragon 2* Cue Analysis	96
6. *How to Train Your Dragon: The Hidden World* Cue Analysis	134
7. Themes Across the Trilogy	174
Conclusion	185
Appendix	189
Chapter Notes	195
Bibliography	197
Index	199

Acknowledgments

I have several people to thank. The first are John Powell and Batu Sener, who have been a joy to work with at 5 Cat Studios. Without their assistance and support, this book would have been impossible to write. Next, my *Film Score Monthly Online* editor Jon Kaplan, whose support has been invaluable. I also received wonderful advice and assistance in the pre-planning stages from the late Gergely Hubai, noted film music author and critic, and Doug Adams, author of *The Music of the Lord of the Rings Films*. I have to thank my school, Oklahoma City University, and my deans at the Wanda L. Bass School of Music, Mark Parker and Mark Belcik, for supporting this project and my application for sabbatical so that I could perform this work. I've gotten to bounce ideas off of two wonderfully brilliant friends in my music theory world, Frank Lehman and Zachary Cairns, the Sandy Koufax and Don Drysdale of the film music theory field. Their insights helped me craft my phrasings in parts of the analysis, and I count myself lucky to consider them as very good friends. Finally, my family—my wife, Patty; my sons Stephen and Theodore; my in-laws, John and Janet Schmitz; and my dad and his wife, Rick and Kim Heine—has been so supportive and have watched the films with me several times. They might be sick of the music, but I'm not. They've given me the space and time to work and immerse myself in the scores and music, and without their day-to-day help, I would never have been able to start, let alone finish a project like this.

Foreword

by Tim Greiving

Great music, like all great art, deserves to be analyzed in detail. Examining it through a microscope—whether that's a technical analysis of the notes or the interrelationships between thematic ideas, looking at historical context or getting direct insight from the artists themselves—reveals *why* it's great, and only makes us appreciate it more and hear it even better. Film music has historically been given short shrift, although thankfully the times are changing, and today academics and musicologists are applying the same methods and serious study to worthy film scores as they've always done with classical music.

John Powell's *How to Train Your Dragon* trilogy followed in the grand tradition of exquisitely detailed, leitmotif scoring that gave us Howard Shore's *Lord of the Rings* trilogy and the blockbuster adventures of John Williams. The music is equally deserving of the granular attention those scores have received from scholars like Doug Adams and Frank Lehman. And just as Powell carried on a *musical* tradition, Erik Heine has picked up this parallel torch of serious study. It's a match made in Valhalla.

Heine is a rigorous but warm and approachable scholar who clearly has a deep well of love for this music. Learning about his personal attachment to it through his own Hiccup, his son, is deeply moving—and that passion pumps real blood into his analysis.

Powell is adamantly not a *literal* film composer—he avoids assigning on-the-nose themes to specific characters—but he is a *logical* scorer, and his drive to compose a musical narrative that deliberately flows and evolves in harmony with the visual story in these films makes the result a potent subject for analysis. Heine has simply articulated the logic to be found in the music, and in doing so he's illuminated and enhanced Powell's hard work.

Like most film composers, Powell wasn't always cognizant of the dramaturgical significance of a particular chord or interval, or how it echoed an earlier part of the score, revealing a hidden connection, or related to some particular Beethoven opera (and so on). He's clearly a very smart and intentional composer, but he was often simply in the flow of a deadline-harried airstream, trying to stay afloat. Still, if Heine finds those connections after the fact, it doesn't mean they weren't there all along. Thoughtful analysis, like this book, finds meaning and assigns meaning in a way that honors the composer's conscious intentions while revealing the more unconscious ones. Great art holds up to that level of scrutiny, and Powell's work is more than sturdy enough.

I'm reminded of something Powell said when I interviewed him about *How to Train Your Dragon 2*: "You look at a painting, and you get something from it if you know *nothing* about the painting—you get something if you know something about the people *in* the painting—if you know about the painter, you get more—if you know about the painter's relationship with the people in the painting, you get even *more*. The value of art can be very two dimensional and just exactly what it is, and it can give us just an instant flash of joy, and that's really all we need. But there are moments that we really do value as a society, and I think time and time again people have valued things that are so layered because they unpick life in a way, or they show you life in all its depths—and the deeper you go, the more you can enjoy."

This book is written in a way that respects scholars while also welcoming non-musicologists alike. It's a book you can curl up in a well-worn chair with, hitting play on the score albums and listening with deep attention, armed with new insights. Like film music itself, Heine's book is a gateway into classical music—full of references and connections to a much bigger universe. If you're a newcomer to that world, or to musical analysis, this book takes your hand and opens it up for you. Powell will be the first to tell you that film music exists on a long continuum with the orchestra music of the past—his own teachers range from Brahms to John Williams—and Heine has found a multitude of enlightening links.

In the end, of course, great film music is inherently *emotional*. That's certainly true of these scores, which soar from euphoric, airborne highs to plummeting losses and then back up again. In taking his academic scalpel to it, Heine hasn't drained the music of its feeling; he's actually exposed even deeper, finer layers of emotion and drama and purpose. To borrow a metaphor from *How to Train Your Dragon*: he hasn't clipped the music of its wings at all … he's simply given it a tool to make the music fly even higher.

Tim Greiving is an arts journalist in Los Angeles who specializes in film music. He regularly contributes to NPR, the Los Angeles Times, *and the* Washington Post. *His work has been published in the* New York Times, Criterion, Variety, The Ringer, Los Angeles Magazine, *and* Vulture. *He has written program notes for the Los Angeles Philharmonic and the Royal Albert Hall, and liner notes for more than one hundred soundtrack albums. He contributes to the visual history program for the Academy of Motion Picture Arts and Sciences, and teaches film music history at the University of Southern California. He is currently writing the first English-language biography of composer John Williams, due to be published by Oxford University Press in spring 2025.*

Preface

My first child was born in late 2006. In May of 2008, he was diagnosed with Rubinstein-Taybi Syndrome. He has gross motor challenges, has cognitive delays, and is non-speaking. While traveling in the summer of 2011 to visit my wife's parents, we were at a hotel, and were searching for something he could watch and enjoy as we were prepping to leave. We came across *How to Train Your Dragon*, and his attention was held for nearly 30 minutes. For a child who had (and still has) only latched on to a handful of programs, this was revolutionary. When we got home, we checked out the DVD from our public library, but it didn't capture him like it did that day. I lost track of the films, as they weren't pertinent to our lives.

Our second child, born in 2015, began to take an interest in the *HTTYD* films after seeing the promo for one while watching Netflix. He quickly grew to love all three of them and brought them back to my attention. In the summer of 2020, we even got to see *The Hidden World* in the theater together—masked, of course—as part of a summer animation series. Having the opportunity to see the film on a big screen was absolutely delightful, particularly the sequence that occurs in the location of the Hidden World.

I began writing for *Film Score Monthly Online* in early 2017 and, in the 2018 November issue, was the lead author on a piece titled "The 12 Best Scores from Remote Control/Media Ventures." The focus of the piece was on great scores by composers who had passed through RC/MV, and not those by Hans Zimmer. My editor, Jon Kaplan, and I thought it would be fun to have a lead author and multiple "additional authors," similarly to how Zimmer's studio, Remote Control, works. One of the scores that I had the opportunity to write about was John Powell's *How to Train Your Dragon*. Spending time with that music was wonderful, and the music stayed with me after I submitted the piece. I found myself listening to it again and again.

Flash forward to early 2020, just before Covid hit the United States hard. I knew I would be able to apply for a sabbatical at my university in the near future but needed to find a project. Through correspondence with Jon, I made an off-handed comment that "someone should write the book on the *HTTYD* music, now that the trilogy is complete." His response was that *I* should do it. Well, without getting in touch with Powell, it would be a lost cause, so Jon got me in touch with Powell's assistant. I had to audition with some writing samples and after some back and-forth emails, I got the job. In order to ensure my analysis was entirely my own, I avoided all media concerning the films except information published in liner notes. Blogs, podcasts, and videos did not cross my path before this project began or during the time of writing.

I was lucky enough to be able to conduct all of my research without needing to leave home in the fall of 2021, through a sabbatical at my university. I received digital access to all three scores and recordings of all cues from the films, and I owned all three films on Blu-Ray. The films were recent enough that I did not need to travel to an archive to view manuscripts or need to document or transcribe cues. During the course of my work, the complete scores for the first two *HTTYD* films was commercially published by Omni Music Publishing, in tandem with Deluxe Edition releases of the recordings by Varèse Sarabande. The printed score and recordings for *The Hidden World* are due to be released in February 2024. The availability of the scores and recordings will greatly enhance this book, as readers can have the printed score open alongside the book, marking theme locations and learning about thematic transformations and manipulations.

The focus of this particular book is as a score guide for the three films rather than a deep narrative analysis of the music in all three films. The contents of this book focus on the final product and not the creation and revisions of the music, the orchestration process, or deleted material. I am a music theorist at heart, so the book contains musical examples and Roman numerals. I hope that even those who are unfamiliar with musical notation and music theory will be able to understand my analysis of the music. Some of the analysis will be narrative, while other portions will dig more deeply into theoretical ideas and concepts. The book opens with a brief chapter concerning musical influences on Powell's *HTTYD* scores, highlighting composers whose music has found its way into these film scores. The second chapter deals with pitch collections and scales, and explains the various materials that Powell uses: six-, seven-, and eight-note scales, as well as pitch-class collections. The bulk of the book deals with the music. The themes, named by Powell, are analyzed in their own chapter, followed by an analysis of every cue from all three films. Every single measure is not analyzed, as that would be unnecessary, but I have tried to foreground the salient features within the cues, and elements that I find exciting and worthy of discussion. Selected themes are then traced across the trilogy, showing how they are used in various situations. Finally, a brief conclusion concerning the music of these three films ends the book's narrative, as I highlight the elements that make this music so loved, as well as any Powell-isms that were used across the trilogy. My goal is to bring deeper insight and appreciation into these films through the musical analysis, for those who are trained musicians and for those who are simply fans of the films and their music. Even though these films are animated and fundamentally geared toward children, they are films for which the potential for visual and aural analysis is rich from several different perspectives.

Becoming immersed in the sound world of Berk and beyond has been an absolute delight. The music that Powell has created is joyous, exciting, and caring, with danger lurking around corners, battle music to support our heroes, and above all, the special relationship between a boy and his dragon, showing his village that the impossible is possible. It's that message that resonates so deeply with me, as my son is often thought to be unable to achieve things, due largely in part to his non-speaking status. I entered this project as someone who deeply enjoyed the music. As I complete it, I exit the project as someone who has the deepest respect for the music Powell wrote, for his music team, and for everyone associated with the projects who created such beautiful and authentic films. I still love listening to the music and watching the films again and again. This book is my open love letter to the music for these films.

Introduction

Great stories deserve great openings, and the opening sequence of *How to Train Your Dragon* is exceptional. We immediately know who, where, what, why and when, and John Powell's music and themes make the action truly come to life—a battle for survival between dragons and Vikings. The success of the *Dragon* films and their music is no surprise to anyone who has seen them. The music is loved by professionals and fans alike, with the score for the first film earning an Oscar nomination. The first *Dragon* film won the International Film Music Critics Association "Film Score of the Year" in 2010, while the second and third films won the IFMCA's "Animated Score of the Year," in 2014 and 2019, respectively. The cue "Flying with Mother" from the second film won "Film Music Composition of the Year" in 2014. With the popularity of the films and music, it seems only natural that someone would write about the music in the films.

The three films are very loosely based on the series of books by Hiccup Horrendous Haddock III and "translated from the Old Norse by Cressida Cowell." In the films, the protagonist remains as Hiccup, his dragon is still named Toothless, and Stoick the Vast is still Hiccup's father and chief of Berk. Hiccup's main character traits—weak, afraid, a hindrance in battle—are all present at the opening of the first film, and through the friendship he forms with Toothless, he learns to overcome these perceived problems, winning his father's respect in the process, first teaching his teenage peers that dragons are kind and thoughtful creatures to be respected, not villainous monsters bent on destruction. Ultimately the entirety of Berk comes around to the same conclusion. The first film opens with a dragon attack on Berk, Hiccup in the way of everything, and almost out of spite, he shoots down the legendary destructive dragon, the Night Fury. Hiccup finds its location and learns the dragon is injured as the shot damaged the dragon's tail. The teens of Berk are taught how to fight, and ultimately slay, dragons, but Hiccup doesn't want to harm the injured Night Fury. Instead, Hiccup befriends it, names him Toothless, repairs his tail, and learns to ride him like a horse, all in secret. Hiccup uses the tricks he learns from Toothless to defeat the various dragons in the training ring, ultimately earning the right to kill a dragon in front of the entire village. Hiccup shares his secret with Astrid, on whom he has a crush, and they ride Toothless together, ultimately coming upon the hive of the Red Death, for which Stoick has been searching. Hiccup refuses to kill the dragon in the arena, with Toothless coming to Hiccup's aid. Toothless is captured and used to locate the Red Death's hive, Stoick disowning Hiccup in the process. Hiccup devises a plan to teach his peers how to train and ride dragons, and they fly together to the hive, where the Viking army is under duress. Stoick releases Toothless, and Hiccup and Toothless defeat and kill the Red Death, with Toothless saving Hiccup's life in the process. The film's conclusion finds dragons and Vikings living together in Berk, with the island's population no longer wanting to kill dragons.

The second film begins five years after the events of the first film. Stoick is ready to turn over leadership of Berk to Hiccup, who maintains he's not ready for that level of responsibility, only being 20 years old. Hiccup would rather map the world with Toothless, the pair working as explorers. In his exploration, he encounters a group of dragon trappers whose hideout has been destroyed by a creature that spits ice. The trappers work for Drago Bludvist, who is building a dragon army to conquer the world. Drago and Stoick have history, as Drago killed all of the other chiefs when Hiccup was a baby. Hiccup attempts to find Drago and convince him that dragons are more like pets, not weapons of war. In the process, he is accosted by a masked rider who turns out to be his long-lost missing mother, Valka, who has created a dragon sanctuary in the nearly 20 years since she was taken away from Berk. Stoick searches after Hiccup, and upon finding him, also finds his missing wife, with whom he reconciles. Drago attacks Valka's sanctuary, drawing out the Alpha dragon, the Bewilderbeast. Drago has a Bewilderbeast of his own and the two fight, with Drago winning. Drago then uses the Bewilderbeast to control Toothless, who is about to kill Hiccup until Stoick throws himself in front of the blast, sacrificing himself for his son. Drago takes Toothless and his army and attacks Berk. The remaining Vikings at the sanctuary ride baby dragons back to Berk, and Hiccup helps Toothless break the Alpha's control. Toothless then rallies all the dragons, as he fights the Alpha. Toothless wins, Drago presumably drowns in the process, and calm is reinstated in Berk. Because of Stoick's death, a new chief must be named, and Hiccup takes the role.

One year later, the third film begins, with all of Berk encouraging Hiccup and Astrid to marry. Hiccup tells of a story from Stoick of "the Hidden World," the source of all dragons, determined to find its location. The young adults of Berk continue their raids on dragon trappers, releasing the dragons and bringing them back to Berk, a human-dragon utopia, at least in Hiccup's eyes. Famous dragon hunter Grimmel the Grisly offers to help the various warlords capture the last remaining Night Fury, Toothless, by using his bait, a female Fury called a Light Fury, due to her white color. Grimmel appears in Berk and threatens Hiccup, provoking Hiccup to relocate. Attempting to find the Hidden World, the village settles on a new island called New Berk. Toothless has found the scent of the Light Fury and makes attempts to woo her, which often fail in spectacular and hilarious ways. Hiccup allows Toothless to go on a date alone, and Toothless and the Light Fury fall in love, finding the Hidden World and taking their place as the Alpha couple. When Toothless fails to return to New Berk, Hiccup and Astrid search for him and find the Hidden World. Hiccup realizes that humans and dragons cannot live together in the Hidden World, and is chased out, saved from harm by Toothless. Grimmel then captures both Furies and takes all the dragons back to his armada. The Berkians battle Grimmel and his armada and win, Grimmel presumably drowning in the ocean in the process. Upon returning to New Berk, Hiccup realizes that he must allow all the dragons to be free to be safe, and after sad farewells, the dragons fly away. Hiccup and Astrid then marry. The film's epilogue finds Hiccup, Astrid, and their two children near the Hidden World, where Toothless, the Light Fury, and their three baby dragons are on a rock, protecting their home. Toothless aggressively advances on the boat until he remembers Hiccup, and begins licking him. Hiccup and Astrid take their children riding on dragons as a final voiceover brings closure to the series.

Introduction

The films are memorable for several reasons, including the 3D animation, the use of camera, and, of course, the music, composed by John Powell. Perhaps the most striking sequences across the films are the flying sequences, and in particular, the "Test Drive" sequence from the first film. Because these are animated films, the camera perspective shown does not need to be realistic. The audience is allowed to see flight from a third-person perspective, both from a distance and near the dragon, and from a first-person perspective, as Hiccup would experience riding Toothless. In her article "Invitation to the Voyage," Sara Ross writes, "In 'The Myth of Total Cinema,' André Bazin made an analogy between the myth of Icarus, which has 'dwelt in the soul of everyman since he first thought about birds,' and the myth of cinema. Just as the desire for super-human mobility predated the airplane, Bazin asserts that humankind yearned to replicate reality well before the invention of cinema. The flying sequence offers a feeling of visual mastery of space that unites these myths."[1] As children, we often pretend that we are flying, arms out and making sound effects while running. Ross expands on Bazin's assertion, connecting it to film sequences, and more specifically, 3D sequences versus 2D animated sequences, stating, "The particular appeal of aerial spectacle may be attributed to the free and rapid movement of the camera in all directions through three-dimensional space."[2] The fact that the camera can move, not just on an X- or Y-axis, but also on a Z-axis is what gives 3D flying sequences additional substance and excitement, as the perspective can change quickly, changing the orientation of the audience. Scott Richmond writes about the involvement of the audience in the flying sequences through his personal experience, saying, "the world unfolding onscreen is not merely an object of fascination, however rapt, but rather a site where my body becomes literally involved in the space of the world onscreen and the (quasi)movement through it. Involuntarily, my body prepares for, hints at, half-executes the as-if motions associated with flying: I lean slightly into turns, gripping armrests and engaging the muscles of my core; I flinch at branches, enacting the opening moves of a full-fledged ducking motion. Not just sensually but viscerally engaged, I become enmeshed in the space of the world onscreen."[3] The interaction of the audience with the visual image becomes enhanced with 3D animation, the audience members placing themselves in the position of Hiccup atop Toothless, turning, ducking, and soaring along with the film. For Ross, the flying sequence is connected to the main point of the film. She writes that the "central narrative quests are connected to gaining the courage to fly,"[4] indicating the need for the protagonist, Hiccup, to overcome his challenges and grow into the adult who will eventually become the chief of Berk. By learning how to fly, Hiccup becomes the first Viking to not kill a dragon, the first to ride a dragon, and the first to share how to tame the dragons with his people. These actions set Hiccup apart from his father, showing a generational shift and presenting a new approach to life.

Powell's music further enhances the flying sequences through its use, and its absence when appropriate, of the *Flying* theme. In the cue "Test Drive," the full version of the *Flying* theme, along with the *Flying Ostinato*, is finally stated. After hours of practice together, Hiccup and Toothless take their first ride, attempting various maneuvers. At one point, Hiccup drops his cheat sheet and the pair descend in a freefall. Powell's music switches from the *Flying* theme to music that is much more dissonant, not triadic, and provides an aural sensation of falling. At the moment that Hiccup regains his bearings, he and Toothless pull out of the dive, inches above the ocean, and the *Flying* theme is stated triumphantly, the audience fully embodying the visual and aural experience. Regarding this sequence, Richmond writes, "As anyone knows who has ridden a roller coaster (or, presumably, done actual stunt flying), our hearts would be in our throats if we were really following the flight of Hiccup and Toothless…. In the cinema, however, this quasi-movement is specified only through visual information. In *How to Train Your Dragon*'s remarkable learning-to-fly sequence, for example, vision and balance tell us very different stories: our eyes tell us that we are skyrocketing at ludicrous speed behind Hiccup and Toothless towards the water, while our inner ear tells us that we are still in our seats in the theater."[5] While Richmond only concerns himself with the visual elements, I would argue that the music enhances the experience far beyond what is possible to see. As an example, the scene can be viewed with the volume muted. As Richmond states, our eyes tell us that we are about to crash, but our inner ears tell us we are seated and not in motion. While none of that information changes with the addition of sound, the music enhances the danger, aurally signaling through cultural codes established over decades that the flight will end in disaster, potentially even injury. But at that last moment, when it no longer seems possible to pull out of the dive, Hiccup and Toothless manage to pull up, skimming the surface of the water, and the *Flying* theme is restated, making us want to cheer, or at least smile. The music is an essential part of the film.

This book is designed to function primarily as a film score guide, directing attention to locations of cues and Leitmotifs, providing close readings of harmony and thematic transformation, and serving as a resource for further study of the music of the films, for study of music in animated films, for the film music of John Powell, and for the wider scope of fantasy and heroic music in film. In the article "Fantasy Music: Epic Soundtrack, Magical Instruments, Musical Metaphysics," Isabella van Elferen writes about the "epic soundtrack," that it was developed most prominently by John Williams in the *Star Wars* films, then stating the epic soundtrack has been used in *How to Train Your Dragon*.[6] She then states, "Howard Shore's score for Peter Jackson's *Lord of the Rings* trilogy is many ways paradigmatic for the genre. Like Williams's scores for Star Wars, the scores to all three films are composed as one overarching musical composition, with consistent leitmotifs identifying characters and situations throughout and thus reinforcing the epic feeling that all the events in Middle-earth are interconnected (cf. Bernanke 2008)."[7] This is also the case for the *HTTYD* films, in that Leitmotifs are used, developed, and transformed across the trilogy based on the narrative needs and situations. As an example, the *Astrid* theme is also a more generalized love theme. Hiccup is in love with Astrid from the opening of the first film, and she is romanticized both visually and aurally. When the two ride Toothless together, the cue is titled "Romantic Flight," and the *Astrid* theme dominates the cue. However, in the second film, when Ruffnut first sees the dragon trapper Eret, the *Astrid* theme, now functioning as the more generalized *Love* theme, is heard as Ruffnut sees Eret's muscles flex, his strong jawline, and utters the words "Me likey," as her language skills are momentarily rendered inert.

The presence of the Irish singer Enya in the first of the *LOTR* films, *The Fellowship of the Ring*, clearly influenced the presence of the Icelandic singer Jónsi across all three *HTTYD* films. Dean DeBlois, who co-directed the first *HTTYD* film and was the sole director of the other two, directed the documentary concert film *Heima* by the Icelandic band Sigur rós. The lead singer for Sigur rós is Jón Þór Birgisson, who goes by the name Jónsi. Jónsi often sings in falsetto with gibberish lyrics in an invented language called "Hopelandic," further obscuring the meaning of song lyrics outside of those fluent in

Icelandic. The effect is that Jónsi's vocals function as another instrument or timbre rather than as a typical vocal line. Enya sings in Elvish in *Fellowship*, another invented language. The connection between the epic soundtracks of the *LOTR* trilogy and the *HTTYD* trilogy is not just limited to instrumental music, but also includes vocal music, wordless or otherwise. Jónsi sings songs in each of the three films, but only one appears in the film's narrative with the other two in the End Credits. The songs are all sung in English, and the song from the second film that appears in the narrative, "Where No One Goes," is derived from the *Flying* theme as Hiccup and Toothless practice new flying techniques together. Perhaps more significantly, Jónsi's voice is used and manipulated when Hiccup and Astrid arrive in the Hidden World, creating a sound unheard through the three films up to that point. The voice serves as another instrument, not singing lyrics, but providing a new timbre to set the Hidden World apart from every other location Hiccup has mapped.

In addition to the epic soundtrack, unusual or "magical" instruments are often used across the three *HTTYD* films. Elferen writes, "As was the case with atmospheric music, the notion of magical instruments and voices in fantasy literature, too, has been taken up by film, television, and game composers…. The 'magic' force of instruments, just like the 'mystic' nature of epic soundtracks, may have powerful aesthetic effects on film or television audiences but does not open fantasy portals and does not cast spells."[8] When these unusual instruments, such as slate and glass marimba, Hardanger fiddle, esraj, sopilka, and Uilleann pipes, are used in the scores of the three films, they are not used because they represent some specific Nordic sound. Instead, each one is specifically chosen for a specific timbre and sound that is outside of the standard orchestration. In an interview I conducted with Powell, he spoke at length regarding these unusual instruments, saying:

> I'm not just writing music in my brain and writing it on paper and then recording it. Everything has to be written and approved before it's played. You're stuck with this issue: you have to produce the music, including all details, up to the level where everyone sitting in the room can say yes or no. So, if I wanted to try something with a player, I could either get one in to do demos, but it's kind of hard to find someone who plays hurdy-gurdy, or something like that, so I would grab samples. And then it's a question of what samples work well with what you're trying to do. The esraj, it's not really an instrument from [Northern Europe], but it's a sound that sounded Nordic to me. It's not to do with any authenticity of instrument, but it's an attempt at the authenticity of the emotional impact of that kind of instrument.
>
> I think I was trying to find unusual instruments, but they were always trying to sound like what I thought felt fair game to that world [of *HTTYD*]. There are frame drums from all over the world. I got 10 guys to play frame drums from India at lots of different levels. Is it significant that they're Indian frame drums? No, it's not. They kind of sound like bodhrans, but that's Irish anyway! We're playing with the idea of "What is the culture?" But they've got dragons, so it's not a real culture!
>
> Bagpipes, sure, but there's all sorts of bagpipes across the world. Irish pipes are very different from the Scottish pipes, which are very different from the Bulgarian pipes. They all have different sets of scales; they all have different purposes. The warpipes in Scotland are very specifically warpipes invented by the British army to frighten the clans. If you had ten pipers, you could hear them five miles away, and it was deliberately to try to tell the clans, "We're coming and we'll kill you if you don't surrender." It's a very deliberate effort of transferring instruments we think of as one thing into something else. I like the idea of using bagpipes as very joyful instruments. A lot of bagpipes are used for funerals, but my childhood was remembering the idea of bagpipes being used for sword dancing, where they jump in and out

of the swords. It's supposed to be a "manly" thing, even though they're wearing kilts, the idea being if your foot slips even a half an inch you'd cut your toe off. You can see the bravado of that kind of culture.

Powell is acutely aware of the power of these different timbres as well as using instruments for purposes outside of the norm, as he discussed with the bagpipes. He is also not attempting any level of authenticity, as he uses the esraj from India, the sopilka from Ukraine, the gadulka from Bulgaria, and the guzheng from China. All of these instruments and timbres form the sound of the world of the *HTTYD* films, a fictional place, as Powell incredulously said, "They've got dragons, so it's not a real culture!" Reality and authenticity are unimportant, exchanged for unfamiliar timbres that can be used to signal "magic." Another "magical" instrument, the slate marimba, is first used in the cue "Forbidden Friendship" from the first film. In it, Toothless and Hiccup become friends, as Toothless allows Hiccup to touch his nose, the famous shot with Hiccup facing away from Toothless, palm open, allowing the dragon to come to him. In the film *Heima*, Sigur rós used a slate marimba to perform a piece derived from the Edda, a collection of Old Norse poetry. The connection is that the instrument provides a sense of music from long ago, the time of Vikings, as well as the general location of countries around the Baltic Sea, the North Sea, and the North Atlantic Ocean. The instrument's timbre is unlike a typical marimba, and is so far outside of normal percussive sounds that it serves to highlight the atypical, or forbidden, friendship between Hiccup the human and Toothless the dragon. In the third film, the slate marimba returns in the cue "Toothless Goes a–Courtin'," also known on the commercial soundtrack as "Forbidden Courtship." The presence of the slate marimba is one of the multiple reasons the cue has that title on the commercial release, clearly connecting it to the "Forbidden Friendship" cue from the first film.

In addition to the trilogy showing Hiccup growing from feeble boy to young chief to father and leader, the films also are concerned with issues of disability, generational gaps, and the relationship to nature. As the films progress, Berk moves from an island attacked by dragons to an island shared with dragons to an island overrun by dragons, forcing the Berkians to find a new home as the resources and space have been exhausted. This specific issue with nature is mostly ignored, as Grimmel is the primary reason for departing Berk, and the film fails to engage with the lack of resources facing the Berkians. However, the issue of Hiccup taming wild beasts is central to the film, as Hiccup does not simply tame Toothless, they become friends. Following Hiccup's attack, Toothless is relegated to a pit with a pond, from which he cannot escape, due to his injured tail. It is because of this specific location that Hiccup is able to keep Toothless hidden from the rest of the village and they can train in private, away from spying eyes. Additionally, Toothless, nor any of the other dragons, does not speak, unlike many animals and creatures in animated films. This provides opportunities for visual spectacles in the films. In her book *Environmental Communication for Children*, Erin Hawley writes, "Uniquely for a children's film and a Hollywood production, the most important scenes in the film lack dialogue, and this privileges the animal's mode of communication, allowing 'wild nature' to 'speak' through movement and non-verbal expression."[9] Toothless not only communicates through movement and non-verbal cues, but because of the sonic space that is permitted, he is also able to speak through the music, an element that Powell takes full advantage of across the trilogy. Many of the flying sequences and battle sequences have little to no dialogue, allowing the music to be foregrounded rather than subservient to dialogue, and these sequences often contain the most memorable music.

Another main feature of the films deals with the generational gap and issues between father and son, as we never see any of the parents of Hiccup's peers. At the most basic level, the older generation speaks with Scottish/Irish/English accents while the younger generation speaks with American accents. Both visually and vocally, the generations are clearly differentiated. At the start of the first film, Hiccup wants nothing more than to make his father proud, rather than disappointed or embarrassed as he seems to do. When Hiccup shoots down the Night Fury and excitedly brags about it, no one believes him. Hawley states, "When he finds the wounded dragon in the forest, he is delighted: 'I have brought down this mighty beast!' he cries, knowing that his father will finally be proud rather than ashamed of him."[10] This moment is then the starting point for Hiccup's rejection of killing dragons and shift to befriending Toothless, even while he maintains a public persona of learning to defeat dragons along with his peers. This public persona grants him access to the Dragon Manual, where nearly every entry concludes with "Kill on sight." Hiccup reading through the manual provides another opportunity for music to be the primary sound source rather than dialogue, as the audience can read the book along with Hiccup. Hawley writes, "Hiccup soon realizes that he must rewrite this knowledge system and lead the adult characters to a more harmonious relationship with the wildness around them."[11] Tying into nature, Hiccup learns that continued battle is unsustainable and that the previous generations need to change their thinking regarding dragons, living together rather than continued fighting and rebuilding. It is only through this effort that Hiccup ultimately gains his father's respect and praise at the end of the first film. The second film continues the relationship between father and son, and introduces the mother into the relationship, taken away when Hiccup was just a baby. Despite (re)-gaining his mother, Hiccup's father is killed, sacrificing himself to save Hiccup. Stoick's death places Hiccup into a position of adulthood and manhood for which he was not prepared, as the chief of Berk ascending to the position left absent by his father. In Stoick's funeral scene, the first half contains more music than dialogue, the cue "Off to Valhalla," but Hiccup's words tell the Vikings that he is not trying to replace Stoick, but that he will be his own leader with his own values, further changing the culture of Berk, and foreshadowing the overcommitment to saving dragons seen at the beginning of the third film.

Disability is also a significant issue across the films. Several characters have prosthetic limbs, most notably Gobber, Stoick's best friend and Berk's blacksmith, for whom Hiccup apprentices. Gobber has a prosthetic left arm and right leg, as well as a fake tooth that is really a rock. When Hiccup shoots Toothless out of the sky, Toothless's tail is damaged and he cannot fly. It is only when Hiccup fashions a prosthetic fin for Toothless that he can get out of the pit and fly, but with the assistance of Hiccup manipulating the tail piece. Hawley states, "The prosthesis only works when Hiccup is flying with Toothless, leading to several of the film's iconic scenes in which the two share the exhilaration of flight. When Hiccup is wounded at the end of the film, leading to an amputation of his leg, the bond between them is complete: the two share an identity as cripples, each with a prosthesis, but when flying together they can transcend these limitations."[12] Hawley's choice of the term "cripples" seems unnecessarily severe, as Gobber is shown as able to do everything that any other Viking can do, and Hiccup only needs a bit of time to learn to walk with his prosthetic lower leg. The characters with the artificial limbs are the only ones who mention them, treating the issue as a matter of fact rather than a disability. Any Viking could have lost a limb while fighting a dragon, which is why it doesn't appear as a significant issue. However, in the second film, the primary villain, Drago Bludvist, is shown to have lost his left arm at the shoulder to a dragon when he was young. Drago then makes it his mission to subjugate all dragons to get his revenge on them and on the world for being disabled. Again, Drago is shown to be able to do everything that any other human can do, but treats his prosthesis as an excuse and not as a fact. Although the horrible trope of the disabled villain (eye patch, scar, absent/artificial limb, etc.) is present in the second film, the concept of living with disability is also treated as somewhat insignificant by the residents of Berk. With all of those issues in mind, Powell's music has to support a number of different scenes and emotions.

I will be using the following system for the labeling of chords in the book: In musical examples, a capital letter indicates a major triad, while a capital letter followed by a 7 indicates a major triad with a minor seventh, or a dominant seventh harmony. A capital letter followed by a "m" indicates a minor triad, while a capital, followed by an "m" and a 7 indicates a minor triad with a minor seventh, or a minor seventh harmony. A "o" indicates a diminished triad, and with a 7, indicates a fully diminished seventh chord. A "ø7" or m7(b5) indicates a half-diminished seventh chord, a diminished triad with a minor seventh rather than a diminished seventh above the root. Chords that contain a slash ("/") indicate chord quality followed by the bass note, which is different than the root (e.g., C/E means a C major triad with E in the bass).

Within the prose, I will use a capital "M" to indicate a major triad, a lower-case "m" to indicate a minor triad, and "Mm^7" to indicate a dominant seventh chord. This is to avoid any confusion regarding words and chord qualities.

I will be using solfeggio (solfège) syllables. Several systems exist for this way of defining pitch, so I will be using "Moveable-do solfège," meaning that whatever note is the tonic pitch will be named "do," and all other pitches will follow. This is in stark contrast to "Fixed-do solfège," where the note C is always "do," regardless of the tonal center.

The pitch C4 represents "middle C," the C in the middle of the keyboard, and appears as a ledger line note below the treble clef staff. The octave above is C5. The figure below provides a quick example of the pitch notation.

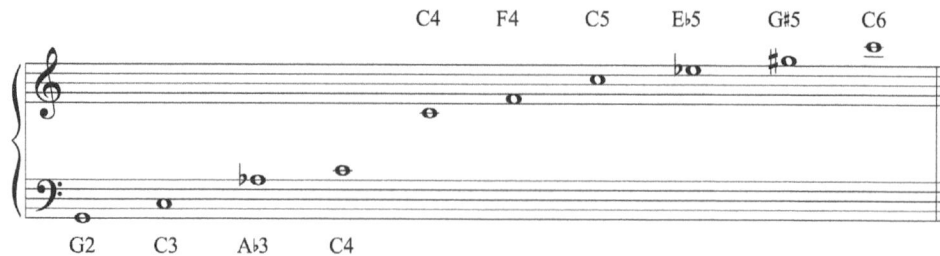

Figure Intro.1. Examples of specific pitches.

Throughout the book, I will place cue titles in quotation marks and theme titles in italics. In each specific film chapter, the cue title and time location are given first, followed by the theme names and location, given in measure numbers. All extended quotations from John Powell come from recorded conversations that we had while I was writing this book.

Let's fly to Berk!

1

Musical Influences on the *HTTYD* Music

Music that accompanies narrative film usually contains influences from somewhere. As the *HTTYD* film series is about Vikings, who lived in a certain geographic region and in a certain time period, it would be expected that the composer would draw on music from the Nordic regions, although likely not from the specific time period. While it may sound promising, music from the 10th and 11th centuries sounds absolutely nothing like most people would expect. In a 2011 interview with Steve Pond, Powell named Carl Nielsen of Denmark and Jean Sibelius of Finland as composers who influenced the music for the first film. Powell stated,

> [The directors] were really very specific a lot of the time. They did want size and depth and emotion. They wanted a feeling of the Nordic musical past. You could say the symphonic musical past was Nielsen, the Danish symphonist. Sibelius. Grieg to a certain extent, although I think he was a little bit more Germanic than he was Nordic. Sibelius was the key. I studied a lot of Sibelius as a kid, and I've always adored his music. So that, plus it was great to have Jónsi do a song at the end of the movie, because I've always liked [moody Icelandic band] Sigur rós. They were an influence as well, even though that seems paradoxical. But there is that in a few cues—heavy, dark guitar textures going on at the same time as large orchestration.[1]

When asked about folk music, Powell responded with, "We looked at all the folk music from the Nordic areas. And I'm part Scottish and grew up with a lot of Scottish folk music, so that came into it a lot. And Celtic music was something that Jeffrey [Katzenberg, CEO of DreamWorks Animation] felt had this very attractive quality to it, and a sweetness, that he thought would be wonderful for the film."[2] From the quote, it's clear that the folk music of the Nordic countries was not selected, with other regional folk music chosen in its place.

Although Vikings were native to Scandinavia, Scottish and Celtic influences are clearly present in Powell's music, resulting in a combination of various styles, rhythms, instruments, and scales in the scores for the *How to Train Your Dragon* films. This section of the book examines the influences on Powell's music, both through specific composers and through the folk music of various geographic regions.

Composers

With Powell naming several musical influences on the score, it makes locating and referencing the source material a bit easier. However, while the name of Jean Sibelius may be familiar to some orchestral music fans, Carl Nielsen's music is less likely to be known by most people in the United States. Trying to distill either composer's compositional style to a bullet-point list of two or three features is an exercise in futility. Both had substantial careers and lived when classical music was undergoing a major shift. Nielsen and Sibelius were both born in 1865, with Nielsen dying in 1931 and Sibelius dying in 1957, although Sibelius didn't actively compose after 1930. Both were alive while Brahms was nearing the end of his career (Brahms died in 1897), both were active while French composers Claude Debussy and Maurice Ravel were using non-functional means of composition, and both were alive in the early stages of the Second Viennese School and the rise of free atonality and serialism from composers such as Arnold Schoenberg and Anton Webern. Sibelius was even alive when Olivier Messiaen and his student Pierre Boulez composed parts or entire pieces based on the concept of integrated, or total serialism, a compositional method where dynamics, modes of attack, and durations of notes are serialized in addition to pitches. Although Sibelius was not an active composer in the final third of his life and never adopted atonality at any level, he was acutely aware of developments in music.

Carl Nielsen

Danish composer Carl Nielsen (1865–1931) was known mainly in his home country during his lifetime, but his works—notably his symphonies—have raised his international profile, with all six performed across the world and recorded by major orchestras. Nielsen's symphonic works are the most applicable to Powell's *Dragon* music, but Nielsen composed across several genres, not just for full orchestra. One of the main reasons that Nielsen was largely ignored by the international community was because his concept of tonality and harmony in his symphonies did not follow conventions of the time. Nielsen scholar Mina Miller writes, "Nielsen employed a range of techniques that expanded the boundaries of tonal practice. Characterized by terms such as 'progressive tonality,' 'emergent tonality,' and 'directional tonality,' these processes are important to the creation of musical form and their presentation in performance."[3] Often when scholars and analysts cannot immediately make sense of a work, it is dismissed. In the case of the reappraisal of Nielsen's music, quite the opposite happens.

Nielsen's sense of tonality and harmony is what sets his music apart from other composers of the period. Daniel M. Grimley argues this point, writing, "For [musicologist Henrik] Knudsen, one of the most immediately striking attributes of the [Third] symphony, and of Nielsen's music as a whole, is its harmonic syntax. What makes Nielsen's music distinctive, Knudsen argues, is its tonal freedom."[4] The concept of tonal freedom is not a quality typically attributed to symphonic writing but is absolutely essential to film music composition, where tonal relationships and closure are less important than in concert music. Powell often modulates within phrases and up thirds to enhance the on-screen tension, and cues have no need to conclude in the same tonality in which they began. In terms of local harmonies, Powell makes significant use of tritone root motion and triads with added notes. Within the functional tonal harmonic system, two major triads a tritone apart cannot diatonically exist in the same key. The interval of a tritone is diatonic in both the major and minor keys, with one member function as the root of a major triad and the other functioning as the root of a diminished triad. Chromatically, the Neapolitan chord, a major triad whose root is the lowered second scale-degree, is a tritone away from the dominant. Concerning Nielsen's music, theorist Harald Krebs states, "Aside from these large-scale usages of semitone and tritone relations, there are many occurrences on levels closer to the surface; their function is usually that of contradicting and hence undermining an established initial key."[5] Keys that are a tritone apart are rarely used in the music of the Classical Era, and only moderately more common in the first part of the Romantic Era. As music progressed into the second half of the nineteenth century, tritone key relationships became more frequent, but still used sparingly. In the twentieth century, composers such as Béla Bartók used the tritone as the foundation of a tonal system, rather than the perfect fifth that had been in use since the seventeenth century. Robert Rival, in his academic journal article "Flatwards Bound," highlights several techniques that give Nielsen's music its "characteristic flavour," such as modulating to distantly related keys, directly modulating within phrases, switching modes within melodic fragments, and the use of ostinatos.[6] The techniques listed by Rival appear across the three *Dragon* films in Powell's music.

Powell also often moves beyond tertian harmony and into chords that are best labeled through the number of discrete pitch-classes contained in each. These harmonies have labels such as tetrachords, pentachords, hexachords, and so on, and are often considered to be atonal, as they cannot be arranged in thirds like tertian harmonies. Krebs writes about Nielsen's music that, "the Sixth Symphony contains even more passages [than the Fifth Symphony] that cannot be fully explained by concepts derived from nineteenth-century practice. Much of the second movement of the symphony, for example, is virtually non-tonal; the first section is based on the non-tonal trichord '016.'"[7] This is one of the reasons that Nielsen's music was dismissed by early analysts, who were looking at models over 100 years old, without taking into account the ways in which harmony had developed over that same time period. For Powell, passages of dissonance, such as those that feature tetrachords and the like most commonly occur in frightening passages, where danger is imminent, or actually occurring. One such example is when Hiccup loses his cheat sheet during their first flight and he and Toothless fall from the sky in the first film. Carl Nielsen's influence is notable across the *Dragon* films.

Jean Sibelius

Jean Sibelius (1865–1957), the composer most closely identified with Finland, was an exact contemporary of Nielsen's, but lived much longer. Powell specifically identified Sibelius in his comments as a Nordic composer, and one whose music he had studied from an early age. While Sibelius certainly didn't single-handedly create Finnish music, he was the composer whose music was most closely attributed with the national music of Finland. Sibelius scholar Matti Huttunen writes, "Nationalist music historians defined Finnish music in a variety of ways. An affinity with folk music, the representation of the *Kalevala* and Finnish landscape, and the expression of the national feelings of the Finnish people were the features most often mentioned as the essence of national art."[8] All of the attributes mentioned by Huttunen appear in Sibelius's compositions, most notably in his tone poems such as *Finlandia*, *Tapiola*, and *The Swan of Tuonela*, but they also appear in Sibelius's seven symphonies. He even spoke of the subject of nationalism in music, saying, "Yes, I do believe in Finnish music, however much the 'experts' may sneer. The sonorous, strangely melancholic monotony, which exists in all Finnish melodies, is so very typical, even though it may strictly speaking be a defect."[9] While it appears to be challenging to describe the salient features of Finnish music, Sibelius felt he had a handle on what make the music of Finland unique.

Despite Sibelius living into the 1950s, he essentially stopped composing in the late 1920s, and largely did not discuss his own music for the last 30 years of his life. He even burned many compositional sketches and writings in 1945. While he was certainly aware of the Second Viennese School, it had no bearing on his compositions, as he had quit composing by that time in history. The forms of the movements of his symphonies, aside from the Seventh, largely follow the eighteenth-century models, but his harmonies and orchestral colors differentiate his music from others. Members of the Finnish Club of Helsinki curate the Jean Sibelius website. They write, "Contemporary composers are interested in Sibelius's ideas of form, the way he manipulates musical time, his ideas concerning colour (which were previously largely ignored), and the way he uses overlapping textures."[10] Of those qualities, the most applicable to Powell's *Dragon* music are orchestral colors and overlapping textures, commonly called counterpoint in the film music world, but better termed as stratification, since stratification means multiple lines occurring simultaneously, but without interacting with each other. Counterpoint implies dependency on musical lines and interaction while stratification does not. Powell's orchestral colors are incredibly diverse, using several instruments beyond the traditional orchestra, many of which are specific to a geographic region or country. Beyond acoustic instruments, Powell also uses electronic instruments and samples to enhance the music, notably through percussive effects, and even runs the voice of Jónsi, the lead singer of Sigur rós, through a filter in a cue in the third film.

Sibelius, like Nielsen, used modes in addition to keys and tonal, functional music, and often used plagal cadences, conclusive harmonic motions of IV-I, rather than authentic cadences with harmonic motions of V-I. These compositional traits led those in the Germanic musical tradition to dismiss and disparage Sibelius and his music, but similarly to Nielsen, Sibelius's music received reappraisal in the later part of the twentieth century, and he is considered to be a major symphonist of the late Romantic Era and into the Twentieth Century with his orchestral music known around the world. Powell's *Dragon* music uses modes far more often than functional keys, and often concludes themes with plagal gestures and cadences. Since Powell had studied Sibelius's music from such a young age, many of those sounds, instrumental voicings, and harmonic progressions had likely become ingrained in his music, making Sibelius an influence on Powell, both consciously and subconsciously.

Ralph Vaughan Williams

"Mention the name Ralph Vaughan Williams and into most people's minds come immediately three words: English, pastoral, and folksong."[11] The two twentieth-century composers most closely associated with England are Benjamin Britten and Ralph Vaughan Williams, and their respective musical styles could not be more at odds with each other: Vaughan Williams, the film score composer, folksong arranger, carol collector, and creator of musical landscapes, and Britten, the opera composer whose music is fueled by dissonance, but not atonality.

Vaughan Williams composed multiple works based on English folksongs, such as the *English Folk Song Suite*, *Fantasia on Greensleeves*, and *Fantasia on Christmas Carols*. One of the features of folk songs is their dependence on modal scales rather than major and minor scales. When modal melodies are harmonized, triads appear in different qualities than would be expected in major or minor keys. In the Dorian mode, for example, the subdominant triad is major and the dominant triad is minor. In a minor key, the subdominant would be minor and the dominant would be major, with the added leading tone. Additionally, Vaughan Williams was not an adherent to common-practice harmonic function, not worrying about typical harmonic progressions derived from Germanic music. Instead, Vaughan Williams scholar James Day writes, "Vaughan Williams's use of harmony in *Pastoral Symphony* is certainly influenced by the way chords are used by French impressionists. This is hardly surprising in view of his studies with one of the two major figures of the movement, Maurice Ravel. The most interesting harmonic feature of the *Pastoral*, though, is the fact that the overwhelming majority of the chords RVW uses are common chords. It is the manner in which he uses them that constitutes a major factor in the work's originality."[12] It is the aspect of *how* Vaughan Williams organizes his harmonies that Powell uses in his *Dragon* music. Like RVW, Powell's harmonies are overwhelmingly triadic, but the way in which he creates his harmonic progressions is inventive and exciting, avoiding many typical common-practice motions and instead choosing alternate paths to reach phrase endings.

For Vaughan Williams, melody was the driver of the music. As a result, the harmonies depended on how they best integrated with the melody. Day states, "The harmony works from the top downwards, not from the bottom upwards…. The result at its best is an amazing monolithic unity of melody, form, texture, rhythm, and harmonic movement; and it is this impressionistic and empirical use of harmony and texture that gives his music its unique combination of solidity and what one can only describe as cosmic vastness."[13] While "cosmic vastness" may be a bit of hyperbole, clearly Day is highlighting the musical elements that combine to make Vaughan Williams's music audibly and unmistakably his. Themes and melodies also seem to be the heart of Powell's *Dragon* scores, and therefore, the music also works "from the top down," working to harmonize the melody. Powell rarely harmonizes his themes exactly the same way. In fact, new harmonization and thematic variation make his *Dragon* scores so exciting. When familiar themes take on new characters, it shows how closely Powell is paying attention to the narrative of the film.

So many of the themes used in the *Dragon* films are modal; very few are truly major or minor. The overwhelming use of modal melodies comes from folk songs, and by extension, from Vaughan Williams's output. Folk songs have a timeless quality to them, rendering them immediately accessible, but also recalling the recent and distant past. Since the *Dragon* films are set approximately 700–800 years ago, these folk songs *could* have been sung by the Vikings we are watching battle dragons. Themes like those for the Warring Vikings and Hiccup are modal and folk-like in construction. They are easily memorable but have the capacity for elaboration and variation. The music of Ralph Vaughan Williams offers a great deal to film composers, and Powell appropriates what is necessary, assimilating it into the rest of his influences for these films.

Maurice Ravel

The musical influence of Maurice Ravel (1875–1937) does not appear in the trilogy until the final film, and is even localized in that film to representing the Hidden World. The music of this location often involves major seventh chords as well as ninth chords.

Ravel scholar Barbara L. Kelly writes, "Extended chords, 9ths and 11ths especially, are integral to Ravel's harmonic language.... He also favoured the diminished octave or major 7th, for example, in the opening and closing chords of *Jeux d'eau*."[14] The ending of 3M12B, "Romance in the Clouds," features a major seventh chord as it initiates harmony for the thematic statement of *The Hidden World* theme. Additionally, full choir and harp enter at this point, with Powell creating a texture reminiscent of Ravel's writing in his ballet *Daphnis et Chloë*. Like Ravel, Powell uses parallel fifths between the root and fifth of the triad in his harmonic motions. Finally, while tritone root motion often serves as an indicator of outer space in film, Powell, like Ravel, uses "the tritone for colouristic purposes."[15] Certainly, outer space does not factor into the *Dragon* trilogy, but flying dragons does fulfill a certain element of fantasy that could be approximated through the use of tritone root relationships. While Ravel's music influence cannot be found across the complete trilogy, it plays a significant role in the final installment.

Sigur rós

The Icelandic band Sigur rós, and their lead singer, Jónsi, play a particular role in the film trilogy. Jónsi contributed original songs to each of the three films, writing and performing them and providing wordless vocals on 4M16B, "The Hidden World," in the third film. Additionally, the cue 2M14, "Forbidden Friendship," from the first film, was temped to a Sigur rós song. In his liner notes to the Deluxe Edition of the *How to Train Your Dragon* soundtrack, film music journalist Tim Greiving writes, "[Director Dean] DeBlois had temped that montage with a track by the Icelandic band Sigur Rós [sic] that features a slate marimba, which 'had a really elemental, very primitive feel to it,' he says. 'It just became married to the visuals for so long that John realized he had to really rise to the challenge of not only meeting it, but besting it.'"[16] Before the making of *How to Train Your Dragon*, in 2002, Sigur rós had performed live music for "Odin's Raven Magic," a musical accompaniment set to Steindór Andersen incanting the text of *Hrafnagaldr Óðins*. In the concert film *Heima*, released in 2007, the band is shown playing a slate marimba on the song "Surtshellir," an instrument that featured prominently in "Odin's Raven Magic."[17] The slate marimba, and its sound, was clearly the inspiration for the cue, as well as the oscillation between *Do* and *Sol*, as heard in "Surtshellir." Powell used the slate marimba, as well as a glass marimba, to create the signature sound of the forbidden friendship between a boy and a dragon. This instrumentation is used in special places in the other two films to specifically recall Hiccup and Toothless's relationship.

A variety of topics were covered in my conversations with Powell. One of these topics was his musical influences, specifically composers, on the *HTTYD* films. His thoughts appear below.

> I've always tried to look for the things in classical music, or the music I grew up with, that felt they had an emotional response in me and see if I can dig them out and pull them in to help the emotional journey that I'm trying to accompany.
>
> I played a lot of Sibelius as a kid in youth orchestras. I studied by listening to the same thing over and over and over, the Violin Concerto in particular. I played a lot of Symphony 2 and [Symphony] 5 as a lot of people have done in youth orchestras, and they were profound experiences. I had an orchestra where the conductor was a magnificent educator as well. He was a way better conductor than a youth orchestra deserved! I remember him trying to explain things to us, never with words, he would just jump around the symphony and get you to play things. Then you'd play this bit and go to another bit where it had been developed, and I certainly sat there

and my head would explode every time he did it, and I suddenly realized, "This is that [musical idea], and he's turned it around, and it's in a triple meter and it's changed."

Eventually I ended up playing the viola, which is, by far, the best place to listen, because you're not worried so much about what you're doing to play, and you're right there in the center, getting a much better orchestral balance rather than being at the end of the first [violins]. If you're in the viola section, you've got the winds right behind you, the brass right behind you, and everybody's around you. You're as close to the conductor's position as anywhere else in the orchestra.

Grieg you could probably say is in there. Brahms. Khachaturian, [laughs] a lot of Khachaturian, Stravinsky as well. The piece that really blew my head off in that orchestra was The Firebird. It was a giant orchestra as well because they were trying to get as many kids in to play, and it was just an incredible thing to feel at such a particular time in your life. I played in some orchestras, Beethoven and things, but nothing quite like Firebird, a piece that I'd never felt such an affinity for before, orchestrally speaking. Everything goes in there. Sibelius is the closest Nordic composer I was using. Russian stuff as well: a lot of Rimsky-Korsakov riffs in there. Sibelius very much in is there, to the point where I pulled loads of bits of parts and sat there and tried to play it on the piano and tried to get his language under my fingers. There is stuff that is something of a recall of those Symphonies, of 2 and 5.

Music of Specific Countries

Scotland

The folk music of Scotland is a significant musical influence on the scores. While not considered part of the Nordic countries by any stretch, the music of Scotland plays a significant role in Powell's *Dragon* music in multiple ways. Beyond the obvious instrumentation use of bagpipes, "prominent musical characteristics found in the traditional music of Scotland include pentatonic modes, double-tonic tunes, cyclical melodies, and the Scotch snap."[18] Although Powell's themes are not pentatonic, many of them are cyclical, meaning that the end of the theme will resolve when the theme restarts. The Scotch snap, a gesture where the downbeat of the measure is short-long rather than long-short or two even eighth notes is prominently featured in the opening of *Hiccup*'s theme, as well as in other locations throughout the scores. "The Scotch snap is a rhythmic cliché of Scottish music that has been misunderstood by composers elsewhere in Europe. Most closely associated with the strathspey, a slow 4/4 reel, this two-note dotted rhythm consists of an emphasized short note on the beat, leading to a longer, off-beat pitch. The snap is also used for special effect in reels and is characteristic of pipe marches. Correct speed and emphasis in the Scotch snap is a marker of traditional performance style, as is the placement of snaps within heavily dotted-rhythm genres."[19] The use of the Scotch snap and Scottish folk tunes, music that Powell grew up with, would have been extremely familiar to him and easily integrated into his music, along with the presence of bagpipes. With a Scottish heritage, it is easy to see how Scottish musical influences found their way into Powell's *Dragon* music.

Ireland

The music of Ireland is distinct from that of England, Scotland, and Wales. However, it is most commonly recognized as an amalgam of music from all those locations, known in the vernacular as Celtic Music. A number of instruments are specific to Ireland, such as the Irish harp, the Uilleann pipes (to be played indoors unlike bagpipes), and drums such as the bodhran. Nicholas Carolan writes, "When French-speaking Normans invaded the country from Wales in the 12th century they found a distinctive Irish harp which seems to have been a development of an earlier instrument. Used in instrumental music, song and recitation performance, and with a lively playing style in which melody was accompanied by the bass strings, the harp remained the chief instrument of Ireland until the 17th century."[20] Much of traditional Irish music is related to the Irish harp.

Many of the folk tunes of Ireland are modal, and "it has been estimated that more than half are in the Ionian mode, followed in order of frequency by the Mixolydian, the Aeolian and the Dorian modes."[21] The use of Ionian (major) and Mixolydian (major with a lowered seventh scale-degree) illustrate that most melodies take on a major-mode nature. Powell's *Vikings* theme is one example of a major (or Ionian mode) theme that does not contain any specific Scottish musical signifiers, making it more Celtic than Scottish.

Dance-like qualities are present in many of the themes in the first film, and many Celtic tunes are based on dance music. Carolan states,

> The reel is performed in a fast forward-moving style, in 4/4 rhythm. The typical bar has eight eighth-notes divided into two groups. The jig, the oldest form of dance music now played, is usually performed at a more moderate speed and in a more relaxed manner. There are several types of jigs, each deriving its name from dance movements, and distinguished from one another by rhythm. The double jig is in 6/8 rhythm, the typical bar having six eighth-notes in two groups. The single jig is also normally in 6/8 rhythm, but the typical bar has two quarter-eighth figures. Single jigs in 12/8 are called slides. The slip jig or hop jig is in 9/8 rhythm and the typical bar has nine eighth-notes in three groups. Some jigs were once ancient marches.[22]

Although the descriptions of the various dances are highly specific, those directions are not always followed in performance. For example, the tempo marking at the start of 3M18, "See You Tomorrow," from the first film, is Tempo di Celtico, with the score stating, "(Film begins with six beats of Scottish drumming)." Scottish drumming, in combination with a Celtic tempo, could be considered as a monstrosity, but for Powell, it's all about combining and synthesizing the various styles and feels into a cohesive score, with interchangeable international elements.

All of these different composers and styles are combined to create the music of a culture of animated Vikings. Berk is on the ocean, so it could be in Ireland, Scotland, England, Norway, Sweden, Finland, or Denmark. No specific geographical markers exist, and, like putting ingredients in a blender and emerging with a new item, the sum of which is greater than its parts, the music of all these different cultures is blended to create the soundscape of the world of the *How to Train Your Dragon* films. Powell spoke with me regarding influences in more general terms as well.

> There are whole sections in the first film that sound really Jewish where I managed to get a Horah in, and it's in an octatonic scale. I remember Jeffrey Katzenberg questioning, "Why does it sound like somebody off–Broadway wrote this music? We're supposed to be in Scotland!" Of course, they're Vikings so they're not really supposed to be in Scotland, but it's all sort of mixed together. At the same time, I was getting requests from Jeffery: "Can you get some of that Enya music in there?" I'd always liked Enya, to tell you the truth, and I love the production. I have a very catholic taste in music, catholic meaning "broad."

All of these musical influences—composers, music from specific geographic locations, various styles—are combined, synthesized, and reconstituted by Powell to create the music of the *HTTYD* films. Powell had to have the proper background and training, both as a student of music and as a performer, in order to draw on the elements of the composers discussed in this chapter and create a new score. As Philip Glass famously said regarding personal style of a composer, "If you don't have a basis [of technique] on which to make the choice, you don't have a style. You have a series of accidents."[23] Powell knew exactly what musical elements needed to be used in creating the sound world of the *HTTYD* films. Knowing the various composers and styles drawn upon makes it easier for an analyst to have expectations and approaches regarding the music, ideas to support, and how the music can be derived from these composers, yet still belong fully to Powell. Every note here is intentional. There were no accidents.

2

Pitch Collections

Film music rarely is written in a single musical style or within the confines of a single type of musical scale. Unlike the vast majority of music from 1725 to 1900, most film music does not strictly adhere to the tonal-functional system of common-practice harmony. Much of the music across the three *Dragon* films contains a clear tonal center and uses primarily tertian harmony but does not follow the "rules" of common-practice harmony, instead operating within its own musical parameters based on the narrative needs of the film, and because Powell often uses modal themes rather than major or minor ones. This short chapter of the book presents the various pitch materials and scales used by Powell across the *Dragon* trilogy. It can be used as a reference for the analysis section of the book, as a basic introduction to pitch materials, or as a refresher for experienced musicians.

Whole-Tone Scale

The whole-tone scale is exactly what it purports to be: a scale comprised exclusively of whole tones (or steps), nothing but intervals of a major second between adjacent scale members. Although any note can serve as the tonal center, only two forms of this scale exist, due to its symmetry. The first is the scale that contains the note C, which will be referred to as WT_0, as 0 represents C in pitch-class notation. The other form of the scale contains the note C♯, or enharmonically D♭. This is referred to as WT_1 because C♯ and D♭ are both 1 in pitch-class notation. Examples of these scales appear in Figure 2.1

The whole-tone scale only contains six notes, so while the scale may appear incomplete, it is not. The six notes of the whole-tone scale are in contrast to the diatonic seven-note scales, which are most common in Western music. Every interval in the

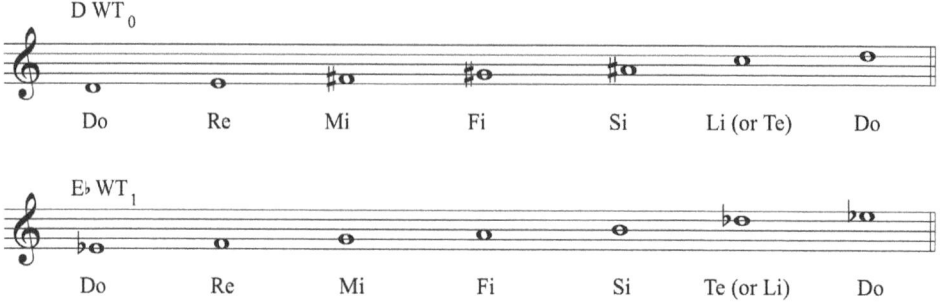

Figure 2.1. Whole-tone scales.

whole-tone scale is a major second, or its enharmonic equivalent, the diminished third. The whole-tone scale does not contain a *Do-Sol* perfect fifth axis like diatonic modes, instead containing a *Do-Fi* tritone axis.

Diatonic Modes and Other Seven-note Scales

The majority of themes across the *Dragon* trilogy are composed in a specific mode rather than the major/minor tonal system. Modes that contain the minor third scale-degree are more common than those that contain the major third scale degree.

Aeolian Mode

The Aeolian mode is the same as what is referred to as "natural minor." The tonic, subdominant, and dominant triads are all minor and leading tones are absent, shown in Figure 2.2.

Figure 2.2. Aeolian mode scale and triads.

Dorian Mode

Dorian mode is very similar to Aeolian mode, but scale-degree 6 is raised by a half step. This makes the subdominant triad major, but changes the quality of other triads, as seen in Figure 2.3.

Figure 2.3. Dorian mode scale and triads.

Phrygian Mode

Phrygian mode is, again, similar to Aeolian mode, but with one alteration. Here, scale-degree 2 is lowered by a half step, as illustrated in Figure 2.4. The tonic and subdominant triads remain minor, but the dominant triad is now diminished.

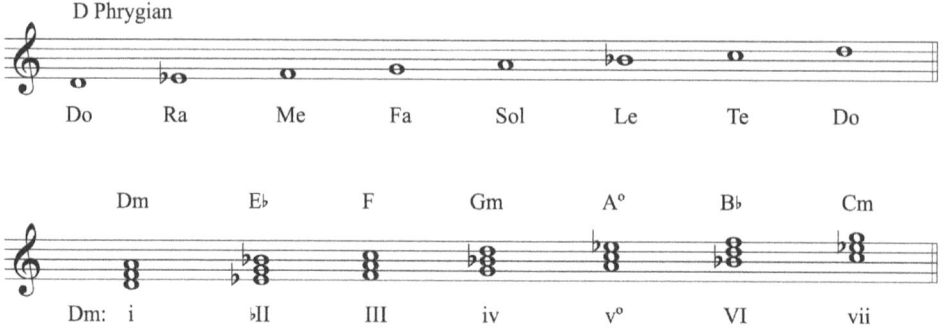

Figure 2.4. Phrygian mode scale and triads.

Harmonic Minor

Harmonic minor uses natural minor (or Aeolian) as its starting point, and raises scale-degree 7 by a half step to create the leading tone to the tonic, the note a half step below. By doing this, the dominant triad is now major, creating more of a drive to resolve to tonic because of the presence of the leading tone, as shown in Figure 2.5.

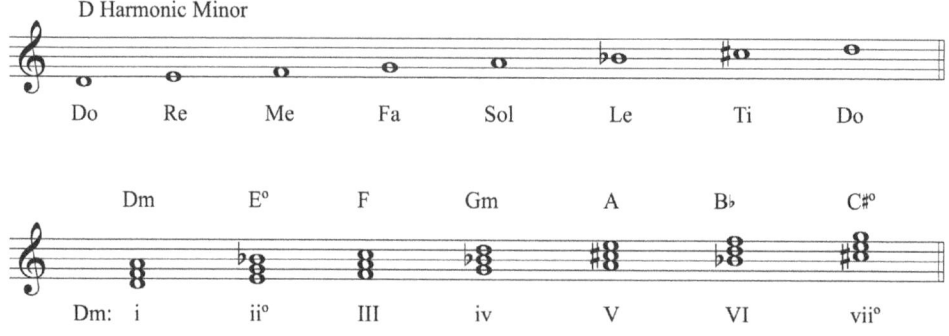

The leading tone is rarely applied to the mediant (III) chord.

Figure 2.5. Harmonic minor scale and triads.

Doubly Harmonic Minor

From harmonic minor, this scale raises scale-degree 4 by a half step, creating a second leading tone within the scale, this one to the dominant. This is not a scale used by most composers of concert music, and its application in the *Dragon* trilogy, when accompanying the main antagonist of the first two films, illustrates it, seen in Figure 2.6.

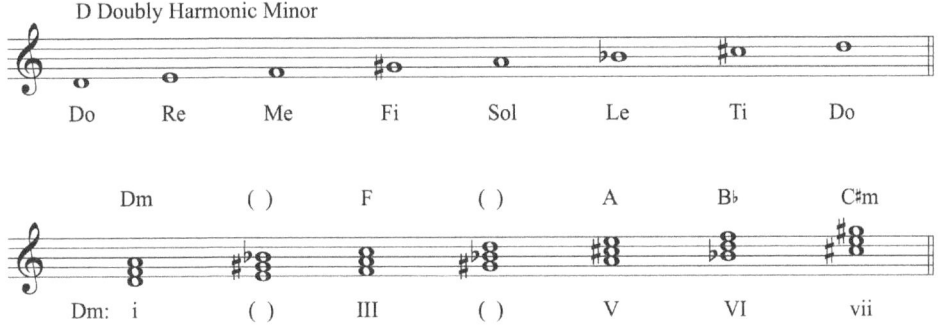

Figure 2.6. Doubly harmonic minor scale and triads.

IONIAN MODE

Ionian mode is the same as the major mode, shown in Figure 2.7. However, when dealing with modal melodies and shifts, it is more appropriate to refer to the scale as Ionian rather than major. In Ionian mode, the tonic, subdominant, and dominant triads are all major, the opposite of Aeolian mode.

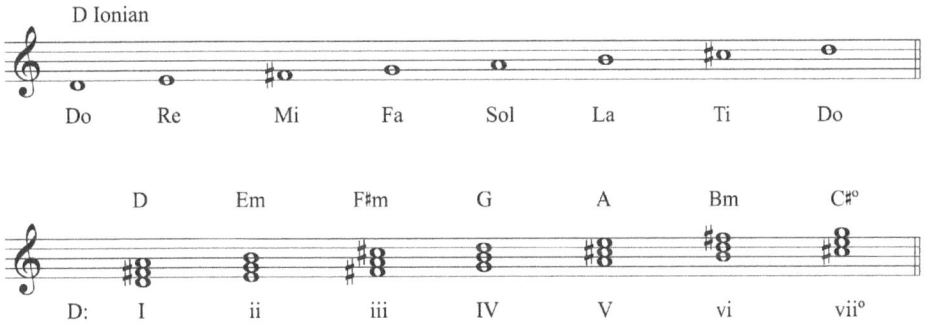

Figure 2.7. Ionian mode scale and triads.

MIXOLYDIAN MODE

Mixolydian mode stakes Ionian mode and lowers scale-degree 7 by a half step, eliminating the leading tone. In making this shift, the dominant triad is now minor and the need for resolution is lessened because the leading tone is absent, as seen in Figure 2.8.

Although Lydian and other modes exist, those scales do not appear with enough frequency in any of the three films to merit explanation here.

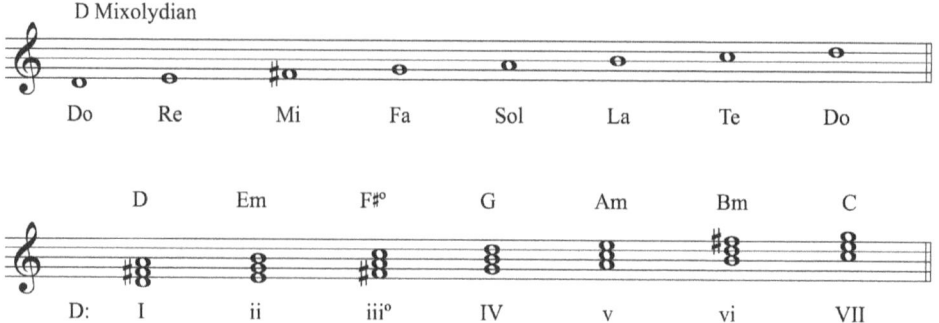

Figure 2.8. Mixolydian mode scale and triads.

Octatonic Scales

Octatonic scales, by their name, contain eight notes that are arranged in a pattern alternating half steps and whole steps. Like the whole-tone scale, the octatonic scale is also symmetrical and can begin on any note, and because of the symmetry, the octatonic scale has a limited number of unique versions. These scales are labeled as (0,1), (1,2), and (2,3), where 0 = C, 1 = C♯/D♭, 2 = D, and 3 = D♯/E♭. Each scale can only contain one of those three half step combinations. All three versions of the scale are shown in Figure 2.9.

Many more triads can be created from the octatonic scale than from a typical seven-note scale. For example, from the tonic note, a major triad, minor triad, and diminished triad can all be found, along with four types of seventh chords, illustrated in Figure 2.10. Octatonic scales can often be found in "action" cues, and in places with

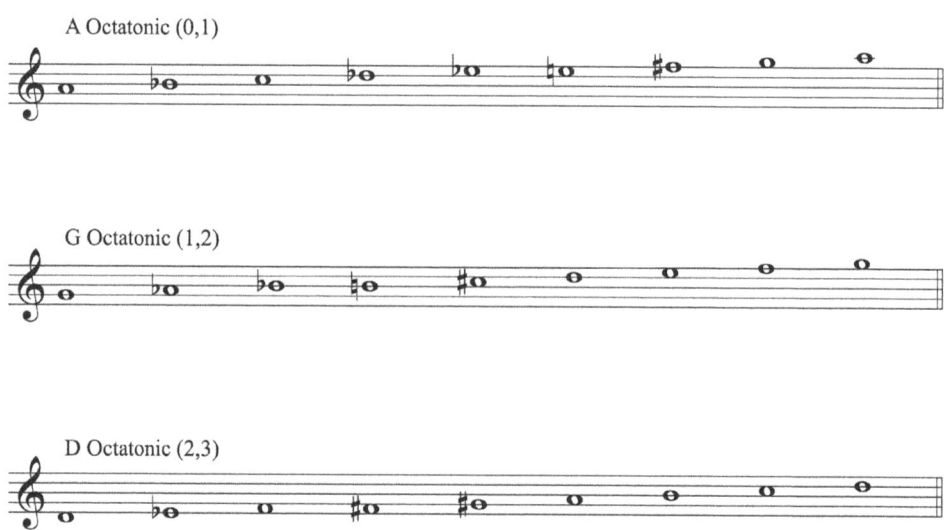

Figure 2.9. Octatonic scales.

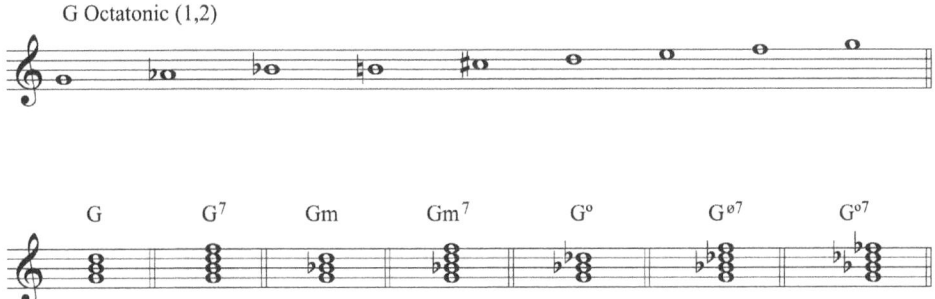

Note: C♯ and D♭ are enharmonic equivalents, as are E and F♭.

Figure 2.10. Available harmonies in the octatonic scale.

rapidly moving stepwise lines. Additionally, chord progressions derived from octatonic scales are used throughout the *Dragon* films, subverting functional harmony and replacing it with a pattern specific to the scale.

Pitch-Class Collections

In the absence of a prevailing tonic or scale, or simply in the avoidance of tertian (triadic) harmony, a composer may use what is termed a pitch-class collection, or a "set," a group of notes labeled according to their most compact form and put into an abstract grouping called prime form. The theoretical system is often called pitch-class set theory, atonal theory, or just set theory. While it can be applied to tonal music, it is most beneficially applied to music without a tonal center, or harmonies that are clearly not triadically based. When Powell uses pitch-class sets in his score, it often accompanies scenes of great tension, anxiety, or trouble.

Although other pitch collections, scales, and methodologies exist in the large world of musical analysis, the materials in this chapter are the most germane to my analysis of Powell's music for the films. I hope that other methodologies will be applied to the analysis of this music in the future.

3

The Themes of the *HTTYD* Trilogy

HTTYD Themes

Flying

The main theme for the *How to Train Your Dragon* films is *Flying*, a theme not titled for a specific character, but an action, most often performed by Hiccup and Toothless. Like the "Raiders March" from the Indiana Jones films, *Flying* often serves to let the audience know that the heroes have accomplished something significant. *Flying* is eighteen measures, split into two parts of eight and ten measures, respectively. The two parts connect without any harmonic problems or difficulties. Both parts of *Flying* are not always heard. Sometimes only the first part—*Flying A*—is heard, while in other instances, only *Flying B* is heard.

The *Flying A* theme appears as a sentence, a typical eight-measure structure where the first two measures are repeated in measures 3–4, and the remaining four measures use clearly related material from the opening two measures. While it appears that *Flying A* concludes with an Imperfect Authentic Cadence (IAC), since it ends on F#, the sentence really contains no true harmonic progression because a pedal D sounds throughout the entirety of the eight measures.

Like *Flying A*, *Flying B* is also a sentence, with measures 15 and 16 essentially repeated in measures 17 and 18, the repetition causing the asymmetry between the two parts of the theme. *Flying B* contains much more harmonic variety than *Flying A*, and the opening two measures use a very familiar harmonic formula of vi-IV-V-I. The second half of *Flying B* is far more atypical. Measures 13–14 use a harmonic progression of vi-iii-V-V/V in D major. In common-practice harmony, we would expect each pair of triads to be reversed: iii-vi, followed by V/V-V, another reversal, which would result in a standard circle-of-fifths progression. What Powell has done here is to keep the expected chords but combine them in an unexpected way. Even the final two harmonies, GM and EM, are not that far afield from common-practice harmony. In fact, this is a common gesture in both film and popular music, often represented by the Roman numerals ♭VII and V, a gesture coined by music theorist Frank Lehman as the "subtonic half cadence."[1] In *Flying B*, these final two chords sound like a half cadence, the music modulating from D major to A major; the last melodic note is *Re* in the key of A major, not *La* in the key of D major. As a further harmonic relationship, GM and EM are chromatic mediants, triads whose roots are a third apart, in this case, a minor third, specifically. In my article "Chromatic Mediants and Narrative Context in Film," I refer to the major chromatic mediant relationship with roots a minor third apart as the "Hero" relationship.[2] The *Flying B* theme is most often used to denote a heroic event or action, whether it is Hiccup mastering his fear in flying Toothless, Hiccup and Toothless victorious in battle, or any similar moment. Powell has both subverted our expectations and simultaneously fulfilled them, quite a remarkable feat.

The melody in the second half of *Flying A* desperately wants to reach the tonic D, and even makes two attempts before falling back down to F#, in the sixth and eighth measures. The reason for this is because *Flying B* finally reaches that upper D, and soars well above it. Powell's melody in *Flying A* is restrained, but in *Flying B*, the unbridled joy of riding a dragon is released, and the melody soars close to a full octave above the

Figure 3.1. *Flying* theme.

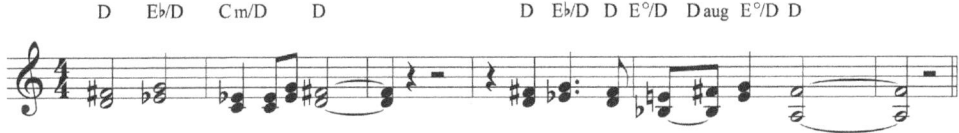

Figure 3.2. Modified harmonization of *Flying* theme.

D that opens it. *Flying B* ends lower than it begins, but higher than either the starting or ending point of *Flying A*. The conclusion of the complete *Flying* theme is open-ended, with more excitement and anticipation to follow.

The opening gesture of the *Flying A* theme appears throughout the film trilogy in various reharmonized fashions. One of these instances appears below.

Flying Ostinato

Related to the *Flying* theme is the *Flying Ostinato*, a two-measure gesture often heard preceding the *Flying* theme and sometimes accompanying it. The ostinato pattern can be used as many times in a row as necessary. As seen in the example, the rhythm is exclusively eighth notes, although sometimes the strings will double up and play sixteenth notes, repeating each pitch of the ostinato pattern.

The melodic line itself descends a full octave from D5 to D4, and the simplified *Flying Ostinato* example shows the straight-line descent. Although the ostinato is harmonically supported with an open fifth D-A, an implied progression of DM-AM-GM-DM, or I-V-IV-I is present through the melodic notes. This is sometimes called a "retrograde" progression, as V doesn't proceed to IV in common-practice rules. We would expect a progression of I-IV-V-I, one of the most common and simplest harmonic progressions in the literature. However, this progression can be seen as two pairs of chord roots descending by fourths: D to A and G to D, with the first chord in each pair separated by a descending fifth, D to G, operating more as pattern-based than typically harmonically based.

Figure 3.3. *Flying Ostinato*.

The descending scale, from D5 to D4, feels as though it is accelerating from the beginning to the end of the ostinato. The opening D5 lasts for 2 beats, along with C♯5. In the second measure, B4 and A4 are one beat each, with the final four notes of the scale as eighth note values. The acceleration gives a sensation of motion, in sharp contrast to *Flying A*, which is harmonically static due to the pedal tone, giving a sensation of hovering rather than flying or being in motion.

Like the *Flying* theme, the *Flying Ostinato* appears in a modified version, most often in the minor mode. In some instances, the descending fifth is kept, *Sol* to *Do*, while in others, the opening leap is adjusted to a descending fourth, *Do* to *Sol*. The minor-mode variation typically indicates that something has gone wrong.

People

Hiccup/Vikings

Powell labels this theme both as *Hiccup*'s theme and as the "fun" *Vikings* theme. I will refer to it as the *Hiccup* theme, but it often sounds when Hiccup is trying to do

3. The Themes of the HTTYD Trilogy

Viking things. The theme is in D Dorian in the example and is an eight-measure theme. Unlike the two parts of the *Flying* theme, this theme is constructed much more like a period, with two equal halves and the same music at the beginning of each half. Unlike a standard period, the *Hiccup* theme does not contain a half cadence (HC) at the end of the first four-measure phrase. Instead, it concludes on an implied subdominant chord. The second phrase ends with an implied i-v7-i progression, a modal cadence that finds the melody ending on tonic, as close to a Perfect Authentic Cadence (PAC) as is possible in the Dorian mode. The theme is typically played in octaves, without accompanying harmonies from the orchestra, leaving only implied harmonies within the melodic line.

Modes can also use chromatic notes just like standard major and minor scales, which explains the F♯ in m. 4 of the example. Although the F♯ is the major third scale-degree of the D scale, it is not functioning in that way in m. 4. The A in the first half of the measure serves as a diatonic upper neighbor and the F# serves as a chromatic lower neighbor, surrounding the chord tone G.

The youthful energy of Hiccup, the son of Stoick the Vast, who is the chief of the Viking village of Berk, is represented in the rhythms of the theme, notably the dotted-eighth-sixteenth-eighth in measures 2 and 6, and the modified Scotch snap, the eighth-quarter figure found at the opening of measures 1 and 5. The technically accurate Scotch snap would be a sixteenth-dotted-eighth figure in simple meter. In the *Hiccup* theme, which is in compound meter, the Scotch snap translates to an eighth-quarter figure in the first half of the measure. Composers of the eighteenth century, including Wolfgang Amadeus Mozart and Ludwig van Beethoven used the Scotch snap to make "rustic or naïve associations,"[3] and Powell seems to be giving Hiccup those same connotations: naïveté for his youth, and rustic for his Viking village. The 6/8 meter gives the theme the feel of a Scottish jig, a lively and energetic dance suitable for the excitable Hiccup.

Figure 3.4. *Hiccup/Vikings/Hiccup*'s theme.

VIKINGS!

The *Vikings* theme is quite long, consisting of five four-measure phrases, plus a repeat of the opening phrases. In the manuscript page reproduced in the Omni score, the cue contains an exclamation point, but I will omit that when discussing the theme. To go somewhat against expectations, the *Vikings* theme is in G Ionian, one of the few major-mode themes in the film trilogy. The complete *Vikings* theme is constructed in Rounded Binary form, and this form is best seen in the unused cue 5M50, "The Vikings Have Their Tea," an imaginary scene Powell scored that focuses on the daintier side of the Vikings from the first film. The opening A section of the theme is constructed as a period, with an HC in measure 4 and a PAC in measure 8. The material in measures 1–3 and 5–7 is nearly repeated verbatim. Following that, each phrase receives its own letter, so a phrase analysis would look like: aa'bcdaa,' and at the larger structural level, would be A|BA,' with the A section containing measures 1–8, the B section 9–20, and the A' section measures 1–4 and 21–24.

The complete *Vikings* theme is very similar to a sarabande, a triple-meter European dance that originated in Latin America, notably Panama and Mexico, in the sixteenth century before reaching Spain and then being exported to Italy, France, Germany, and England.[4] In the sarabande, the stress is on beat 2 of the measure, rather than beat 1, with beat 2 most commonly having the duration of a dotted quarter note, as in measures 2 and 3 of the *Vikings* theme. Sarabandes are found in nearly every instrumental suite by Johann Sebastian Bach, and nearly 150 years later, Claude Debussy used the dance form again in his own piano works.

Each phrase of the *Vikings* theme has its own distinct character. The a and a' phrases of the *Vikings* feature a very clear harmonic progression, using only diatonic chords in G major. The ascending melody, rising over an octave from D4 to G5, shows the vastness of the Vikings' lands, as well as the size of the burly explorers themselves. The melody also shows a return to home, with the first phrase ending B-A (*Mi-Re* in G major) and the second ending A-G (*Re-Do*), illustrating that even those these are explorers, they always return home when finished. The b phrase of the theme focuses on the dominant harmony, D, while the c phrase directly modulates to B♭ major in measure 13 before concluding in G minor, the relative minor of B♭ major, in measure 16. Finally, the d phrase begins in G minor, briefly shifts to B♭ major, and ends on the dominant of the home key of G major, ready to restart the opening measures and reach a final conclusion.

Most commonly, Powell uses just the A section of the theme; full statements of the *Vikings* theme are rare. However, like the *Flying* theme, sometimes just the B section of the *Vikings* theme is used without the A section preceding it. The presence of eighth notes on the downbeat of nearly every measure allows Powell to vary the theme as the narrative provides. In the

Figure 3.5. *Vikings* theme.

introduction to the published score, Timothy Rodier writes, "When the composer needs to show heroism through the music, he alters the 8th notes into dotted 8th notes/16th, which gives the theme a swashbuckling sound. Changing the 8th notes also gives specific characteristics to the melody, i.e., dotted 8th to 16th transforms the music to sound Irish, where 16th to dotted 8th is more Scottish."[5] On occasion, the *Vikings A* theme appears in minor, with melodic and harmonic variations. Like the *Flying* theme, the minor-mode *Vikings A* theme highlights something amiss with the Berkians.

The presence of the Scotch snap and use of Dorian mode in *Hiccup*'s theme places it against the *Vikings* theme, in Ionian mode and without the Scotch snap figure. Essentially the two themes are Scottish versus Celtic, younger generation versus older generation, Hiccup against his father. Powell uses the salient features of these two themes to place Hiccup outside of the adult Vikings. While not musical, the adult Vikings all have Scottish or Irish or English accents, while the teenagers have American or no accents. Even though dialogue is not music, it is another aural indicator of the generational and ideological gap in Berk.

Warring Vikings

The life of a Viking is not all fun and games. Many times, the Vikings of Berk are at war, most often with dragons, at least in the first film. The *Warring Vikings* theme shows the side of the Vikings that is unrefined, hypermasculine, and stubborn. Unlike the lilting dance feel of the *Vikings* theme, the *Warring Vikings* theme is in a standard 4/4 meter, often accompanied by march-like figures, and concludes open-endedly. The theme never gets more than a fourth above or below the tonic note that opens the theme. The melody is constantly undulating, only repeating the opening note, and based on the typical harmonization, is in E♭ Dorian even though scale-degree 6 is melodically absent. This theme is short, at only four measures, and because of its ending, is often immediately repeated a fourth higher. *Warring Vikings* is used during fight sequences or fight preparations while the *Vikings* theme is commonly reserved for calm and celebration.

Figure 3.6. *Warring Vikings* theme.

Hiccup and Astrid's Love Theme

At the start of the first film, Hiccup is clearly infatuated with Astrid. She, however, thinks Hiccup is sort of a doofus and a lost cause, much like everyone else in Berk. She is also visually shown to be a tough Viking warrior, despite being female. In fact, she is the only female warrior that we see throughout the films aside from Ruffnut, who is mostly present for comic relief (Valka is not really depicted as a warrior). To highlight Astrid's warrior nature, she is first shown in the film walking with an explosion behind her, the ideal girl in Hiccup's narration. It is a moment that never fails to make me laugh, playing on the trope of the masculine action hero walking away from an explosion created through his actions.

The complete *Love* theme, which is rarely heard in the film, is 20 measures and is divided into two unequal parts of 9 and 11 measures. The first part can be classified as a sentence as measures 4–5 are melodically shifted down a third from measures 1–3, and measures 6–7 are using a similar harmonic shape but with a completely different, and much faster, harmonic rhythm. Measures 8–9 feature a typical cadential progression leading to an HC in measure 9.

The first half of this theme contains some unusual rhythmic content that makes the theme feel as though it is in the wrong meter. In the opening measures, the tonic triad arrives on beat 2 in the measure of 3/4, but the measures that follow place the emphasis on the downbeat. The shift of accent from measure to measure is highly atypical. Also atypical is the fact that the downbeats of those two measures are harmonized with chords other than the tonic. Had the entire passage been harmonized with the F major tonic triad, the melodic B♭ would be treated as an appoggiatura, a non-chord tone approached by leap and resolved by step in the opposite direction. Additionally, appoggiaturas appear on strong beats, so the B♭ fits all requirements of the definition. The melodic G, harmonized by a C major triad, would be treated as a passing tone, moving stepwise from A to F. Passing tones can appear in strong or weak metric positions, although weak beats (or unaccented passing tones) are more commonly found throughout the literature. Astrid, of course, is an atypical female character, in that she doesn't need a male character to show her a path forward. Instead, Hiccup needs Astrid to find his way, a sort of archetypical character reversal, and her strength and atypical nature manifests itself in the opening measures of the theme.

The second half of the theme feels as though it could end in measure 14 with a plagal cadence (PC). However, it the melody leaps up an octave, like Hiccup's heart, before returning to its original octave, and finally ascending to conclude an octave higher than where the theme began in measure 1. The cadence at the end of the theme—IV-(I⁶)-ii⁷-I—is quite uncommon due to the lack of dominant harmony, as the final tonic is approached by predominant chords, IV and ii. The stepwise descent of the bass line is met with melodic leaps of thirds and fourths. Although Hiccup is the son of the chief, Astrid clearly is the dominant voice in the relationship.

Figure 3.7. *Love* theme.

The final harmonic progression is notably similar to the final cadence in another love theme, the aria "O soave fanciulla" from Giacomo Puccini's opera *La bohème*. "O soave fanciulla" ends Act I of the opera, and as the main couple, Rodolfo and Mimi, exit the apartment building, their final word, "amor," (the word "love" in Italian) is repeatedly sung over the harmonies FM, Dmm^7, and CM, or IV-♯i7-I in C major. In *La bohème*, Mimi is fated to die. In *How to Train Your Dragon*, Astrid is fated to help Hiccup become the best version of himself, both for her and for the village of Berk. As a result, the harmonic progression is not exactly the same, nor is it in the same key, but the harmonic reference to *La bohème* is certainly no accident.

Although this is called the *Love* theme, this theme can also refer to the character of Astrid, like the *Hiccup* theme refers to Hiccup. However, the theme is used to represent love in other characters, namely Ruffnut for Eret in the second film, so it cannot be called the "*Astrid* theme," even though it is often used in that fashion to identify when Astrid is the primary character within a portion of a scene.

Everything Else

Dragon Tune

The *Dragon Tune* is a lengthy, slow-moving theme that contains nothing but minor triads and diminished harmonies until the final measure of its sixteen measures of melody. The basis for the scale of the *Dragon Tune* is D doubly harmonic minor. Harmonic minor features a leading tone, *Ti*, rather than the subtonic *Te* of natural minor or Aeolian. Doubly harmonic minor builds on harmonic minor, and replaces *Fa* with *Fi*, creating leading tones to both *Do* and *Sol*. As a result, all G♮s are chromatic to the scale, as is the B♮ in measure 13 of the example. Like the largest of dragons, who move slowly, the harmonic rhythm for the *Dragon Tune* is exceptionally slow. The final harmony, a dominant seventh over the tonic pitch, prepares the *Dragon Tune* for a repeat back to its beginning. These dragons are scary, ready to fight the Berk Vikings, and their melody is typically played by bass instruments and brass for an extra characterization of fear and power. Unlike the other themes for this film, the sixteen measures of the *Dragon Tune* do not parse easily into four-measure phrases or two (un)equal halves. Instead, chromatic lower neighbor notes and the rhythmic gesture of long-short-short-long, seen in measures 3, 5, 6, 7, 9, and 11, are the primary materials used. This theme is essentially an example of *Fortspinnung*, a German term that essentially means "the spinning out of motives," or more precisely, motives deriving from previous motives. It is not difficult to see the lower neighbor gesture in the opening two measures that is then rhythmically contracted to create the gesture in measure 3. From that point on, each measure is derived from earlier in the theme until its conclusion, where the melodic leaps reach their maximum size.

In our conversation of the music, Powell and I discussed composing music for villains or antagonists. His thoughts appear below:

> They're ALWAYS the easiest to do! I probably fall into the same kind of world every time. Again, they're Vikings, so they have a common language, and the villains are probably not going to be too different from each other, really. The idea of "good and bad" is such basic storytelling. The problem with the score is always, you have to do "dark music," or music

Figure 3.8. *Dragon Tune.*

that's different. "The Other." It's a kind of xenophobic way of telling stories or supporting storytelling. Xenophobes would say, "This person is not of our family, not of our tribe. They are different, so they sound different." Hollywood has done that, endlessly, forever, but so does storytelling. It just does. It's a little tricky to tread that line. Yes, the language of the scales and things, of course, contributes. A lot of those scales have more tension in them. The tension of a kind of Arabic scale is just implicit to, unfortunately, the Western audience, but it isn't to people who listen to that music all the time. It's like saying Ligeti or Penderecki is the go-to for horror music. That upset me because I actually see a lot of that music intended to be, and is, very beautiful, even though it's all tension. That's the problem with the physics of music: what is resolved and what is unresolved? What resonates and what pushes against itself? There's the commonality in Hollywood of doing that, and I really couldn't avoid it. The other way to do it would be, if you were in the right kind of world, you could have a very complex Romantic sound for the people that you like, and you could have a very simple and undeveloped sound for the people you don't like. Or, do it the other way around. It's about finding enough of an opposite sound to give clarity so that you can achieve the storytelling need, which is darkness and light.

If you think of Toccata and Fugue in D minor by Johann Sebastian Bach, where's the bad guy in that? It's not there. It's drama. There is no bad guy. There are the tensions of the world and transitioning from nothing to life and life to death, and that's all in there, in my opinion. It got co-opted, at a certain point, to sound "Gothic," and something like a bad guy would play, and I always thought, "That's a shame!" Why is the bad guy playing that? It's an amazing piece of music. Everyone would react to that piece as incredibly impressive and incredibly knowing of the human condition, and yet we've damned it to being the bad guy.[6]

Fate Theme

The *Fate* theme accompanies Hiccup's realization that his fate is to become a dragon rider and to make peace with dragons, not war with and kill them. Like the *Hiccup* theme, the *Fate* theme is also in a minor mode. Because the theme is harmonized with both G major (containing B♮) and B♭ major (containing B♭), the mode fluctuates between D Dorian and D Aeolian.

The *Fate* theme is eight measures long, clearly dividing into two equal halves. The opening two measures are essentially repeated in measures 5–6, giving the theme a period-like structure. However, the chord that ends the first phrase is B♭ major, which has a Roman numeral of VI in D minor. This is not a cadence by any definition, nor is the final cadence in measures 7–8, ending B♭ major followed by G major, VI-IV in D minor. The use of the major triads at the ends of the two phrases gives a false sense of half cadence, particularly at the end, where the G major triad is chromatic in D minor.

Melodically, the theme spans an octave from A3 to A4, or *Sol* to *Sol* in D. The melody often ascends from D4 to A4 before coming back down, and C4 commonly serves as a lower neighbor to the D4. The dotted rhythms here are much more conventional than the Scotch snap that identifies the *Hiccup* theme, giving the music a Celtic feel. Similar to the *Vikings* theme, the *Fate* theme does not feature consecutive notes that are the same; it is constantly in motion, undulating from *Do* to *Sol* and back down again. Hiccup's fate, and the fate of the population of Berk, are fully connected.

Figure 3.9. *Fate* theme.

Action Motif

The *Action Motif* is a one-measure gesture repeated again and again. It always has the same rhythm, as shown in the example, and usually has the same pitches. Like the *Warring Vikings* theme that naturally wants to be repeated higher, it is common to hear the *Action Motif* transposed up after three or four statements. Rather than a perfect fourth, the *Action Motif* is normally transposed up a third.

The melodic content comes from the C Octatonic (0,1) scale, and uses only four notes: C, D♭, E♭, and E. The opening leap, from C to E, is a major third, but that interval is quickly extinguished and replaced by the downward shift to E♭, and ultimately

Figure 3.10. *Action Motif.*

the descent back to C, via the D♭. The *Action Motif* is used to accompany intense action scenes across all three films but is used most commonly in the first film.

Calming Motif

The *Calming Motif* almost always occurs in the same key: D major. I am placing it in that key because the opening melodic gesture is clearly in D major. However, the melodic G is harmonized with an E♭ major triad, the Neapolitan or ♭II chord in D, and the melodic E is harmonized with a C major triad, the subtonic or ♭VII chord in D. The chord roots and the melodic contour surround the tonic D and the melodic pitch F♯, giving the *Calming Motif* something of an exotic character as Hiccup is the only one who can calm the dragons, a unique trait among the inhabitants of Berk.

Figure 3.11. *Calming Motif.*

HTTYD2 Themes

The second film takes place five years after the end of the first film. Hiccup is now 20, and his father is ready to turn over the responsibility of leading Berk to him. Dragon trappers, and their boss, Drago, threaten Berk and its new way of life. With new enemies, new characters, and new battles to fight, *How to Train Your Dragon 2* contains eight new themes.

People

Hiccup the Chief

The second film finds Hiccup at the age of 20, knowing that soon he will face the responsibility of being chief of Berk once his father, Stoick the Vast, relinquishes the

3. The Themes of the HTTYD Trilogy

position. The bounciness of the fun *Hiccup/Vikings* theme is replaced here by longer melodic lines and a range of two octaves. The tempo is slowed and the style is much more sober and much less naïve. In contrast to the D Dorian modality of the *Hiccup* theme, *Hiccup the Chief* is in D major, with the occasional intrusion of D Mixolydian when C♮ is introduced.

The theme is loosely periodic, with the first four measures very closely corresponding to the next four measures. However, a cadence is not present at the end of the first four measure phrase, as the only chord roots used are D, E, G and C, or I, ii, IV and ♭VII in D major, all tonic functioning chords (as the Em/G chord is used in a passing motion). As the theme nears its conclusion in measure 8, an authentic cadential progression is anticipated, but instead of reaching the expected authentic cadence, the final harmony is B major, a chromatic chord in D major, and one that would have the unexpected Roman numeral of VI in D (or V in E). Even stranger is the chord that precedes it, an F half-diminished seventh chord, which would function as ii°7 in E♭, not E. The tritone root motion places the ending of this theme in a very different location than the opening, showing Hiccup's growth, not just from the first to second film, but from the beginning of the second film to its conclusion. More locally, the inconclusive ending on B major allows the cue to move on from this theme in a different direction very smoothly and easily where additional music can easily link up and progress, as these themes are rarely used without music preceding or following them.

Figure 3.12. *Hiccup the Chief* theme.

Drago's Tune

The first film in the trilogy didn't have a human enemy. Instead, Hiccup had to convince his father, along with the rest of Berk, that they could live with the dragons rather than fight them. It took work, and after Hiccup's rejection by his father, Hiccup earned his father's respect and trust, and the village accepted Hiccup's views. In the second film, Drago Bludvist, who commands a dragon army, threatens Berk's way of life, attempting to steal all of Berk's dragons and even temporarily turns Toothless against Hiccup.

The theme initially appears in the cue "War is What He Wants," but the complete *Drago's Tune* occurs in "Meet Drago." It is in C doubly harmonic minor, with the presence of some additional chromatic pitches, and the absence of the leading tone, B, until the second half of the theme. The opening gesture arpeggiates a C minor triad, while the second statement outlines a F♯°7 chord, here functioning as a common-tone diminished seventh chord, with C and E♭ as the common tones between the two harmonies. The next four measures are all centered around C; the melody first sustains an E♮, making the triad C major, then restates itself, pushing down to E♭, returning to C minor. The chromaticism, along with the melodic rhythm, sounds more exotic than just a simple major-to-minor parallel motion, almost as lulled into a trance.

The second part of the theme melodically outlines an incomplete B°7 chord even though the melodic pitches are each harmonized with major triads, certainly an atypical musical illustration. As the theme nears its conclusion, it contains a chromatic harmonic progression leading to the half cadence—♭II-V—while the melodic line's final two-note gesture descends stepwise—F-E♭, C-B♭.

Like the *Dragon Tune* from the first film, *Drago's Tune* is the longest and most chromatic of the themes introduced in the second film. It shares the doubly harmonic minor scale with the *Dragon Tune*, and its melody is typically played by low-ranged instruments. It is meant to sound ominous yet enticing, angry yet soothing, like the character of Drago, who can subjugate nearly any dragon.

Figure 3.13. *Drago's Tune*.

Drago Riff

Drago's fury, ire, and wrath is heard in the two-measure *Drago* riff, often accompanying moments where Drago subjugates dragons. The short and separated sixteenth-note triplets sound harsh because of the space between each one. Since the

Figure 3.14. *Drago* riff.

riff exists outside of a tonal center, the riff is frightening, as the notes could go anywhere since they do not belong to a tonic. However, the *Drago* riff subjugates the notes into a pattern of repetition, like Drago to dragons.

Valka's Tune

Hiccup had always been told his mother, Valka, was dead, killed by dragons, but she has been alive all the time, protecting dragons and creating her own dragon sanctuary. Her theme is first introduced in the cue "Should I Know You?" and this statement of her theme is in G Dorian. Her theme leaps from *Sol* to *Do*, swirling around *Do* in eighth notes before descending stepwise to the first note of the theme. The Dorian mode provides a sense of majesty to *Valka's Tune*. She is not only the long-absent wife of the chief of Berk, but she is also the queen of the dragons in her sanctuary.

Valka's Tune is a four-measure phrase that is repeated, but the contour and rhythm of the theme makes it unique. The harmonies all fit diatonically into the Dorian mode, and by concluding each four-measure phrase on *Sol*, it allows for both a tonic resolution as well as the opportunity to propel into the next phrase, be it a thematic restatement or something new. The presence of both minor tonic and dominant, along with the orchestration, give the theme a sense of majesty, nobility, and pathos.

Figure 3.15. *Valka's Tune*.

Everything Else

Map the World

Map the World is not the main theme in *How to Train Your Dragon 2*, but it does accompany Hiccup when he explores, and it eventually leads him to his mother. The theme prominently features throughout this film. The map Hiccup makes with Toothless enlarges their "known" world, and introduces new characters and new enemies. *Map the World* is unusual in that it is a ten-measure theme grouped as four- and six-measure phrases, respectively. The theme is in C Aeolian and uses harmonies exclusive to that scale. The 6/8 meter, the soprano timbres, and the soft dynamic all contribute to make this theme longing, searching for something … unknown.

Figure 3.16. *Map the World* theme.

The theme is structured as a period without a clear internal cadence. At the beginning of the second phrase, measures 5–6 feature a slight variation on the theme, both melodically and rhythmically, and the music leads to a half cadence in measure 10, a typical place to restart the theme and potentially structure it as a compound period or move in a new melodic direction.

Lost and Found

Lost and Found is the main theme of *How to Train Your Dragon 2*, significantly featured in the cue "Flying with Mother," the memorable montage scene. The first time *Lost and Found* is sounded, in "Hiccup and Toothless Attacked," a complete statement of the first part of the theme is heard, but it is rather skeletal and without much melodic decoration. The theme represents many elements of the film: Hiccup being taken and leaving Toothless behind, Hiccup finding his mother, and Stoick and Valka making up for lost time, among others. The ability to fit different situations makes it one of the most commonly used themes in the second film, as well as being used opportunistically in the third film. There's a sadness to the melody, but also a sense of grandeur, because it concerns not just loss, but also the gain of something new.

The first part of the theme opens in E Aeolian with two four-measure gestures that are very closely related and begin exactly the same. The first hint of oscillating between two tonal centers occurs in mm. 7–9, where the music modulates to G Ionian at the start of the third phrase of the first part. However, the G tonal center is fleeting, as the first part ends on the subdominant chord in E Aeolian in mm. 12–13.

The second part of the theme, mm. 14–19 floats between the E Aeolian and G Ionian, so that when the theme ends on a half cadence in the original E Aeolian mode, it feels like a modulation, even though the music has only briefly left the tonal center.

3. The Themes of the HTTYD Trilogy

Figure 3.17. *Lost and Found* theme.

The incomplete nature of the ending of the theme allows for multiple possible narrative interpretations based on this theme's title.

Good Alpha

The *Good Alpha* theme is initially presented in the cue "Valka's Dragon Sanctuary." In this instance, it serves to highlight the gigantic Bewilderbeast as the Alpha species of dragon, to which even Toothless acknowledges. Ultimately, this theme will come to be associated with Toothless at the end of *How to Train Your Dragon 2*, as he fights and defeats Drago's Bewilderbeast after getting out of its control, with the rest of the dragons deferring to Toothless as the new Alpha.

This theme is majestic, and exclusively stepwise in its melody. The minor dominant harmony, which often oscillates with tonic, is another way in which the power and respect of the Alpha is realized. The theme is six measures long and repeated, often with a restatement sounding a third higher. Toothless, by virtue of his breaking free of Drago's Bewilderbeast's control, has the ability to not only save Berk, but also be redeemed for killing Stoick while under the control of the Bewilderbeast. Hiccup may have assisted Toothless, but Toothless plays the role of the hero in this final battle.

Music theorist Scott Murphy discusses the harmonic relationship between the major tonic and minor dominant triads, positing that the oscillation between the two signifies wonder and transcendence.[7] The size and scope of the Bewilderbeast in Valka's Sanctuary certainly inspires wonder and awe, a dragon beyond comprehension. When Toothless, a small dragon but full of heart and loyalty, attacks Drago's Bewilderbeast, it seems beyond comprehension that all the dragons would side with him over the large dragon, but they follow Toothless. It is a moment of wonder when the dragons assault the Bewilderbeast in order to save their humans, and the harmonic content of this theme speaks to that wonder.

Figure 3.18. *Good Alpha* theme.

Courting Song

The *Courting Song* is sung when Stoick finds Valka and rekindles his relationship with her. He is not angry that she has been gone; instead, he is thankful that she is alive. It is

Figure 3.19. *Courting Song*.

a song that takes them, and us as the audience, back to the start of their relationship. The tune itself is in the style of a traditional folk song, using only four different harmonies throughout the entire song, which is composed in a rounded binary form.

Indicative of a folk song, the melody repeats itself quite often, and rhythms are consistent and recurring. Cadences occur at the end of every four-measure phrase. The contrasting middle section of the rounded binary ends on a half cadence, preparing the return of the original material, and the song closes with an authentic cadential progression—ii^7-V-I—and a PAC.

HTTYD: THW Themes

The final film in the trilogy, *The Hidden World*, concludes everything exceptionally well, giving a new life to Hiccup, to Toothless, and to all the dragons while defeating the last "big boss." Hiccup has matured into the role of the chief of Berk after only one year, and he and his friends continue to rescue dragons from trappers. Several new themes are introduced in this film, such as the *Love* theme for Toothless, the theme for the film's villain, Grimmel, and the majestic theme for the titular Hidden World. Since Powell already had two films of themes on which to draw, he did not introduce as many new themes in this film as in the second installment, but the smaller quantity allows for more development and transformation.

People

Grimmel's Tune

Like the antagonists of the previous films, the theme for Grimmel is the longest of any theme introduced in *The Hidden World*, and like the *Dragon Tune* and *Drago's Tune*, *Grimmel's Tune* is also the most chromatic of any theme introduced in this film. In fact, *Drago's Tune* and *Grimmel's Tune* contain multiple similarities in terms of rhythm and chromaticism, and this connects the two human villains across the films. Grimmel is more sophisticated, more conniving, and more strategic than Drago. As a result, *Grimmel's Tune* begins in one tonal center, but ends in a far different one.

The first part of *Grimmel's Tune* is centric to B♭, and based on the initial harmony, B♭ minor or B♭ Aeolian is somewhat implied. The harmonic rhythm in this first part, which is six measures, is slow, with each harmony lasting one measure. The only chord diatonic to B♭ minor is the opening tonic triad; all other harmonies in this part are chromatic—E°, B♭M, D♭Mm,^{7} and D♭m. The melodic theme has a certain slinkiness to it that highlights Grimmel's forethought and elusiveness. By ending the first part of the theme on a chromatic chord, Powell refutes expectations for its resolution, and immediately resolves up a half-step to a D minor triad, an unconventional harmonic motion.

As the second part of the theme begins, the harmonic rhythm accelerates. Like the first part of *Grimmel's Tune*, the only chord belonging to this new tonic of D minor is the

Figure 3.20. *Grimmel's Tune.*

opening triad. The remaining chords—D♭m, F♯m, Cm, A♭m, and E♭Mm⁷—are all chromatic. The serpentine nature of *Grimmel's Tune* is fully realized as the final note of his theme is enharmonically the same as the first note of his theme, one octave higher. Trying to assign Roman numerals to *Grimmel's Tune* would not elucidate any of the inner workings of the music. Instead, harmonic expectations and conventions are constantly defied, as the melody has slowly climbed over the course of the theme, knowing full well that it would end where it began, as planning is an essential trait of Grimmel.

Heroes

The group of teenagers with whom Hiccup trained are now all in their early 20s. Hiccup, Astrid, Snotlout, Fishlegs, Ruffnut, and Tuffnut form a team that raids the ships of dragon trappers, rescuing and bringing the dragons back to Berk. In the third film, this team gets their own theme, the *Heroes* theme, and like so many of Powell's themes, it has both an A and a B section.

The *Heroes* A theme, in F Aeolian, opens like a sentence, with a two-measure melodic idea that is repeated and elaborated upon. However, the second two-measure group is harmonized quite differently, making the relative mode of A♭ Ionian (major) the emphasized tonal center. Like a typical sentence, the A theme ends after eight measures, except it neither ends with a standard cadence, with an Imperfect Authentic Cadence, nor in a standard place, with the cadence arriving on the downbeat of measure 7. The second half of the A theme contains much more melodic activity than the first half, and also continues the triplet sixteenth-note accompaniment in the violins, arpeggiating gestures that are exciting and worthy of battle. The *Heroes* A theme does not feature swashbuckling rhythms. Instead, it is more reserved and deliberate, although hints of chromaticism show that the heroes can be impulsive.

The structure of the sentence is also used for the *Heroes* B theme, which begins in D minor. The *Heroes* B theme is curious, as melodically it uses both Dorian mode and melodic minor, while the harmonization is based in the functional minor mode. The

3. The Themes of the HTTYD Trilogy

Figure 3.21. *Heroes* theme.

opening two measures, like before, are repeated and varied. The melody of the next two measures contains a similar contour to measures 5–6 from the *A* theme. However, the harmonies between the two locations are quite different, allowing the audience to know which part of the theme is being used. The conclusion of the sentence is unusual in that the final harmony arrives early, in the seventh full measure rather than the eighth and final measure of this portion of the theme.

Perhaps one of the most curious ways that the theme is constructed lies in the opening gesture of each part. The opening of the *Heroes A* theme contains a descending perfect fourth, from F to C, outlining *do-sol* in F. Following the anacrusis, *Heroes B* opens with an ascending melodic leap from D to F and back down to D, *do-me-do*. While the group of young Berkians can be considered heroes, they are not fully ready, evidenced by Valka overseeing their raids along with the atypical harmonic conclusions to both parts of the *Heroes* theme.

March of the Warlords (The Other Bad Guys)

Grimmel is the primary antagonist, but he aligns himself with a group of largely nameless warlords and their armies. As a result, Powell wrote a short theme to differentiate

Figure 3.22. *March of the Warlords.*

them from Grimmel, called the *March of the Warlords*. Like so many themes in the film trilogy, this one is constructed as a sentence, but with half as many measures. The opening gesture, an ascending half-step in sixteenth notes, leaps up a third and steps down, filling in the space. The following measures repeats and slightly varies the opening, with the leap up a fourth before moving down. The second half of the sentence features fragmentation of the opening two measures, with just the ascending half-step in sixteenth notes, gradually rising before the first violins enter, and creates contrary motion with the second violins, who have been playing the melody throughout the theme. The sentence ends on a minor seventh chord; a cadence does not occur, but through the use of the sustained harmony, the theme reaches its logical termination.

The harmonies defy a single tonal center, with neither the opening B nor C making sense as a tonic. Because a functional harmonic progression is not at work in this theme, the music can go nearly anywhere. It is the ascending half-step that holds the theme together in the absence of a clear tonal center. In the article "Chromatic Mediants and Narrative Context in Film," I argue that the pair of minor triads related by chromatic mediant with roots a major third apart is the "Vader" relationship.[8] This relationship represents evil but is not the ultimate evil, as even Vader serves Emperor Palpatine. In this film, the *March of the Warlords* has a more significant name than the role that they play in the film, which is why Powell gave it the alternate name of *The Other Bad Guys*.

Everything Else

Furies in Love

The *Love* theme for Hiccup and Astrid was introduced in the first film. Its initial presentation found Hiccup admiring Astrid from afar, and Astrid wholly unimpressed with Hiccup. Of course, their relationship evolved, and they marry at the end of *The Hidden World*. Toothless gets a love theme in the third film, and his arc mirrors Hiccup's, but much more rapidly as he falls in love with the Light Fury.

In the early stages of the film, *Furies in Love* is introduced, bit by bit. Each time, more of the theme is revealed, but it isn't until "Romance in the Clouds" that the full theme is sounded. In the theme's pure form, C Dorian is the opening modality and the theme is structured as a sentence, with the first two measures repeated in the succeeding two measures, with only small cosmetic melodic adjustments. The large-scale harmony

3. The Themes of the HTTYD Trilogy 51

has an alternation of C minor and F major, the Roman numerals i and IV in C Dorian. The second half of *Furies in Love*'s sentence, beginning in measure 5, finds the two furies kissing. The first "kiss" motive contains a tonicized progression of ii°7-I in B♭ major, confirming their love, while the restated motive contains another tonicized progression of iv7-V7-I, now in G minor, allowing for the melodic theme to remain in B♭ and continue to soar. These tonicizations should not be read as though the two furies are not in love. It is quite the opposite—the shifting tonal motion allows for the theme to continue, to leap an octave and soar into the air, their hearts leaping, before finally concluding on a G dominant seventh chord, the dominant in the home tonality of C. *Furies in Love* is a magical theme with a unique rhythmic profile and breathtaking harmonic motion to convey the love between the two remaining Furies, Light and Night.

Powell had quite a bit to say concerning how the *Furies in Love* theme was introduced, bit by bit, in the first half of the film. He said:

> Believability is basically zero on all films, until it's not. We're watching something, and at any point, you could say to yourself, "Dragons don't exist. What am I watching?" When films work, your believability is being suppressed. The analysis of what is real and what isn't has to be suppressed by a stronger idea. I was thinking, I can't crack on with a giant romantic theme as soon as we see the Light Fury. We have to be behind the audience a little. If the film composer is ahead of the audience, it's very irritating. It's manipulative. You feel like, "I know. I don't need you to tell me this." I was trying to think, "What is the audience feeling at this moment?" The most I would have felt at the first moment is, "Oh! Maybe he likes her," and that's all. Realistically I would have tried to write the theme where I needed it to be complete, and that's the place where they're in the clouds, so that's where it gets written. Then you go backwards and find the other places, and then you try and reduce it and reduce it so it grows to the right place. Then you're never ahead of the audience and you're building the scaffolding to get to the arrival where it pays off so it feels suddenly new.

Figure 3.23. *Furies in Love* theme.

John Williams is the master of that. *E.T.* is the perfect example. You get to the end of the film and you see it completed. And all the way through the movie you see it, but never all the way quite full and complete and it never really is as satisfying. The danger would be if he started earlier, and if he reached the musical and emotional climax to soon, where's he going to go from there? He very smartly always tries to go to the important place where the theme needs to resonate in its biggest and grandest form, and then build towards that. It's just development and the idea to not give everything away, but that's the antithesis of symphonic form! The functionality of it is, "Don't manipulate the audience." If you poke the audience in the wrong way, they'll just snap out of the film.

[Director] George Miller said this to me: "We have to keep the audience on the wave." He's Australian, so a surfer. "If you go too fast, they'll fall off the back. Too slow, they'll slide down the front and there's no momentum. It's about keeping them on the perfect part of the wave without it cresting over or pushing them forward or pushing them back." I do believe in that. I'm probably guilty of not doing it enough or too much, but ever since working with George, I've tried to be aware of where I am as a normal audience member. If the music can support the story without me noticing, as an audience member, as in, "a little later than I thought it," then the music can help you say, "Yes, that's how I feel, and that music is perfect for how I feel about this."

The emotional moment I have: understanding something, or falling in love with a character because of something they've just said, or realizing the character is broken. All of those moments need to be scored in resonance with what I'm thinking as an audience member, not what the film is trying to tell you. It's hard, because sometimes as a composer you have to provide clarity. The other side of that is sometimes you need to say to an audience, "Yes, this is important. In case you're wondering, yes, this is important." And you try not to say too much, and that's when shifting or change is good. Change can just be starting a cue. Change can be stopping a cue. Any change is good when it's clear to help you know the beats of the story, the moments where the story is shifting. If you can do something that also supports not only the change, but the emotion you have as an audience member realizing something has changed. It's a long-winded way of saying, "Don't do too much!"

Light Fury Motif

The first hint of a potential love theme occurs at the end of the opening cue, "Rescue Mission." This softer and gentler musical gesture, the *Light Fury Motif*, is used throughout the film, as the two furies are trying to feel each other out, almost in flirtation. While C♯ major is functioning as tonic, the other harmonies, F♯m and Bm, do not originate from the same C♯ modal scale. In fact, the scale is much closer to C♯ Phrygian, but with a raised third scale degree, or perhaps even F♯ minor. However, the tonic is clearly

Figure 3.24. *Light Fury Motif.*

not F♯, as the C♯ major triad provides stability. Needless to say, the *Light Fury Motif* sounds magical in its musical construction and defies a single Roman numeral analysis, as it should.

Village Hymn

The village of Berk must be relocated due to the incredible number of dragons it houses, along with Grimmel's attack. Powell wrote a *Village Hymn* and in its initial statement, it is scored for strings alone: violins I and II, violas, and cellos (no basses), a traditional string quartet, but with an entire section rather than a single player on a part. This hymn is only seventeen measures long (16 measures plus a resolution) and is constructed as a period with a half cadence in the middle and an Aeolian cadence at the end. Each four-measure idea concludes on a major triad, somewhat surprising for a melody in Dorian mode, but Powell doesn't confine the harmonies to the Dorian mode. Instead, he uses multiple forms of minor modes—Aeolian, Dorian, and harmonic minor—to harmonize the melody.

The *Village Hymn* serves as both an *alma mater*-like melodic statement, paying homage to the seven generations of Berkians who lived there, and as an elegy for a village that is no longer sustainable in its current circumstances. The theme is typically at

Figure 3.25. *Village Hymn.*

a dynamic of *piano* and marked *dolce* (meaning "sweetly"), and the music rarely rises above the soft volume. The theme is a solemn reminder of all that has occurred in Berk, and all that will change and start anew in New Berk.

The *Village Hymn* is a spiritual relative of the English folk song "Dives and Lazarus," a tune famously set by Ralph Vaughan Williams as *Five Variants of 'Dives and Lazarus.'* That folk tune, in B Aeolian, features major triads at the end of each two-measure idea of its eight-measure theme, sharing proportionalities with the *Village Hymn*, and concludes with an Aeolian cadence at its end. Of course, the melodies are quite different, but the solemn treatment and the modal harmonization of the melody highlights the shared qualities between the folk song and Powell's theme.[9]

Fate Tune

The first film in the trilogy presented a *Fate* theme associated with Hiccup; his fate was to learn to tame dragons and become a dragon rider. In the third film, a new *Fate Tune* is introduced that tells of the legend of the Hidden World, the source of all dragons, who are fated to leave Berk for their own secret and safe location.

The *Fate Tune* is lengthy and its melody is often broken between various instruments in the orchestra, rather than being played by a single instrument as so many of the themes are. The fluctuation between the relative minor and major keys of C minor and E♭ major makes this theme special among the themes in the trilogy, as no other themes feature this oscillation. The *Fate Tune* is thirty measures long and can be parsed into two even halves, with a questionable half cadence on the downbeat of measure 8 (questionable due to the local tonality), and an authentic cadence as the theme's conclusion featuring a tritone substitution, D♭M for GM. Both cadences could potentially be heard in F minor, but the internal cadence in measure 15 finds the harmony shifting from the CM cadence chord to Cm, creating the feeling of nullifying the cadence, a pause that isn't really a pause.

The fluctuation between the keys, combined with the questionable cadences, create a sensation of not wanting to let go. Hiccup holds on to the idea that everyone, humans and dragons, will move to the Hidden World for as long as he can. It is only when he visits the location that he realizes he doesn't belong there, and instead

Figure 3.26. *Fate Tune.*

hopes Toothless and the rest of the dragons will stay in New Berk by their own choice. Of course, the dragons will choose the Hidden World, but Hiccup's hope remains in the form of the half cadence at the theme's conclusion. By giving the theme an 'open-ended conclusion, Powell allows for the possibility of further interaction and engagement between Hiccup and Toothless, which is what we find in the final scene of the film.

Fate Riff

The *Fate* riff is much like the *Action Motif* in that it is largely accompanimental rather than melodic or thematic. However, it is significant enough to be thought of thematically, like the *Flying Ostinato*. The *Fate* riff is a ten-beat pattern that naturally repeats the pattern over the span of two measures of 5/4. However, the *Fate* riff most often appears in measures of 6/4 meter, meaning that the pattern will sound four times over five measures, skewing the expectation of four-measure phrases. Because the start of the *Fate* riff is metrically displaced in every instance, the music gives the impression of being more arbitrarily constructed than it actually is.

With Powell's writing, though, another layer can usually be found. As the *Fate* riff appears in the film, the violins and violas all play the *Fate* riff in three octaves. At a glance, it appears that the cellos play the same thing, another octave lower. However, the pattern in the cellos repeats in every 6/4 measure; it is three eighth notes shorter and contains different notes than the *Fate* riff. The cello part will occur five times during the four statements of the *Fate* riff, further contributing to the disorientation and faux-random pitch construction of the theme.

Figure 3.27. *Fate* riff.

Sex Riff

The *Sex* riff is a four-measure theme that is used when Toothless is wooing the Light Fury, and is the foundation of the cue "Toothless Goes a–Courtin'." The harmonic rhythm significantly increases in the second half of the *Sex* riff, as the first two measures each contain a single harmony. As the harmonic rhythm increases, so does the syncopation in both the rhythm and the melody. The theme is playful and the articulation is light, as indicated by the *staccato* notes. The end of the riff, despite being harmonized

Figure 3.28. *Sex* riff.

as V-I in F major, prepares a circular return of the opening measure, as the notes A and F are not only *Mi* and *Do* in F major, but *Sol* and *Me* in D minor, the key of the *Sex* riff.

Courting Riff

The *Courting* riff often accompanies the *Sex* riff or is used in lieu of it. Its derivation is from the *Sex* riff, and it maintains the same harmonies.

Figure 3.29. *Courting* riff.

The Hidden World

The title theme from the third film is arguably the most familiar from the film, even though it may not be the film's primary theme. Like so many of the themes in the trilogy, this one is modal, in F Aeolian, and adheres strictly to the mode. The complete theme features three complete statements of the eight-measure theme, which is constructed as a sentence, with the first two measures repeated in the next two measures. The second phrase of the theme performs as expected, except for each of its conclusions, only one of which arrives on a true cadence chord.

The *Hidden World* theme is majestic, with its opening ascending leap of a perfect fifth recalling regal horn fanfares, along with several large leaps in the bass line, including instances of octave leaps. The Aeolian mode provides the theme with a sense of timelessness and gravitas appropriate to accompany the source of all dragons, and the "welcoming home" of Toothless, the Alpha Dragon. The subtonic chord, a harmony often used as a substitute chord for the

Above and following page: Figure 3.30. *The Hidden World* theme.

dominant in the minor mode, E♭ major in F Aeolian, is nearly absent in this theme. The dominant chord, here C minor, is treated as just another minor triad, with G featuring prominently in the bass as an arpeggiation of the C minor tonic triad. When the mediant chord, A♭ major, appears in the theme, it typically appears in first inversion, sounding more like a minor dominant chord rather than a major triad. Root position major triads are entirely absent in this theme, yet another way that *The Hidden World* theme and its location are set apart from other themes in the film trilogy.

4

How to Train Your Dragon Cue Analysis

1M2alt—This is Berk (0:00:01–0:06:05)

3–14—Flying A (F major)
16–24—Hiccup/Vikings (F Dorian/Aeolian)
25–33—Flying B (A-flat major)
42–49—Hiccup/Vikings (B-flat Aeolian)
50–53—Warring Vikings (E-flat Aeolian)
54–59—Hiccup/Vikings (B-flat Aeolian)
61–70—Vikings B/C/D (B = F Aeolian despite harmonization;
   C = G-sharp major; D = F-sharp Dorian)
72–79—Hiccup/Vikings (B Dorian/Aeolian)
80–83—Warring Vikings (B Aeolian)
88–91—Warring Vikings (C Aeolian)
92–95—Warring Vikings (F Aeolian)
98–107—Love theme (A-flat major)
109–117—Vikings A (B-flat major)
118–123—Vikings A (B-flat major)
140–143—Warring Vikings (G Aeolian)
152–167—Dragon Tune (D doubly harmonic minor)
168–183—Dragon Tune (D doubly harmonic minor)
184–191—Warring Vikings variation (D Aeolian)
192–204—Heroic Dragon (G Mixolydian)

The film's opening cue is nearly its longest, as Powell treats this cue like an opera overture, introducing many of the themes heard throughout the film. Quite unusually, the cue opens with horns playing the *Flying A* theme over a pedal F as the moon logo of Dreamworks fades in. Typically, the studio logo has its own short thematic statement, but it is foregone in lieu of Powell's music. The performance marking, "Warmly," indicates that the music should be played with tenderness, not aggression; Powell rewrote this opening section, as the original opening was thought to be too forceful. The *Flying A* theme remains incomplete and segues into a gentle statement of the *Hiccup* theme, played softly by the solo bassoon. This theme adds harps and choir to its accompaniment, further reinforcing the gentle nature of the music and the idyllic presentation of the life of the Berkian Vikings. In his 2021 American Musicological Society Annual Meeting presentation, Dan Obluda focuses on the harmonic motion and oscillation between the triads Fm and B♭M, a relationship that emphasizes nature. He states that as we hear the "rustic" version of the *Hiccup* theme, we see cinematography that foregrounds the natural environment and exciting camera motion.[1] The ranges of both opening thematic statements are lower than typically used throughout the film in order to provide contrast with the upcoming larger orchestration and octave displacement of the subsequent theme, as well as supporting the action-taking nature of the Vikings.

The *Hiccup* theme is completed and moves directly into the *Flying B* theme, where the theme is played by the pennywhistle, implying a Celtic feel to the music. The orchestration continues to grow, but the dynamic remains relatively soft. Berk is still an idyllic place, despite its description through Hiccup's voice-over narration. It is only when Hiccup states the real problem with Berk that the music immediately becomes more intense—faster and louder—and the action shifts from idyllic to battle.

At this shift, measures 37–39, Powell uses a gesture similar to one found in Gustav Holst's "Mercury" from *The Planets*, namely tritone root-related triads. Mercury was the messenger of the gods, indicating that he could fly by wearing winged shoes and a

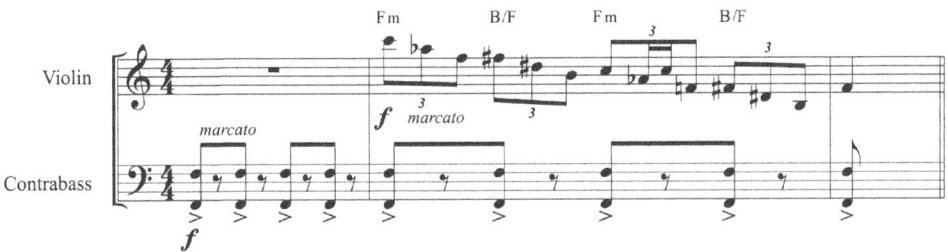

Figure 4.1a. 1M2, measures 37–39, tritone related harmonies.

Figure 4.1b. Holst, "Mercury" from *The Planets*, measures 1–3, tritone related harmonies.

winged helmet, and as shown on screen, dragons can fly. The tritone-related gestures are shown in Figures 4.1a and 4.1b.

In Figure 4.1b, the example from "Mercury," two triads whose roots are offset by a tritone, B♭ major and E major, rise through the string parts, jumping an octave with each statement. The alternation of major triads a tritone apart is a gesture synonymous in film music with outer space, certainly a topic with which the god Mercury, who could fly, would be appropriate. Powell takes this gesture, shown in Figure 4.1a, and uses two triads whose roots are offset by a tritone, F minor and B major, and uses them to descend two octaves in just one measure, one octave for each statement, as the audience is about to see the dragon attack. The alternation of minor and major triads does not imply outer space, but the rhythm and the tritone root motion can easily be referenced back to Holst, as the dragons can also fly, and often swoop down to snatch food and attack their prey and enemies.

The cue reaches its first exciting moment in measure 42 as the *Hiccup* theme is reintroduced in horns, upper woodwinds, and Uilleann pipes, followed by an immediate restatement by the *tutti* orchestra. A new theme, the *Warring Vikings* theme, is then introduced in the low woodwinds, low brass, low strings, and piano. The parts are marked *pesante*, giving even more force to each note beyond the *forte* dynamic. The *Hiccup* theme returns, followed by a codetta that repeats the final measure of his theme. Here it is passed around the orchestra, becoming less forceful, more detached, and sillier with each statement.

As the Vikings, notably Stoick, Berk's chief, fight back against the dragons, the *Vikings* theme is introduced. Curiously, the opening section of the *Vikings* theme is absent, unused until later in the cue. Instead, the B, C, and D sections of the theme are used here, modified to fit into minor modes rather than their more expected and typical use in major. Despite the use of the minor modes of Aeolian and Dorian, many of the harmonies are major triads, imbuing the music with a sense of fight and nobility, and of timelessness, all of which are further reinforced through the presence of the men's choir in this passage.

The *Hiccup* theme returns yet again in the horns and trumpets, now in B Aeolian, and at its loudest dynamic of *fortissimo*, supported by "Hom hah!" articulations in the men's choir, as the catapult is hoisted. The Vikings of Berk are doing what they do best. The immediate restatement of the *Hiccup* theme is timbrally different, played only by the flute; success is not imminent with Hiccup involved.

The *Warring Vikings* theme returns in rhythmic augmentation, in synchronization with launching of the catapults. The immediate restatement of the *Warring Vikings* theme, which becomes typically used throughout the films, is a perfect fourth higher, expected based on the ending of the theme, and enhances the drama and tension.

Through the explosions and destruction occurring all across Berk, the *Love* theme is introduced. Astrid is the girl of Hiccup's dreams, but the visual introduction of the character is anything except romantic. Astrid is seen walking toward the camera, explosions occurring behind her, in what will come to be a running gag across the trilogy. The typical action trope of the male hero walking away from the explosion is turned on its head through the use of a female character, romantic melodies, and higher timbres. Astrid is no damsel in distress; she is a warrior, an action hero, respected by her peers and the adults of Berk, and is visually introduced like the stereotypical male action hero in contrast to Hiccup and his immature body and skills. The theme, marked *con affetto*, is a gentle, affectionate theme, completely working against the image in the film. Because Hiccup is narrating, he is paying attention to Astrid and not the ongoing battle in which he finds himself, a common problem with Hiccup. Only the first half of the *Love* theme is used here, a major-mode theme, which then moves directly into another major-mode theme, the *Vikings A* theme, its first statement in the film, initially played by a solo clarinet, then by the horns, but the horn statement is interrupted as Hiccup accidentally knocks out a Viking with a catapult, his lack of skill on full display.

A long thematic break occurs in measures 124–139. The melody in these measures is dominated by a lower neighbor gesture of a half-step. In the themes heard so far, nearly every lower neighbor is a whole step—in the *Hiccup* theme and in the *Warring Vikings* theme. The bass line in measures 125–132 also operates with neighbor motion, but upper neighbors in measures 125–128, then lower neighbors in measures 129–132, and still half-steps in all instances. The descending triplet arpeggios in the woodwinds are reminiscent of the tritone passage from earlier in the cue, but the root motions are in thirds and fourths instead of tritones. All of these elements combine to make the music familiar, yet without a clear thematic recall. Narratively, Gobber tells Hiccup to "stop being all of … this," as he points to Hiccup. The Vikings of Berk do not think very highly of Hiccup, and it would not be appropriate to associate this exchange with a specific theme. But the music needs to remain in an appropriate style to connect to the next theme. Powell does a terrific job of staying out of the way in this section.

A quick statement of the *Warring Vikings* theme, in rhythmic augmentation, is sounded before a grand pause and the introduction of the warpipes to signal a more serious dragon attack. It is at this point that the *Dragon Tune* is introduced. Marked "Barbaric," we hear Hiccup's narration: "Killing a dragon is everything around here." Through this statement and the music, it is clear that the dragons are the antagonists of this film, destroying the things the inhabitants of Berk love. The *Dragon Tune* is stated in full twice, taking destructive and ominous actions against the village. Finally, a seemingly confident Hiccup is accompanied by a variation of the *Warring Vikings* theme, harmonized exclusively with major triads. As Hiccup heads into battle, a major-mode variation of the *Dragon Tune* that I will call *Heroic Dragon* is sounded, seen in Figure 4.2, and this theme concludes the cue.

Figure 4.2. 1M2, measures 192–204, *Heroic Dragon* variation of *Dragon Tune*.

The passage from measure 184 through the end of the cue is extraordinary, as Powell takes two themes and transforms them both, but unites them through harmony and expectation. At this point in the cue, we expect to hear the *Warring Vikings* theme twice, with the restatement a perfect fourth higher than the original. In measure 184, the *Warring Vikings* theme begins in D Aeolian. When the restatement presumably begins in measure 192, it is in G Aeolian. That expectation is fulfilled. Even the harmonies in measures 184–185—DM-GM-FM-B♭M—nearly correspond to the harmonies in measures 192–193—GM-CM-B♭M-DM. This theme ultimately results in an Aeolian cadence in D in measures 201–202, followed by a brief cadential extension to keep the music from reaching a full stop.

How does Powell create the *Heroic Dragon* variation in spite of the clear melodic and thematic differences of the *Warring Vikings* and *Dragon Tune*? The opening note in both themes here lasts for the entire measure. After that, the contours and rhythms are similar, leading the audience to think this is yet another transformation of the *Warring Vikings* theme. It is only at the sixteenth notes that an astute listener might notice the rhythmic similarity to the *Dragon Tune* rather than the *Warring Vikings* theme, and then make the connection beyond the *Warring Vikings* theme. A comparison of the *Dragon Tune* and *Heroic Dragon* music is illustrated in Figure 4.3.

A typical opera overture doesn't introduce every theme present in the work, and neither does Powell in this cue. Only part of the *Love* theme is heard, and the *Flying Ostinato* and *Fate* theme are both absent. However, these absences should be expected. The second part of the *Love* theme hints more at a romantic relationship between Astrid and Hiccup, a relationship which is nowhere close to that point at the opening of the film. Hiccup and Toothless have not met, so the *Fate* theme is not relevant, nor is the *Flying Ostinato*. Likewise, Hiccup has not learned how to calm a dragon, so the *Calming Motif* is absent here as well. Even though both parts of the *Flying* theme appear, they are used only during the opening studio credits portion of the cue rather than the Berk

Figure 4.3. Comparison of *Dragon Tune* and *Heroic Dragon*.

battle, but their inclusion is necessary, as the *Flying* theme should be considered as the primary theme of the film trilogy. The truly amazing ways in which Powell connects the themes in this cue, as well as the amount of thematic content, offer an exciting model for beginning a film.

1M6—Anybody See That? (0:06:08–0:07:22)

12–16—Vikings A (F-sharp major)
19–22—Warring Vikings (G Aeolian)
23–24—Warring Vikings (C Aeolian)
30–44—Hiccup/Vikings (C Aeolian)

The full cue, as written, does not appear in the film. On the album, the cue begins with string harmonics and bowed glass marimba and waterphone, creating an eerie and mysterious effect. In measure 5, a B major/E♭ major polychord is played in the violas and cellos, adding to the dissonance and opaqueness of the music.

When the cue begins in the film, in measure 10, it begins on an F♯ minor triad, a harmony much simpler than what appeared in the first nine measures. The F♯ minor triad becomes an F♯ major triad, and leads into the *Vikings A* theme, as Hiccup believes he has taken down a Night Fury, a very rare and fearsome type of dragon, his first step in becoming a full-fledged Viking. No one else is around to see it, and the first phrase of the *Vikings A* theme is interrupted by dissonance, a D major/A♭ major polychord. The two triads are a tritone apart, yet Powell does not use them to convey a sense of outer space. Instead, the polychord functions to support the miraculous achievement of Hiccup.

As Hiccup runs to tell the rest of the village of his accomplishment, we see Stoick and hear the *Warring Vikings* theme in G Aeolian. The previous polychord, in light of the new tonal center, is quite remarkable, as A♭ major is the Neapolitan chord, which has a predominant function, and D major is the dominant. Both functions are heard simultaneously, predominant and dominant, before correctly resolving to G minor, the tonic. The expected restatement of the *Warring Vikings* theme occurs a fourth higher in C Aeolian, but only the first two measures are used as the harmony becomes static, sustaining a G/D open fifth. This open fifth functions as the dominant into the C Aeolian statement of the *Hiccup* theme, which is used for the remainder of the cue. The excitement and bounciness of the theme is at its peak as Hiccup's excitement at capturing a Night Fury can hardly be contained.

The statement of the *Hiccup* theme in measures 30–33 is *tutti*, but the restatement in measures 34–37 is harmonized in C minor, using the Roman numerals i-III-VI-iv, i-III-VI-iv-i. These harmonies are all diatonic to C minor/Aeolian, and they all serve to prolong the tonic function, meaning that the harmony doesn't truly progress. A unison *tutti* thematic statement is essentially without harmony, meaning it too does not have a harmonic progression. Powell finds two highly different ways to accomplish the same task, keeping the familiar melody but altering the accompaniment.

1M7A—War Room (0:09:17–0:09:55)

1–2—Warring Vikings *inverted* (E Aeolian)
2–3—Vikings (E major)
4–6—Warring Vikings *inverted* (E Aeolian)
8–10—Warring Vikings (E Aeolian)

Figure 4.4. Vaughan Williams, *Symphony No. 5*, movement I, measures 205–207 (transposed); 1M7, measures 1–2; *Warring Vikings* theme, transposed and rhythmically altered.

A solo horn call, reminiscent of one in the first movement of Ralph Vaughan Williams's *Symphony No. 5*, opens this cue. It is a rhythmically altered and melodically varied Warring Vikings statement. A comparison between the Vaughan Williams excerpt and the opening horn call appears as Figure 4.4.

Three themes are heard in quick succession: the varied *Warring Vikings*, the opening of *Vikings A*, and the full *Warring Vikings* theme. When the *Warring Vikings* statement is used in full, it is played by bassoon and cello, with wordless men's choir and snare drum accompanying the theme. The orchestration immediately indicates the militaristic nature of the cue, as the Vikings are creating a battle strategy against the dragons. Hiccup does not belong in the war room, which is why the opening horn call is something of an incorrect *Warring Vikings* statement; too short, incorrect melodic contour, entering at the wrong time. Through the dialogue, it has been made clear that Hiccup is an issue for the Vikings of Berk, causing problems that others need to solve. He needs to be watched (or babysat), even though he should be able to function on his own as a teenager. The war room percussion shows how far away Hiccup is from being a true Viking.

1M7B-C—Training Out There (0:11:16–0:14:45)

3–4—Flying Ostinato (E Aeolian)
7–10—Warring Vikings *inverted* (E Dorian)
11–13—Warring Vikings *inverted* (B-flat major)
13–18—Vikings A (G major)
19–26—Fate theme (D Aeolian)
70–73—Warring Vikings (F-sharp Aeolian)
74–77—Flying Ostinato highly varied (D Aeolian, shifting to chromatic)
78–84—Flying Ostinato (A Aeolian)
86–90—Flying A reharmonized (unclear)
98–103—Flying Ostinato (G Phrygian)

Like 1M6, this cue is also abbreviated in the film. The opening of the album version of this cue features the first hint of the *Flying Ostinato*, but here, it is in E Aeolian, and the intervallic content is wrong, largely because it begins on *Me* in E minor, the note G, and not *Do* or *Sol*. As Stoick tells Hiccup of days gone by, the *Warring Vikings* theme is inverted and played in rhythmic diminution, twice in E Dorian, then a third statement in B♭ major, a jarring tonal center a tritone away from E. These are not current stories, hence the modified statements of the *Warring Vikings* theme. All of this material is cut from the film.

When the cue enters in the film at measure 13, it opens with the first phrase of the *Vikings A* theme in G major, ending with a half cadence. The third of the D major triad, F♯, is lowered to F♮, and the first statement of the *Fate* theme enters in D Dorian. The harmonization is different than when the standard theme is sounded, and as a result, this statement doesn't end with any conviction, segueing into the moment where Hiccup discovers Toothless. The *Fate* theme is not fully realized here, as Hiccup still believes he needs to kill the Night Fury to win his father's approval, which is not Hiccup's true fate.

As Hiccup comes across the injured Toothless, the music becomes much more ethereal, beginning in measure 31, using a technique of bowing instruments usually struck or strummed, such as the marimba, gong, and guitar, and combining this with violin harmonics. The resulting sound is quite unusual and unexpected; no one in Berk has ever seen a Night Fury. Hiccup peeks at Toothless from his hiding spot, and a chromatic cluster of notes slowly ascends through a glissando to the highest possible pitch on the violin. This dissonance is accentuated through the sustained chromatic notes in the strings and woodwinds, the stopped horn notes, and continued percussion. To further highlight the unfamiliarity, Powell uses harmonies from the Octatonic (0,1) scale as Toothless moves his foot, followed by an E♭M/BM polychord in the strings, measures 58–62. This is the polychord from the opening of "Anybody See That," the portion that was ultimately cut from the film. Further dissonance is added through a CMmm^9 chord in the woodwinds in measures 60–62, almost creating the complete Octatonic (0,1) scale, with the note B replacing A in the scale in this harmony. The chord resolves to an F♯ minor triad as Hiccup resolves to slay the injured Night Fury. The *Warring Vikings* theme enters, as Hiccup is about to become a "true" Viking through slaying the dragon. As Hiccup raises the knife, we hear a harmonic passage of Em-Dm-Fm-Am-Fm. The minor chromatic mediant relationships, particularly the Fm-Am pair, traditionally indicates evil or antagonism in film music. One reading of this progression is that Hiccup slaying Toothless would be an act of evil, one unnecessary and unprovoked. As Toothless looks at Hiccup, knife raised, we hear the minor version of the *Flying Ostinato*, indicating following through would be a poor choice. When Hiccup determines he can't kill the dragon, the *Flying A* theme is heard, but transformed and with the "incorrect" harmonic support, shown in Figure 4.5. The music provides a hint of what's to come in their relationship, but it is not yet ready to flourish.

Toothless is quite agitated and lunges at Hiccup. With the dragon's eyes visible, the gadulka and hurdy-gurdy are used to play the *Flying Ostinato* in G Phrygian, a familiar melody on unfamiliar timbres and in an unfamiliar scale. The Night Fury, the most

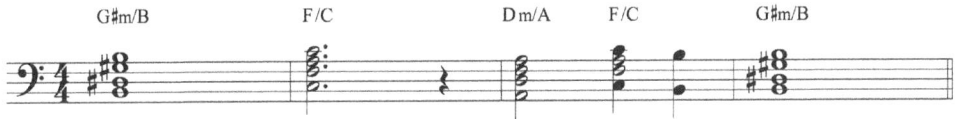

Figure 4.5. 1M7B-C, measures 86–89, reharmonization of *Flying A*.

mysterious of all dragons, is viewed in full by Hiccup. Additionally, the Hardanger fiddle plays a descending scalar line in G—D-C-B-A♭—that doesn't belong to a typical diatonic mode, but can fit into the Octatonic (2,3) scale. Unusual percussion, such as the surdo, brekete, and waterphone, assist in creating this foreign soundscape; no one has been left alive by a Night Fury before, nor has anyone seen one up close and lived to tell about it. A new relationship has begun to be forged between Hiccup and Toothless due to Hiccup's benevolence.

2M8—Hiccup Comes Home (0:15:11–0:15:29)

2-9—Dragon Tune (C Aeolian)

This is an extremely short cue, only nine measures long, with a C pedal sounding throughout the cue. Melodically, the cue uses the opening of the *Dragon Tune*, but is harmonized with Cm, GM, Gm, and Am, as opposed to a single tonic chord, as it appeared in 1M2.

2M9—Dragon Training (0:16:52–0:19:58)

2-10—Warring Vikings variation (A Aeolian)
59-61—Warring Vikings *inverted* and variation (D Aeolian)
76-79—Warring Vikings (A Aeolian)
80-83—Warring Vikings (D Aeolian)
92-106—Dragon Tune (G doubly harmonic minor)

Hiccup, Astrid, and the rest of the teenagers get the opportunity to begin training to learn to kill dragons in battle. Their teacher, Gobber, introduces the teens to a Gronkel by simply putting them in harm's way and having them receive "on-the-job" training. The prelude to the training shows the teens entering the arena, accompanied by the *Warring Vikings* theme, as turning them into adult Vikings is the goal of the training. As the realization of what's about to occur sets in for the teens, the horns play a descending A Phrygian pentachord over the A minor harmony in measures 20–21, adding depth and a bit of uncertainty to the impending fight.

An intense four-measure repeating pattern begins, seen as Figure 4.6, growing in dynamics, range, orchestration, and intensity until the Gronkel bursts out of its cage to loud percussion drums and bagpipes. The music in this section, measures 24–51, is not thematic, but the melodic leap of a perfect fifth and the harmonies are somewhat reminiscent of the *Dragon Tune*. As the teens battle the Gronkel, the *Warring Vikings* theme is played twice in succession, first in A, then in D with a new harmonization, but it is clear that the Gronkel has the upper hand, as the music tries to initiate the *Dragon Tune*, and successfully does so in measure 92, starting with the fourth measure of the theme. The conclusion of the *Dragon Tune* finds Hiccup pinned while the music plays a D♯°7/E chord, a highly dissonant harmony. Gobber hooks the Gronkel and drags it back to its

Figure 4.6. 2M9, measures 24–27, ostinato pattern.

cage, and the harmony ends, leaving only the sustained E. As Gobber drops the door latch, imprisoning the Gronkel, the E drops to E♭ and the cue concludes. Hiccup can come down from the stress of the fight, which is reflected in the pitch descent.

2M10—Wounded (0:20:41–0:22:03)

6–10—Flying A (D major)
21—Flying A (interrupted) (D major)
23–27—Flying A (F major)

This cue remains at one tempo, one marking ("Mystical"), and uses a single thematic element—the *Flying A* theme, but consistently reharmonized. The long and sustained notes in the strings and winds, combined with the chromatic flourishes in the woodwinds and harp, conjure the support of Hiccup watching the injured Night Fury try to fly with its injured tail. Each attempt is unsuccessful, but something changes over the course of the cue: Hiccup offers the dragon a fish, which it accepts, marking another step in their relationship. The cue ends in F major, a minor third higher than where it started in D major, a chromatic mediant relationship typically associated with heroism in film. Together with Toothless, Hiccup will become the film's hero through friendship with the dragons rather than war.

2M11—The Dragon Book (0:23:16–0:25:33)

1–5—Flying A (D major)
6–10—Flying A (D major)
15–23—Dragon Tune (D doubly harmonic minor)
24–30—Flying Ostinato (D Aeolian, but raised third sometimes)
34–39—Warring Vikings (A Aeolian)

The same reharmonized *Flying A* theme heard in 2M10 opens 2M11, again in D major. Hiccup looks through the Dragon Book to find information on the Night Fury. As he flips through the book, nearly every entry ends with "Kill on sight." The *Dragon Tune* enters in measure 15 with a normalized rhythm (no dotted rhythms or values less than an eighth note), only reaching the midpoint of the theme. When Hiccup reaches the Night Fury entry in the book, a varied form of the *Flying Ostinato* is played by the dulcimer in measure 24. The scale used here is quite unusual—D Phrygian, but with F♯ rather than F♮. This is the same type of scale used by the Hardanger Fiddle back in 1M7B-C. This portion of the cue dissolves on an A♭ major triad as the action shifts to Stoick searching for the dragon nest out in the ocean, not just a shift in location, but also a shift in generational thought. We hear the *Warring Vikings* theme played by the esraj in A♭ Aeolian, a new and unfamiliar timbre, followed by militaristic percussion before the cue ends on an E♭m^{add9} chord that accompanies a flash of light; something *is* out there, yet to be found.

2M12—Hiccup Focus (0:25:43–0:27:42)

1–8—Action Motif (starts on C)
2–9—Dragon Tune (C doubly harmonic minor)
10–14—Action Motif (starts on E)
12–14—Warring Vikings variation (E harmonic minor)
23–26—Action Motif (starts on E-flat)

33–34—Dragon Tune (G-sharp doubly harmonic minor)
35–39—Warring Vikings (F Aeolian)
41–46—Action Motif (starts on G)
41–43—Warring Vikings variation (D melodic minor)
42–46—Action Motif (starts on B)
47–49—Warring Vikings (E Aeolian)
55–56—Action Motif (starts on C)
58–66—Action Motif (starts on C-sharp)

Like 2M9, this cue also deals with the teenagers battling a dragon in a "safe" chaperoned environment. Unlike 2M9, this cue just drops the audience into the action without preparation, beginning with the *Action Motif* on C. Combined with the percussion, the *Action Motif* serves as an ostinato to support the *Dragon Tune*. At measure 10, when the *Dragon Tune* is interrupted and left incomplete, the *Action Motif* rises a major third to begin on E. The intensity and stakes are now higher than they were just moments ago, and when the "Nut Twins," Ruffnut and Tuffnut, pause, tritones are sounded on C-F♯ and A-E♭ as a whole-tone scale gesture cascades down through the orchestra.

The *Action Motif*, along with the percussion, resumes at measure 23, now beginning on D♯. Hiccup's questions to Gobber interrupt the music, and as he is forced to reengage with the dragon, we hear a 6:4 polyrhythm between the woodwinds and strings. Hiccup is asking questions that are viewed as unnecessary, reflected in the polyrhythm, instead of just fighting like everyone else. Astrid gets Hiccup's attention and the *Action Motif* resumes on C. She fights the dragon, accompanied by the *Warring Viking* theme, and after the dragon bites at them, the *Action Motif* once again returns, now on G. Hiccup asks what he should do, to the opening of the *Warring Vikings* theme, but only the opening, as Hiccup is not a Viking. Additionally, the harmonization and pitch content are highly modified to further demonstrate Hiccup's lack of maturity. As the training course falls apart, the music alternates AM and E♭M triads, chords a tritone apart, raising the stakes.

The *Action Motif* returns one final time, beginning on C♯ in measure 58 and ends when Astrid hits the dragon. The musical point of arrival is in measure 68, a C quintal chord—C-G-D—a chord with fifths as the primary intervals rather than thirds. The cue ends on a V^7 chord in C, but what is most remarkable about the ending is the musical support of Astrid's command posed to Hiccup: "Figure out what side you're on!" She is concerned that Hiccup is too worried about not harming the dragons, but by not taking action against them, it leaves the rest of the crew vulnerable to attack. Powell does something remarkable here with the music, shown in Figure 4.7. First, a descending line

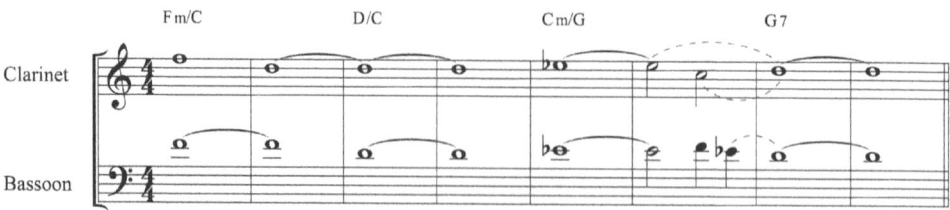

Figure 4.7. 2M12, measures 72–79, approach to final D from above and below.

in the clarinet and bassoon sounds, leading down to D. However, the bassoon breaks off from the doubling just before the end, and the D is then approached both from above, by the bassoon's E♭, and below, by the clarinet's C. Meanwhile, the first violins play an ascending line from C to F. As they reach the final harmony, GMm^7, the dominant chord in C, contrary motion is heard in the different parts, and the cue ends without full cadential closure, giving Hiccup something to think about with respect to Astrid's question. The subtleties present at the end of this cue show a composer with fully able to support the narrative in multiple ways and through multiple techniques.

2M13—Offering (0:27:43–0:28:29)

1–3—Flying A (starts on G)
3–6—Flying A (starts on G)

"Offering" is another very short cue, similar in sound to 2M10 with its unusual percussion sounds. In this cue, the Octatonic (1,2) scale is used, further altering the thematic statement of *Flying A* at the opening of the cue. As Hiccup offers the Night Fury a fish to eat, a G minor triad emerges through arpeggiation. The Night Fury sees the fish and approaches Hiccup.

The harmonies near the conclusion of the cue are Gm-EM-Gm, chords derived from the Octatonic (1,2) scale, but chords that are also related by doubly chromatic mediant. The two chords share no common tones and are quite distantly related as they do not exist in any single diatonic scale. This relationship, and harmonic oscillation, are extraordinary and foreshadow the upcoming cue where Hiccup and Toothless become friends.

2M14—Forbidden Friendship (0:29:03–0:33:11)

8–23—Flying Ostinato elements (B major)
40–42—Flying Ostinato elements (B major)
58–59—Flying Ostinato elements (D-flat major)
62–63—Flying Ostinato elements (D-flat major)
68–75—Flying B ending (F major)
76–109—Flying Ostinato (D-flat major)
76–97—Flying A opening (augmentation) (D-flat major)
116–132—Vikings A (B major)

"Forbidden Friendship" is a fabulous cue. The scene is beautiful, the music uses the glass and slate marimbas, the *Flying Ostinato* is properly introduced with hints of the *Flying A* and *B* themes, and the harmonic relationships are exceptional. The way the cue builds from beginning to end, sustaining the energy and introducing hints of the *Flying* theme through harmonies and melodic fragments, shows Powell's compositional skills at their finest. The particular types of marimbas used here give rise to the "forbidden" part of the friendship because a marimba is typically made of wooden bars, but the slate and glass bars used on these marimbas create a timbre that is somewhat foreign and magical, highlighting the nature of the relationship between a boy and a dragon. Powell spoke with me concerning the specific marimbas used in this cue. His comments appear below.

> The slate marimba was something that Dean introduced me to. He said, "Have you heard this song?" He was saying, "I wish we could use something very 'earthy' in this [scene]," like something Jónsi had done with Sigur rós, and then he played it for me, and that was the key.

There's aren't any instruments except the few they have in Iceland and in Los Angeles they have slate marimbas and glass marimbas that they made years ago. There's a couple of guys in LA who started finding and making strange and wonderful instruments in the 1960s, and they've always been useful for scoring.

The cue opens with a trichord of F♯-A♯-B, (015) in set theory nomenclature. The trichord is essentially a "stinger" to accompany Hiccup jumping back as Toothless, the name Hiccup has given the Night Fury, eats the fish that Hiccup has offered, his retractable teeth appearing. The two glass marimbas then enter in measure 4, playing B and F♯, establishing the tonic as B, with the slate marimbas entering in measures 8 and 10, respectively. The D♯ is not introduced until measure 20, confirming B major as the key. In measures 24–39, Powell uses a highly conventional harmonic progression—vi-ⁱi6-V in B major—then repeats it, delaying the tonic resolution until measure 40. In this passage, Toothless regurgitates the fish to share with Hiccup and insists he take a bite. The tonic resolution in measure 40 is when Toothless smiles, imitating Hiccup's facial motion after he pretends to eat the fish, as they bond.

As Hiccup reaches out to try to touch Toothless, Toothless becomes skittish and flies away. This moment introduces the first chromatic chords of the cue in measures 43–47—AM-EM-G♯m-C♯M, or ♭VII-IV-vi-V/V in B major—a four-chord pattern that is expected to be repeated. Instead, Toothless makes a spot to sleep in and looks up at a bird able to fly. Powell changes the harmonies to AM-EM-F♯m-A♭M, using the F♯m triad to pivot to the new key of D♭M, an enharmonic whole step higher than B, as Toothless aspires to fly again. These harmonies are shown in Figure 4.8.

Hiccup begins drawing a picture of Toothless's face in the dirt, and the sopilka plays the end of the *Flying B* theme, beginning in measure 68, as Toothless comes over to investigate. As Toothless watches, the *Flying A* theme and the *Flying Ostinato* are sounded together for the first time. Toothless then uproots a tree and draws Hiccup's face in the dirt, surrounding him in the portrait. Once the wide shot is revealed, the violins enter with the *Flying Ostinato* in measure 98, and the music reaches its loudest point thus far in the cue. Hiccup learns that if he steps on the lines that Toothless has drawn, Toothless will growl at him, so Hiccup spins around, avoiding touching the lines. Powell accompanies this with the progression seen in Figure 4.9.

Figure 4.8. 2M14, measures 43–52, Toothless wants to fly.

Figure 4.9. 2M14, measures 110–116, altered *Flying Ostinato* leading to *Durchbruch*.

The final chord in the passage, the BM triad, is chromatic to B♭m, representing a magical moment, something of a breakthrough (in German, *Durchbruch*), as Toothless is waiting right behind Hiccup, the closest he's allowed Hiccup to get thus far. In his survey of Beethoven's late style, Michael Spitzer paraphrases German philosopher Theodor Adorno's *Durchbruch* as "the eruption of suppressed musical forces engendering a new spark of life."[2] When the B major triad is sounded, the *Flying Ostinato* stops, and we primarily hear vocals, quite literally the sound of life. A solo female voice sings a rhythmically augmented version of the *Vikings A* theme as sustained notes and harmonies are used throughout the rest of the cue. Hiccup turns his face away from Toothless, open palm outstretched, allowing Toothless to move forward to touch his hand. The *Vikings A* theme never reaches its conclusion, ending on C♯, *Re* in B major; Hiccup will become a new type of Viking, one that lives with dragons rather than fighting against them. The cue has come full circle, returning to B major, and ending on an open fifth of F♯-C♯, the dominant in B. Hiccup and Toothless have felt each other out and chosen to be friends rather than enemies. Their connection is still fragile, as neither the *Vikings* theme nor the harmony reach their respective tonic closures. Powell takes the audience on a journey worthy of a blossoming friendship, a new life for both Hiccup and Toothless. Regarding the solo voice at the end of the cue, Powell said, "Voices are the ultimate tool, I think, for connection, so if you're asking 'why would I choose that sound,' it's a sound that is the most intimate of musical instruments ever to exist. It's your mother singing to you. It's the sound of somebody singing while you're inside the womb. It's the breath of a lover. It requires no instrument, there's no technology. It's our oldest instrument, as it were, for connecting with that language."

When Toothless approaches and touches Hiccup, it is a very special and intimate moment. Powell chose to score this intimacy with the solo female voice. As Powell said, the voice is the only instrument that does not need an external object to produce sound. It is a moment shared only by Toothless and Hiccup, and that moment of acceptance is best musically illustrated through the use of the voice.

2M15—New Tail (0:34:17–0:37:00)

    6–22—Fate theme (D Aeolian)
    23–25—Calming Motif (D major)
    28–31—Calming Motif (D major)
    35–36—Calming Motif (D major)
    48–57—Hiccup/Vikings (A Dorian)
    58–66—Hiccup/Vikings (in parallel fifths) (A Dorian)
    75–82—Hiccup/Vikings (A Dorian)

Hiccup has resolved to help Toothless fly again by fixing his injured tail through the use of a prosthetic one. As he leaves the group of teens listening to Gobber's tale of how he lost his hand, the cue opens with the distinctly uncommon sounds of the slate marimba, hurdy-gurdy, and yayli tambur. Hiccup is off to perform an unconventional task. The sopilka then plays the *Fate* theme, followed by the Uilleann pipes, adding to the uncommon sounds of the music as Hiccup begins to obtain the necessary hardware to fabricate a new tail piece for Toothless.

In order to get close to Toothless, Hiccup once again presents Toothless with a basket of fish to eat, but when Hiccup mentions the "smoked eel," stopped horn enters in measures 25–26, musically signaling "NO," as Toothless growls and pulls away. Hiccup throws the eel away, and the *Calming Motif* is stated twice. The *Calming Motif* is sounded a third time, but with the highest melodic voice beginning on A rather than the expected F♯, as Hiccup tries to hold down Toothless's tail in order to hook up the prosthetic tail. Toothless feels Hiccup and pauses. The music uses the melodic A as a way to pivot into A Dorian, and the sopilka plays the *Hiccup* theme in A Dorian. Hiccup doesn't realize that Toothless is no longer occupied with eating and senses what is happening, so when Toothless takes flight, Hiccup is caught unprepared, and his theme is once again played, but by Uilleann pipes and strings, a much larger and louder group than the sopilka. The sopilka and pennywhistle play the *Hiccup* theme in parallel fifths, the only such instance in the film. Hiccup and Toothless are flying together, but not as they should. After a brief scare, the *Hiccup* theme returns in the woodwinds and strings, with full orchestral accompaniment, as Hiccup delightedly shouts, "It's working!" Toothless throws Hiccup off his tail and the cue comes to a close with the final measure of the *Hiccup* theme played by bassoon and cello.

3M16—Teamwork (0:37:09–0:37:47)

    3–8—Action Motif (starts on C)
    11–18—Action Motif (starts on E)

"Teamwork" shifts the action back to the training arena. After an ascending flourish of augmented and diminished triads, the music arrives in C, where the *Action Motif* is briefly sounded, then fragmented before returning in earnest in E and following a similar trajectory to the initial statement in the cue. As the teens look fearful, a pentachord consisting of notes from the Octatonic (0,1) scale is sustained, while the harp plays from the same scale; only the A♭ is outside of the Octatonic (0,1) scale. As Hiccup throws water at the Pziiffelback in an unsuccessful attempt to quell the two-headed dragon's fire breath, the woodwinds play a full chromatic scale run and the arrival harmony is a septachord, missing only C from the Octatonic (0,1) scale. Dissonance abounds in this cue and very few major or minor triads are heard.

3M17—Charming the Pziiffelback (0:38:31–0:38:53)

    3–9—Calming Motif (D major)

Since Hiccup's water toss completely missed the mark, he has no choice but to attempt to calm the dragon using the technique he learned with Toothless. As the Pziiffelback roars at Hiccup, 12 horns play a (016) trichord—A-B♭-E♭. The first violins arpeggiate up through a D augmented triad, and the orchestra arrives on a D major chord, initiating the *Calming Motif*, which is sounded in full. Hiccup shows the eel to the dragon, accompanied by stopped horns, throws it, and as it lands, an F♯° triad is played in the trumpets over the D major triad sounding in the strings. As the door closes on the dragon, both harps arpeggiate a D major chord, signaling the danger is over.

The cue has a feel of exoticism to it, particularly in the opening orchestration and the resolution of the augmented triad to the major triad. The *Calming Motif* uses chromatic chords, including the Neapolitan, a major triad a half-step above tonic, another reference to exoticism. This musical gesture recalls Maurice Jarré's score for *Lawrence of Arabia*, another film located in an exotic place, particularly because of the use of I-bII-(bVII)-I harmonic motion.

3M18—See You Tomorrow (0:39:03–0:42:55)

5–10—Flying Ostinato variation (A major)
5–10—Flying A (A major)
17–24—Fate theme (D Aeolian)
24–30—Fate theme (F Aeolian)
36–42—Flying Ostinato (C major)
45–54—Fate theme (B-flat Aeolian)
72–79—Flying Ostinato (D major)
74–79—Flying A (D major)
79–87—Fate theme (D Aeolian)
87–93—Fate theme (F Aeolian)
106–111—Warring Vikings (B Aeolian)

From the opening marking of "Tempo di Celtico" and the use of the sopilka and dhol, this cue is very clearly meant to have a Celtic/Irish feel to it. However, the Scottish bass drum is present, and the score states, "Film begins with six beats of Scottish drumming," indicating something of a mishmash between the Celtic and Scottish styles. The opening rhythms, notably the eighth-triplet-sixteenth figures at the front of the measure, convey the Celtic feel of the cue.

This cue serves as underscore to a montage where Hiccup and Toothless work on training and trusting each other through activities such as flying together and begins in A major. As a result, the cue is dominated by the *Fate* theme, highlighting Hiccup's fate to become a dragon tamer and not a dragon killer. In the opening scene in the forest, we hear the *Flying Ostinato* and the *Flying A* theme, both of which are interrupted and come to a sudden stop as Hiccup falls off Toothless, the music being somewhat comedic. In Hiccup's second attempt, solo sopilka plays as the melodic instrument and Hiccup and Toothless crash again moments after they are shown flying; no themes are present in this attempt. Measure 14, the end of the first four-measure phrase of the second attempt, is a fascinating measure, as none of the five triads used in the measure are diatonic in A major—EbM-FM-CM-GbM-EbM, resolving to A major in measure 15. Measure 14 is the fourth measure of the four-measure phrase, so the chromatic harmonies used are very surprising. Those harmonies can all be derived from the Octatonic (0,1) scale, with the addition of F, so, octatonic plus an extra note. The F only appears in the F major triad. Additionally, two separate tritone relationships are present, from CM to GbM and from EbM to AM, as the four-measure pattern restarts. The shift from diatonic major to "octatonic plus" is sudden and short, accompanying the crash. Just as soon as the octatonic scale arrives, the music returns to A major in the following measure.

As Hiccup checks on Toothless following the crash, the *Fate* theme is played in the horns as Toothless rolls around in the grass, not unlike a puppy. Hiccup deduces that the particular type of grass has soothing properties and the montage cuts to the training arena, where Hiccup uses the grass to calm a dragon. The *Fate* theme is restated, up a minor third, from D to F. The Female Village Elder takes note of Hiccup's progress, his friends are amazed, but Astrid thinks he's up to something.

The montage then cuts back to Hiccup and Toothless in the forest, with the return of the sopilka melody and style from the opening of the cue. Once again, Hiccup uses a technique (scratching by the dragon's ear) to sedate a dragon in the training arena, and the music pauses. The *Fate* theme is initiated by the trumpets in B♭ Aeolian as everyone moves to Hiccup's table in the mess hall, leaving Astrid frustrated. Hiccup is now viewed at the best warrior rather than Astrid. Back in the forest, Hiccup learns that Toothless will chase the reflection of a light, much like a cat would do, and employs this back in the training arena with the Terrible Terror. Once again, Powell uses harmonies belonging to a single octatonic scale, this time Octatonic (1,2)—D♭M-GM-EM-B♭M, and again using tritone-related pairs—to break away from the diatonic nature of the themes, as the Terror attacks Tuffnut's nose. Astrid is told that Hiccup "is better than you ever were," and she takes out her frustrations in the forest, throwing her axe at trees, a reference to male rage here for Astrid because she is a warrior. Powell uses the Octatonic (1,2) scale and again cycles through the harmonies GM-B♭M-EM-D♭M, breaking away to a DMm^7 chord. The scale change and interruption of the octatonic harmonic cycle coincides with her noticing Hiccup. The music resumes in the style of the opening of the cue, and the sopilka re-enters as Hiccup is saddling Toothless.

The return of the *Flying Ostinato* and the *Flying A* theme coincides with Hiccup and Toothless practicing flying while tethered to a post at the edge of a cliff. As they become untethered due to a gust of wind, the *Fate* theme returns in the horns in D. As Hiccup sneaks Toothless into Berk, the *Fate* theme repeats in the bassoons in F, a gentler timbre than brass instruments. Astrid approaches Hiccup, telling him he's acting even "weirder than normal," and as Hiccup tries to hide Toothless, the music goes through the same octatonic harmonic cycle as was used in the training area earlier in the cue, with this cycle again ending on D♭M, but using that ending as the progression into a perfect authentic cadence through a V/V-V7-I harmonic progression in B major, using the chords D♭M-F♯M-BM. Most film composers try to avoid cadences when possible, as a cadence means "stop." Powell had thoughts regarding the use of cadences in film music, which appear below:

> Cadence is a dangerous thing to do in film music. If all music is the conceit of tension and release, if you're trying to create tension to tell a literal story rather than a musical story, you have to be careful where you release. Hence, cadences feel weird if you do them for no real reason. I don't get back to the end of the movie having developed and then recapped, and then come back to certain keys, unless it's felt useful to have built something and then get back to a certain key, but it would have to be in a short enough time frame for an audience to feel the returns. Modulations are very significant if it indicates a move in the story. There are all these things in classical music that are used for storytelling reasons within a story that is so unspecific where a classical composer to afford to find his way back to the tonic. I'm not able to because I know the audience would never remember that because there are a whole bunch of other things that we have to go through. I do try it sometimes, but often you end up being flummoxed by the extra bits that you have to try and do in between.

The tonic B major chord coincides with the cut to the boats where Stoick has been leading the search for the dragon's nest. The *Warring Vikings* theme is played in the bassoons, almost as a lament, since their search was fruitless, and once again, the final note, here a B, is approached both from beneath, in the bassoons, and above, in the violins. Stoick will eventually have to choose sides. Will he choose to fight dragons until his demise, or will he listen to Hiccup, and work alongside the dragons? Astrid posed this same question to Hiccup, but with Powell using the same gesture at the conclusion of a cue, he is relating what was clearly stated to Hiccup as foreshadowing for Stoick.

3M20—Test Drive (0:43:27–0:45:55)

4-11—Flying Ostinato (D major)
12-19—Flying A (D major)
20-28—Flying B (D major)
31-38—Flying A (D major)
54-57—Flying Ostinato (E major)
58-67—Flying B (E major)
68-70—Flying Ostinato (E major)

Finally! The complete *Flying* theme is heard without interruption, with its appropriate harmonization and the *Flying Ostinato* accompaniment, and in its expected key of D major. When the *Flying B* theme is reached, Hiccup and Toothless descend to fly inches above the water. At the conclusion of the full theme, they hit a rock and the theme has to restart, as does their flight. As it begins anew, they initiate an ascent, straight-up into the air. At this point in the cue, we expect to hear the complete *Flying* theme again, but at the end of the *Flying A* theme, Hiccup drops his cheat sheet, and the theme is interrupted by impending disaster. Following a B♭ major triad, the brass play a (0123458) septachord, a dissonant harmony which climbs chromatically higher over four measures. The strings play a chromatic cluster, and glissando to each instrument's highest note over the same four measures, 40–43. All of the dissonance is to highlight and exacerbate the predicament in which Hiccup finds himself.

As Hiccup spins out of control, measures 44–48, the lower timbres of the orchestra play a pedal D. The brass instruments play all three major triads where C is a member—CM, A♭M, FM—over the D pedal. C is the subtonic in D, a whole step lower, and Hiccup is falling through the air, literally beneath Toothless. Toothless swoops down and gets under Hiccup, who reaches for the harness. The music in these measures, 49–54, is exceptional. Harmonically, the music in measures 49–51 alternates between F major and D major, a pair of chromatic mediants whose root relationship indicates Heroism. In measures 52–53, the single harmony is G major, and in measure 54, it resolves to E major. G major and E major have the chromatic mediant relationship of Heroism. Underneath these chords, bass instruments previously playing the pedal D begin ascending, almost through the Octatonic (1,2) scale. The notes ascend through two octaves: D-E-F-G-A♭-B♭-C-D. C is the one note outside of the octatonic scale; it should be C♯ in order to complete the scale, but Powell opts for the C to avoid the C♯-G tritone. Despite completing two full scale statements and ending on the starting note, Powell uses the D as a lead-in to the upcoming E major harmony as a Chromatically Modulating Cadential Resolution (CMCR). In this instance, the music is not driving toward a cadence, but the arrival on E major clearly feels like a new key area, met with success and celebration. Figure 4.10 illustrates the music of this passage.

Figure 4.10. 3M20, measures 47–54, spiraling and recovering.

The *Flying B* theme, which was delayed back in measure 39, prior to the fall, enters in measure 58, as Hiccup and Toothless pull out of their fall and swoop between the rocks and the ocean. This is a triumphant and celebratory moment, and as such, is represented both visually and musically. The cue ends with Hiccup triumphantly shouting in excitement, and Toothless shooting a celebratory fireball out of his mouth, accompanied by the *Flying Ostinato*. They fly through the fireball, Hiccup slightly singed, and the most exciting cue thus far in the film comes to a close.

The soot-covered image of Hiccup is one that is famous, pulled from the 1927 film *Wings*, the first film to win the Oscar for Best Picture. Sara Ross writes that this final shot, "ends things on a comical note as Toothless flies Hiccup right through the path of his triumphant puff of flame, a shot that echoes David's flight through the smoke of a fallen Fokker in *Wings*. The overall effect is an intense illusion of spatial mastery that ties this flourish of 3D spectacle to the character's acquisition of the skills and trust needed to truly become one with his dragon."[3] The visual comedy shows that although Hiccup and Toothless have flown together, they are far from being comfortable, but are working to become a team. The soot-covered face following a fiery explosion is a comedic technique used throughout animation history, commonly in Looney Tunes shorts, as just one example. The character is never truly harmed, but is shown to have been through fire. For Hiccup, this is both literal and figurative. Literally, Hiccup just flew through a fireball, but figuratively, he's been through the fire in order to tame Toothless, to build a prosthetic tail fin, and through several attempts to fly with Toothless as a team. The soot-covered face is more than just comedy.

3M21—Not So Fireproof (0:46:39–0:47:10)

41–49—Flying B ending (G major)

This cue's use as written versus its use in the film is quite different. In the film, the first 30 measures are cut, making this cue only 19 measures long as used in the film. As the little dragon swallows its own fireball and staggers around drunkenly, Hiccup says, "Not so fireproof, are you?" This is the point where music enters in the film, and the melody shown in Figure 4.11 is played; the flute melody is closely related to the *Dragon Tune*.

While not exactly the same, the general contour and intervallic leaps are similar to the opening of the *Dragon Tune*, but this variation is far less menacing and dissonant, as it is harmonized with both major and minor triads, as opposed to the *Dragon Tune*, which is harmonized by a single minor triad for its opening measures.

As the little dragon curls up next to Hiccup, the end of the *Flying B* theme is played by flute and violin I, and is significantly reharmonized. Hiccup says to himself, "Everything we know about you guys is wrong." He has come to the realization that not just Toothless can be friendly, but all dragons can be friendly, if treated correctly, and Hiccup wants to share this radical new idea with the rest of Berk. The use of the reharmonized *Flying* theme here indicates that the taming of dragons moves beyond Toothless to all dragons.

3M22—This Time for Sure (0:49:39–0:50:17)

6–15—Hiccup/Vikings (B-flat Aeolian)
16–19—Warring Vikings (E-flat Aeolian)
20–23—Hiccup/Vikings (B-flat Aeolian)

Much of "This Time for Sure" recalls the start of the action in "This is Berk." "This Time for Sure" opens with the familiar F minor and B major triads, alternating in a descending fashion as in the opening cue, and leading into a statement of the *Hiccup* theme. In this cue, the tritone related triads support the awkwardness of Stoick

Figure 4.11. 3M21, measures 30–36, flute melody and transposed *Dragon Tune*.

instead of Hiccup, and the dragon fighting is done by the teenagers in the training arena, rather than the Vikings of Berk. Following two statements of the *Hiccup* theme, the *Warring Vikings* theme is used as Astrid is confident that she will be the one to defeat the Gronkel this time. As she leaps over the obstacles to engage the Gronkel, she sees Hiccup has put it to sleep; the final two measures of the *Hiccup* theme are used, and the cue ends.

3M23—Astrid Finds Toothless (0:51:57–0:52:30)
    8–13—Flying Ostinato (G Aeolian)
    16–23—Flying Ostinato (G Aeolian)

Astrid finally learns Hiccup's secret, and postures aggressively at Toothless, who rushes to attack her. Hiccup protects her, but the *Flying Ostinato* is sounded in G minor in the gadulka to indicate Toothless's anxiety, the minor-mode statement and unusual timbre accentuating Toothless's self-preservation instinct. Powell also uses lots of Brazilian percussion—brekete, repinique, and surdo—with the brekete marked "Brutal!" at one point. As Toothless backs down and Astrid scampers toward Berk, the *Flying Ostinato* is again sounded in G minor, but in the lowest octave of the violins; no one is flying.

3M24—Astrid Goes for a Spin (0:53:30–0:54:13)
    1–16—Hiccup/Vikings (D Aeolian)
    32–41—Hiccup/Vikings (C Aeolian)

The first person that Hiccup needs to convince of his plan to tame dragons is Astrid, as she's learned his secret. Before she can return to Berk to tell the village of Hiccup's Night Fury, Toothless swoops down and picks her up. Reluctantly, and stuck high in a tree branch, she agrees to Hiccup's plan of going riding on the back of the Night Fury. Before the cue begins, Toothless gives Astrid quite the side-eye as she mounts him, frustrated at having her near him. The animation is quite humorous.

The cue opens with a fully harmonized version of the *Hiccup* theme in D Aeolian, using Dm, FM, GM, and B♭M triads. First, Toothless ascends rapidly in an attempt to get Astrid to fall off his back, then does an inverted dive, again to try to throw her off, pulling up just before crashing into the water. Right before Toothless touches the water with his wings, a fully chromatic wedge of sixteenth notes is played in the violin I and II parts. This wedge highlights both the excitement of riding a dragon, and the frustration of Toothless at sharing himself with Astrid.

The music then moves into a new section, measures 18–31, that recalls 3M18 "See You Tomorrow." This section, like in "See You Tomorrow," is in A major, but the chromatic chords are wildly outside of the key—E♭M, FM, A♭M, and B♭M. Hiccup's line to Toothless during these chromatic chords is, "Thanks for nothing, you useless reptile." The (faux) annoyance that Hiccup feels matches Toothless's frustration. Neither one can remain in the diatonic key, and the chromatic chords are wholly necessary.

As Toothless pulls out of the dive, the *Hiccup* theme returns, now in C minor. Toothless hears Astrid apologize, saying, "I'm sorry," and starts to behave more appropriately, or at least, more like Hiccup wants him to behave. Toothless momentarily stops misbehaving, and the cue ends, segueing into "Romantic Flight."

3M25—Romantic Flight (0:54:14–0:56:06)

1–13—Love theme (B major)
13–29—Love theme (B major)
30–37—Flying Ostinato (A-flat major)
41–60—Love theme (D-flat major)

The cue opens with a nearly complete statement of the *Love* theme in B major, as Astrid opens her eyes and begins to relax. The only instruments in this opening are a solo violin, two harps, and female choir, clearly romantically idealized orchestration. The *Love* theme is restated an octave lower in the horns, with accompaniment from woodwinds and strings. Other than the final cadence to the theme, its use is complete here. As Astrid's confidence grows, so too does the orchestra. She throws her outstretched arms in the air, and the flute and violins take the melody as the brass momentarily drop out.

The end of the second statement of the *Love* theme leads into a modified version of the *Flying Ostinato*, altered to fit the triple-meter of the *Love* theme. In this cue, the ostinato must be adjusted to fit into the triple meter of the *Love* theme. The entrances of the choir highlight the Aurora Borealis that Astrid sees while soaring above the clouds, and as the clouds break, the *Love* theme returns, now in D♭ major, an enharmonic whole step higher than at the start of the cue, as she is now thoroughly enjoying the ride and the company. She sees Berk from above, smiles, and Toothless looks back at her and smiles. Astrid then gives Hiccup a loving embrace, and the theme receives a proper ending in D♭. Of course, the music cannot come to a sudden halt, so there's a short codetta at the end of the cue, one which uses a prominent C♭ in the harp as Astrid notes that both the flight and Toothless are "amazing!" This chromatic note punctuates the fact that Astrid can hardly believe how Hiccup was right, and how her attitude toward dragons has changed so quickly. Although Astrid is certainly not "in love" with Hiccup yet, it is the beginning of that emotion. They have gone from adversaries to friends and will go far beyond that in the upcoming films. The romance is not present quite yet, but the seeds have been planted through the use of chromaticism.

3M26B—Dragon's Den (0:57:07–0:58:42)

13–33—Dragon Tune (E-flat doubly harmonic minor) *partially not in film*
34–42—Flying A opening (starts on E-flat)
46–49—Flying A opening (starts on F)
70–80—Dragon Tune (D doubly harmonic minor)

"Dragon's Den" is another cue where much of the opening was cut from the film; the cue begins in measure 23 in the film. In the music cut from the film, the *Dragon Tune* is sounded in E♭ in extreme rhythmic augmentation in the low brass and contrabass. Once the music enters in the film, the *Dragon Tune* has already begun, the cut beginning the middle of the theme. Toothless descends into the den, and a highly modified melodic and harmonic version of the opening of the *Flying A* theme is heard, also in E♭. It is difficult to hear these statements in the film, as they are buried in the texture in the trombones, the melodic notes part of the harmonic fabric. As Toothless, Hiccup, and Astrid watch the food "being dumped down a hole" from behind a rock, the modified *Flying A* theme is heard again, now in F, a whole step higher, and much more audible.

The intensity is greater, the thematic content clearer, as they are now surrounded within the dragon's nest.

A Gronkel, the last to share its take, drops a fish out of its mouth into the hole, and the tuba plays a B1, an exceptionally low note. Just then, something emerges from the pit; its jaws clamp down and it eats the Gronkel. The musical reaction is extraordinary. An octachord of (01234678) is played in the low brass, bassoons, and low strings. This is for the giant Alpha dragon of the nest, the Red Death. The gasping reaction of Hiccup and Astrid sounds one beat later, as the violins, violas, and horns, play their highest note, with the marking "high 'shriek.'" While this isn't quite mickey-mousing the on-screen action, it is very close, and certainly represents and supports the on-screen action.

The Red Death sees Toothless and tries to eat him. As Toothless, Hiccup, and Astrid escape the den, the opening of the *Dragon Tune* is sounded in the horns and trombones in D, with a flurry of accompaniment—eighth notes in the strings and triplet eighth notes in the woodwinds. It is meant to sound somewhat chaotic, as all of the dragons are chasing them out of the den, and all three of our heroes are nearly killed.

3M26C—Let's Find Dad (0:58:51–0:59:54)

    3–8—Flying A (E major)
    15–28—Love theme (A major)

Astrid suggests to Hiccup that they reveal the location of the dragon's den to Stoick, but Hiccup refuses in order to keep Toothless protected and hidden from the rest of Berk. A more regularly reharmonized version of the *Flying A* theme is used in E major, concluding with an Aeolian cadence—CM-DM-EM. Hiccup and Toothless are not yet free and in the open, which explains the modified version of the opening of the *Flying A* theme.

Astrid accepts Hiccup's position and asks what to do. The *Love* theme sounds, this time on harmonium, a new timbre, representing a new part of their relationship, as Astrid first punches Hiccup for "kidnapping" her, then kisses him, "for everything else." As in "Romantic Flight," only the final phrase of the *Love* theme is absent; there is no closure here, as Hiccup must go to the Kill Ring in the morning and he's faced with a decision about revealing his relationship with Toothless to all of Berk.

4M27-28—Kill Ring / Stop the Fight (1:00:31–1:04:55)

    2–11—Vikings A (G major)
    4–6—Flying Ostinato (G major)
    12–23—Dragon Tune (E doubly harmonic minor)
    51–53—Vikings A (E major in horns)
    55–57—Flying B (C Aeolian)
    62–66—Dragon Tune (C doubly harmonic minor)
    68–71—Flying Ostinato (E major)
    93–98—Flying B ending (B major)
    115–126—Flying Ostinato variation (G doubly harmonic minor)

A sort of Richard Wagner-esque style permeates the opening of the cue, which begins with a bit of a prologue to the scene, as Stoick proudly tells the village that his son is about to become a Viking. The *Vikings A* theme is nobly stated in the horns, accompanied by a new harmonization for the occasion, but is interrupted for a measure by Astrid asking Hiccup what he's going to do. When she asks the question, the opening of the

4. How to Train Your Dragon *Cue Analysis*   81

Figure 4.12. 4M27–28, measures 2–11, modified *Vikings A* theme.

Flying Ostinato is sounded, reminding us of Hiccup's feelings for Toothless, and truly, for all dragons. As the *Vikings A* theme continues, it is harmonized differently than expected, showing the Hiccup is going to be a different type of Viking than the adults of Berk. The new harmonization is shown in Figure 4.12.

As Hiccup dons his Viking helmet and walks out into the ring, a varied treatment of the *Dragon Tune* is heard; this will be unlike any kill ring fight ever seen. As the door begins to be unlocked, an F♯/C tritone is heard throughout the orchestra and a Monstrous Nightmare, a fire-breathing dragon bursts out of the door. The orchestration in this part of the cue is not thick, as the music is not primarily action based. The orchestra sounds a G°7 chord, a dissonant harmony that finally resolves up to an A♭°7 chord, heightening the tension as Hiccup places his shield on the ground and attempts to soothe the dragon. Consecutive fully diminished chords are synonymous with the "villain-ties-the-heroine-to-the-railroad-tracks," and the "will she/won't she be saved" question. Powell is using this old trick here to accomplish the same type of narrative question, namely, will Hiccup actually fight the dragon. Hiccup removes his helmet, declares to the dragon that he's not "one of them," and Stoick stands and orders the fight to be stopped. Buried in the horns in measures 51–53 is a rhythmic variant of the *Vikings A* theme opening in E major. The entire village is present to watch this fight, but they cannot believe their eyes, that one of their own would lay down his shield and not fight the dragon. The final note of the opening gesture of the *Vikings A* theme, the C♯, is absent in the horn part, but it is the root of the C♯°7 chord that is heard at the end of the gesture.

Action music is finally used in this cue, beginning in measure 55, as the dragon attacks Hiccup upon seeing Stoick rushing to the ring. First, a modified fragment from the *Flying B* theme supports Toothless hearing Hiccup's cries for help. Then, a modified fragment of the *Dragon Tune* in C is heard as Toothless climbs out of his hiding spot. The Monstrous Nightmare continues to attack as Hiccup evades it. A highly modified *Flying Ostinato* statement is heard as Toothless runs through the forest, since he cannot fly properly without Hiccup's assistance. To break up the action, Stoick opens the gate, and Powell uses a syncopated gesture, not to synchronize anything to the picture, but to break up the dragon attack from the other action in the scene.

Toothless finally arrives in the ring, and the modified *Flying Ostinato* is presented canonically in the strings. Once Gobber recognizes the second dragon as a Night Fury, a newly-harmonized statement of the end of the *Flying B* theme is present in

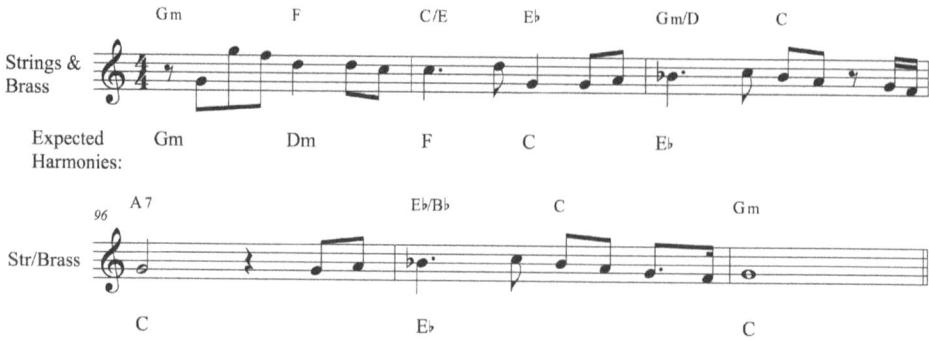

Figure 4.13. 4M27–28, measures 93–98, Modified *Flying B* theme as Toothless protects Hiccup.

measures 93–98, shown as Figure 4.13, as Toothless fights the Monstrous Nightmare and is clearly protecting Hiccup. Toothless does his job, intimidating the dragon, but Hiccup tries to get Toothless to leave before he is hurt by the Vikings.

A moment of decision is imminent, as the orchestra plays a unison G♯°7 chord for six measures, at one point even introducing an F minor triad against it in the brass. Toothless protects himself, and seeing Stoick advancing with an axe, tackles him and prepares to kill him. Hiccup screams "No!" and Toothless stops. But in showing momentary "weakness," the Vikings ensnare Toothless in a net, and the *Flying Ostinato* is played in G doubly harmonic minor, the scale used for the *Dragon Tune*, with a marking of "Devastating." Stoick declares, "Put it with the others," and the cue ends on a D major triad, a half cadence in G. Notably, Stoick refers to the dragon as "it" and not "him." He is not willing to entertain Hiccup's notion that dragons can be friendly and tame, but in ending the cue on a half cadence, it allows for the possibility that Stoick could, one day, be convinced to see things differently. For now, however, that will not happen.

4M30—Not a Viking (1:05:33–1:06:28)

3–11—Dragon Tune (A doubly harmonic minor) *not in film*
12–19—Flying Ostinato (A Aeolian)
24–29—Warring Vikings (E-flat Aeolian)

After professing little faith in his son, then praising him for his training, Stoick rejects Hiccup, both as a Viking, and more horrifically, as his own son. Once again, this is a cue for which the opening was not used in the film, instead beginning in measure 12 and omitting the statement of the *Dragon Tune*. As Hiccup mentions the island of the dragons, referring to it as "their island," the music enters. Stoick cannot believe what he is hearing, believing his son is "siding" with the dragons over his own people. The *Flying Ostinato* initiates the cue's beginning in the film as Hiccup tries to convince his father of the folly of attacking the island. The bass line descends from A, and we expect a descent down to D, as would be the D Aeolian pentachord, but at the moment of arrival of the expected D, Stoick pushes Hiccup to the ground, and the bass arrives on E♭ instead, never reaching the D. Stoick's mission will end in failure.

Stoick then tells Hiccup, "You're not a Viking. You're not my son," followed by the entrance of the *Warring Vikings* theme in E♭. What is fascinating about this entrance is the timbres and octaves used. Only horns, violins, and cellos are playing the theme; horns and cellos begin on E♭3 while the violins begin on E♭6, three octaves higher. Everything in between is absent. While Stoick is off to war, he leaves his only son feeling hollow, empty, and miserable, and the spacing and orchestration of the *Warring Vikings* theme illustrates Hiccup's emptiness. The cue segues into "Ready/Confront."

4M31—Ready / Confront (1:06:28–1:07:49)

    4–7—Warring Vikings (E Aeolian)
    8–11—Warring Vikings (A Aeolian)
    15–25—Flying B (D major)
    26–29—Warring Vikings (E Aeolian)
    35–43—Fate theme (E Aeolian) *not in film*
    43–47—Fate theme (B Aeolian) *not in film*
    51–58—Vikings (A major) sounds like chorale
    62–73—Dragon Tune (E-flat doubly harmonic minor)
    77–79—Dragon Tune (D doubly harmonic minor)
    80–82—Dragon Tune (F doubly harmonic minor)
    83–84—Calming Motif (starts on F)
    89—Calming Motif (starts on E)
    91–94—Warring Vikings (A Aeolian)
    93–96—Dragon Tune (E doubly harmonic minor)
    96–100—Warring Vikings (A Aeolian) *not in film*
    101–105—Calming Motif (starts on D-sharp) *not in film*

Preparations begin to sail to the island of the dragons for an all-out war. As a result, the *Warring Vikings* theme is performed in a militaristic fashion, with two snare drums playing. The expected repetition of the theme occurs up a perfect fourth from E to A Aeolian, but this statement is tonally adjusted in order to conclude back in E, almost like an answer to a fugue subject. The addition of bagpipes to the second statement reinforces the militaristic style of the music, reaching back to the instrument's original musical function.

Toothless is chained and bound, raised up to lead the way to the dragons' island through his sense of smell. The *Flying B* theme is used, slightly melodically altered, and with a completely new harmony that sounds very awkward in comparison to the correct harmony. This wrong harmony perverts the joy that Hiccup and Toothless have flying together, and is shown in Figure 14. Stoick has rejected Hiccup and enslaved Toothless, so while the theme may be recognizable, the harmonization is not. The ships set sail, accompanied by the *Warring Vikings* theme in E Aeolian, and as they dissolve, indicating the passing of time, all that remains is the harmonization of the theme. The Vikings of Berk are headed to war, perhaps for the final time.

The music in measures 32–47 is not included in the film as Astrid and Hiccup discuss what they're going to do to help Toothless. As Hiccup proclaims that he wouldn't kill a dragon, the cue re-enters, and the *Vikings A* theme enters in A major, in a very gentle version. When Astrid says that she thinks Toothless is frightened now, the music uses the same descending A Phrygian pentachord as was heard in "Dragon Training." There, the Phrygian pentachord was used to indicate anxiety about what might emerge from a door in the first day of training. Here, the anxiety is again present, but now is it much more specific to Toothless and Hiccup and rescuing the dragon. The musical texture

Figure 4.14. 4M31, measures 15–24, *Flying B* theme altered negatively.

thickens as Hiccup says he'll probably do "something crazy," and the scene changes to the Vikings on the ships.

As the ships enter the fog, the *Dragon Tune*, rhythmically augmented and normalized, is sounded in measures 62–73. The score indicates the marking as "Bleak," and the wordless choir does not instill hope. Gobber speaks to Stoick, asking about the plan, or if there even *is* a plan. The theme is soft and a bit elegiac, as Stoick, if he follows through with his plan, will lead all the Vikings to their demise. Suddenly, Stoick hears a sound and the theme stops. Toothless then hears a sound, and the opening of the *Dragon Tune* is played twice, much more forcefully than before, first in D, then in F.

The action then cuts back to the Kill Ring, where Hiccup plans on releasing the dragons and flying on them to the island with the rest of his pals. This scene opens with the *Calming Motif* to indicate Hiccup's plan, since he does not overtly state it. After everyone gets a turn to say something, Astrid asks, "So what is the plan," accompanied by the *Calming Motif* once again, indicating the plan to calm and use the dragons to fly through music and not dialogue.

The action returns to the ships one final time and the low strings play a stripped-down version of the *Warring Vikings* theme in A Aeolian. Rather than repeat the theme up a fourth, the theme is repeated in A. As the first *Warring Vikings* statement is sounding, a bowed waterphone plays the opening of the *Dragon Tune* in E, a perfect fifth higher. This technique is very similar to the opening of a fugue, where a subject is presented, and the answer is sounded a perfect fifth higher. In a fugue, the subject and answer are essentially the same musical idea. Here, the ideas are different. In fact, they are oppositional, implying that one will ultimately be the winner. Unfortunately, the music begins to fade out before the *Dragon Tune* is fully heard on the waterphone, so ultimately, this final section of the cue is unused in the film, but the thoughtfulness and musical technique shown by Powell is extraordinary. Despite being omitted from the film, this part of the cue can be heard in the recording.

4M33-34—Relax / Stroke / Hell (1:11:48–1:12:54)

16–20—Calming Motif (starts on F-sharp)
22–26—Warring Vikings (F Aeolian)

The previous cue fades out into sound effects, and as the ships near the island, the sound effects grow louder. We quickly figure out that it is the sound of the dragons inside the cavern on the island, a noise similar to cicadas—loud, constant, buzzing. But as Stoick jumps out of the ship onto the rocks, the sound stops.

When the cue begins, the film cuts back to the Kill Ring, as Hiccup is trying to coax the Pziiffelback out of its cage. We hear two sustained chords in measures 2–6, C major and D major, a harmonic relationship that often indicates protagonism in film. Here, Hiccup has clearly become the leader of the teenagers and is taking charge of the situation, foreshadowing to his later transformation into the chief of Berk. The next pair of chords in measures 8–9, C major and E♭ major, form a chromatic mediant relationship indicating heroism. Again, Hiccup is the hero of the film (although one could argue it's really Toothless). As Snotlout begins to pet the Pziiffelback on its snout, a variation of the *Calming Motif* is used. Here, an ascending whole step is used rather than the familiar half step, as Hiccup's ideas are used by other Berkians. The wordless choir and harps make this section of the cue sound magical, and the teens are able to view dragons in a far different way than the adults; the magic is in the younger generation.

The scene cuts back to the dragons' island, where the Vikings are sharpening spears and preparing other weapons. This cut is accompanied by a *Warring Vikings* statement in the brass at a dynamic of *fortissimo*, and accompanied by percussion, further enhancing the militaristic nature of the Vikings. This cut highlights the generational difference between the adults and teens of Berk. The softer, magical-sounding music for the teens and their treatment of dragons is juxtaposed with the loud warring music of the adult Vikings. The generational gap has never been wider. Stoick states, "No matter how it ends, it ends today!" As he finishes his statement, the music arrives on a G♭ major triad, the Neapolitan of F, the tonality of the previously heard *Warring Vikings* statement. The rest of the cue is unused in the film, which is too bad because it is harmonically interesting, but sound effects prove to be scarier and more effective here as the rocks launched by the Vikings crack open the side of the mountain, and we wait for the dragons to emerge.

4M35-37—Over / Less Okay (1:14:11–1:20:27)

17–48—Dragon Tune (C doubly harmonic minor)
49–64—Dragon Tune (E-flat doubly harmonic minor)
83–90—Warring Vikings (E major)
91–98—Warring Vikings (E-flat Mixolydian)
110–117—Vikings A (C major)
118–127—Fate theme (B-flat Dorian)
134–143—Vikings (C-sharp minor)
144–147—Action Motif (starts on E)
148–153—Warring Vikings (F-sharp Aeolian)
154–155—Warring Vikings (E-flat)
154–159—Action Motif (starts on A-flat)
160–161—Warring Vikings (F Aeolian)
172–190—Dragon Tune (F-sharp doubly harmonic minor)
194–196—Dragon Tune variation (A)
196–204—Flying Ostinato (B-flat minor)
207–211—Flying Ostinato (D minor)

86   The Music of the *How to Train Your Dragon* Trilogy

215–218—Flying Ostinato (D major)
215–222—Flying A (D major)
223–232—Flying B (D major)
234–241—Flying A (D major)
257–258—Flying Ostinato (E major)
259–269—Flying B (E major)

The entrance of this cue is buried in the sound effects of the crumbling of the mountain, but once the strings and woodwinds enter with loud eighth notes in measure 5, music is audibly present. The music cycles through three four-measure phrases, all based in C minor. As the giant Red Death emerges from the mountainside, the *Dragon Tune* is sounded in the brass in rhythmic augmentation. The notes are elongated because of the actual size of this dragon as opposed to the dragons that the Vikings are used to fighting.

As they see the Red Death, the Vikings scatter; it's something they've never seen before, and Gobber instructs the men to "get to the ships!" Stoick exclaims, "No," and the *Dragon Tune* begins again, this time up a minor third in E♭ to intensify the action and raise the stakes. Now that the Red Death has fully emerged, it could do real harm to the Vikings and kill them all. The dragon breathes fire at the ships, laying waste to them, and leaving them all unusable. Toothless remains captive atop the main ship, Stoick forgetting about him. Stoick and Gobber agree to run a diversion to allow the men to flee to the other side of the island. As they begin to attract the Red Death's attention, the *Warring Vikings* theme is sounded in E♭, but with major triads harmonizing the theme, recalling a similar passage near the conclusion of "This is Berk." This is a heroic action and a heroic harmonization of the theme, illustrated in Figure 4.15. But just as things appear to be working for Stoick, the Red Death looks at him, the heroic harmonization disappears, and the music sustains an F♯ minor triad in measures 103–106.

Just as things look their bleakest for Stoick, the teenagers arrive, having flown dragons from Berk. The music celebrates their arrival with the *Vikings A* theme in C major. This is the first time that the *Vikings* theme has been specifically played to accompany the teens of Berk and not the adults. A new generation of Vikings, with different values and beliefs, is emerging. In fact, the complete *Vikings* theme, with all four sections,

Figure 4.15. 4M35, measures 83–89, *Warring Vikings* theme harmonized heroically.

excluding a definitive ending, are used here, one of the very few locations in the film where that occurs.

Hiccup flies off from the rest of the group, and a variation in C♯ minor of the *Vikings A* theme begins; Figure 4.16 shows this variation. Both the pitch content and harmonization are different and distorted. The rest of the teens fly around the Red Death to keep it distracted and allow the Vikings to reach safety. However, as they all end up facing the Red Death, the *Action Motif* begins in E. The teens apply their training, looking for the "blind spot," but because of the number of eyes the dragon has, it doesn't have a blind spot. A statement of the *Warring Vikings* theme leads Hiccup to jump from Astrid's dragon and onto the sinking ship where Toothless is in chains. The action intensifies, as does the music. Themes are shortened to only fragments, with two measures of the *Warring Vikings* theme heard along with the *Action Motif* in measures 154–155. The rhythm changes from eighth notes to triplet quarter notes, as Fishlegs and his dragon crash to the ground, the slower-feeling rhythm indicative of falling, but not a total free fall.

The Red Death then tries to stomp on Fishlegs while Snotlout hammers at its eyes, but the dragon bucks Snotlout off its head. The dragon is winning this fight, and Powell uses the *Dragon Tune* to assert its dominance at this point in the fight. The music reaches an F♯°7 chord, and the Red Death destroys the ship where Toothless is. As Toothless become submerged in the water, still chained and unable to break free, a variation on the *Flying Ostinato* is used; Toothless is in trouble. Hiccup tries to free him underwater but cannot hold his breath long enough. Stoick reaches down and pulls Hiccup to safety.

Stoick then dives back down, and the *Flying Ostinato* sounds again, this time in D, and using mode mixture—Phrygian with a major third scale degree. The music sounds an open fifth D-A, changing to a tritone, D-G♯, and Stoick frees Toothless from his chains. As Toothless emerges from the water, the music is synchronized with the action on-screen, and the *Flying Ostinato* and the *Flying A* theme are used together, both in D major with the previous tritone resolving. Stoick's decision to free Toothless was still debatable, as indicated by the presence of both the B♭ and E♭ in the *Flying Ostinato* after he saved Hiccup. The reemergence of Toothless from beneath the water is a celebratory moment, and we are

Figure 4.16. 4M35, measures 134–143, minor-mode *Vikings A* theme.

meant to cheer both his safety and Stoick's freeing of him, coming around to see what Hiccup sees. Stoick even apologizes to his son, telling him, "I'm proud to call you my son." The *Flying* theme begins again as Hiccup and Toothless soar into the air, still in D major. The teens continue the aerial attack on the Red Death, and the harmonies alternate between B♭M and DM, a chromatic mediant relationship indicative of magic. Astrid and Snotlout try to avoid being sucked into the dragon's mouth, and this trouble and terror is musically represented through the use of polychords, A♭M against DM and CM against DM, then BM against DM. This section is reminiscent of "Test Drive," where Hiccup loses his cheat sheet and falls off Toothless in their "test flight." The DM triad represents Toothless and the fighting teens of Berk while the other triads represent the present struggle against the Red Death. After Toothless shoots a blast at the dragon, polychords continue, with DM against FM, and the bass line climbs up, using the same near-octatonic ascending scale motion as in "Test Drive." The end of the scale finds the music reaching E major, just as before. This time, instead of Toothless pulling up ahead of the water, he catches the falling Astrid and delivers her to safety, fully trusting her. The moment coincides with the return of the *Flying Ostinato* and the *Flying B* theme. As they dive to attack the Red Death, Hiccup notices that the dragon has wings. An F♯ major triad is the last thing heard in the cue, lasting four measures, and with an exciting rhythm that feels outside of the 4/4 meter. Toothless hits the Red Death with another blast, and the cue ends, segueing directly into the next cue.

Figure 4.17 shows the markings, tempos, meters, and tonal centers for the complete cue.

Measure	1	49	77	99	108/109	118	122	130	134	144
Marking	Energico				Heroic					
Tempo	q = 203				q = 130					
Meter	3/4				2/4–4/4					
Tonal Center	C minor	E♭ minor	E major	G minor	C major	G major	B♭ major	C minor	C♯ minor	"E"

Measure	148	154	160	170	191/192	194	198	200
Marking				Faster	Tense	Appassionato		With Desperation
Tempo				q = 206	q = 198	q = 100		q = 122
Meter				3/4	3/4–4/4	4/4		4/4
Tonal Center	F♯ minor	A♭ major	F minor	F♯ minor	F♯ minor	F♯ minor	B♭ minor	B♭ minor

Measure	204	207	248	257	269
Marking	Lento	Subito allegro			End Cue
Tempo	q = 71	q = 125			
Meter	3/4	4/4			
Tonal Center	C minor	D major	Polychords	E major	

Figure 4.17. Breakdown of 4M35–37 by measure, marking, tempo, meter, and tonal center.

It would be impossible to continually increase the tempo to match the increase in the visual intensity, so Powell has a number of techniques to heighten the intensity beyond just tempo. (*See From the Composer*) The first tempo change sees the tempo decrease, but also finds the meter changing from simple triple meter to simple quadruple. Then, in measure 170, the music returns to the initial meter and slightly faster than the initial tempo. A large slowdown occurs in measure 194, cutting the tempo in half, accelerating, and then shifting even slower a few measures later. The *lento* marking serves as a moment of sustain, making the return to *subito allegro* seem much faster than the previous marking, "With Desperation," even though only a minuscule three beats per minute separates the two.

The constant shifting of tonal areas is also essential to keeping the forward momentum throughout the cue. The longest time that the music remains in a single tonal center is at the beginning of the cue, forty-eight measures. The start of the cue establishes the tone and pace of the cue, so it is only natural to establish a tonal center and remain there for some time at the outset of the cue. While forty-eight measures may seem like a long time, because of the tempo, this initial tonal center lasts approximately one minute, or 1/6 of the cue, which isn't truly that much time. These tonal areas that are in motion and shifting are an integral part of the overall pacing of action cues for Powell.

Locally, the key areas rise by seconds or thirds, with the one exception being the motion from G minor to C major in measures 99–109, and back to G major in measure 118. Modulating up a third, most commonly a minor third, is one of Powell's most common techniques to raise the tension and stakes in the music. Looking at the key areas, as they change with the tempo, the following key areas arise: Cm–CM–F♯m–B♭m–Cm–DM–EM. The key areas circle from Cm back to Cm, before ascending in major seconds (whole steps) from C minor to D major and ending in E major, a major third higher than the opening of the cue. As the music shifts to D major, Hiccup and Toothless enter the fight together, bringing hope to the Vikings of defeating the Alpha. From the opening tonal area of C minor, the motion to D major is an ascending major second, as well as switching mode from minor to major. The fear present at the start of the cue is replaced with hope and optimism.

Although the tempo appears to be cut in half at measure 194, the extremely fast triple meter at measure 170 gives the aural impression of 12/8 meter, not 3/4, where each full measure of 3/4 feels more like a single beat of 12/8. In this scenario, a single beat (dotted-quarter note) would be at 137, so the slowing doesn't feel quite as severe as it might look on the page. Additionally, the sound effects of the Red Death's foot largely cover the music, and few measures later, the big heroic moment occurs. The tempo "downshifts," but does so in conjunction with a visual pivot so that we don't notice the music slowing, and when the big moment arrives, it feels like an acceleration in tempo. It's a phenomenal technique applied by Powell, and one that he uses throughout the film series.

Powell spoke at length about his approach to scoring action scenes and sequences. His thoughts from our conversation appear below:

> There are three impressive pieces I love. First is "The Young Person's Guide to the Orchestra" by Benjamin Britten. In the fugue at the end, there's this point where it goes to an incredibly slow cross-rhythm version of the Purcell [theme on which the piece is based] while all these other things are still going. That always impressed me so much! It always blows my mind when I listen to it. It's the idea of winding everything else up, and then it feels like the camera

pulls back and you see a mass of energy, and within that energy you see the shape of this bigger message. Given that everything in the piece is based on the same thing we're hearing incredibly slowly over the top. There's never been a greater piece of music to show people what music can do in the hands of a genius.

Then, there's John Williams scoring the scene in the Indiana Jones film where he's under the truck; it's the fight where he's falling off the truck. [author's note: this is the "Desert Chase" cue from *Raiders of the Lost Ark*] It's gets faster and faster and faster, and you think, "Where is he going to go?" And it's like, he goes into fifth gear, and the car feels like, "Is it going to get it?" So, the music slows down, it goes into 3, or he changes meter in a kind of way that resets. I remember really clearly hearing this idea of a reset. It shows determination and gives that feeling that we're on the last bit of this [sequence]. Which is why, if you do it in the wrong place, if you do it too early, you're screwed. You have to do it in the right place, where it seems to fit.

The other one that I've studied endlessly, and I always talk to younger composers about, is the Barn Dance from *Seven Brides for Seven Brothers*, which is a five- or six-minute sequence entirely based on "Bless Your Little Hide." The orchestrators or arrangers from MGM, or whoever did it, are just … it's the most incredible piece of development. It gets higher and faster for five minutes, but it can't, because it doesn't. How I describe it is: you go up the stairs this way, you get to a landing, and then you turn, and you go up steps that way. And in turning, it allows you to shift. It's the sort of barber's pole thing, where you can't see [how it works]. Those are very hard to do, and they can get repetitive. Whereas trying to find the moments to turn and shift, it's about tempo, key, intensity, meter. Meter and key are very important to those. There are action films where it's fast and just gets faster all the time, more hi-hats, more drums. We've all done that because that's what filmmakers want.

If you get a chance to do these scenes, and they don't keep cutting them on you, which is one of the big problems, you're trying to craft a nine-minute action scene, and it's basically five sections, and then it's suddenly seven minutes and they've cut one of those sections out. That's one of the reasons I don't like doing live-action movies, because that happens a lot in action scenes, whereas in animation they have to be more careful. They can't just cut two minutes out of the scene, but they can speed it up. So, what I tend to do is work on these long scenes a little slow, because I know that they'll get trimmed and tightened and tightened. I often forget that and we end up at the scoring stage with music that's almost impossible to play because the only way to keep my synchronization with the film that keeps getting cut is to get faster and faster, so you do end up with things that are almost impossible to play. Thank goodness the studio musicians are incredible.

The Barn Dance—that's the kind of thing where I sat with that and looked through it a million times to learn how they did that, and what happens there, and by looking it over and over again, I think the instinct of how to shift and where to shift came to me. The hardest thing is actually understanding the structure of the scenes so that you head for the right places to shift, and finding the right places to shift and the right moments. If you get that right, then you aren't working against what the director is feeling about the scene. Then you can really find the steps and how to turn and hide the shifts in such a way that you pick up more and more intensity without just getting faster and higher.

The cue "Over/Less Okay" is the first cue that is truly an action cue from beginning to end and all of Powell's techniques are on display as he is able to maintain the necessary level of musical intensity for six minutes. In studying music from composers of both concert and film music, Powell was able to isolate the necessary elements to write excellent action music, which is a hallmark of the composer, generally speaking, as well as the *HTTYD* trilogy.

4M38—Wings (1:20:27–1:21:39)

7–18—Dragon Tune variation (B doubly harmonic minor)
24–32—Warring Vikings (E Dorian)
33–40—Heroic Dragon (A Aeolian)
41–46—Warring Vikings (E Dorian)

A dissonant octachord (01234689), played by the woodwinds and brass opens the cue as Toothless hits the Red Death with a fireball. The dragon then rises and opens its wings. Powell's music is wholly dissonant in this portion of the cue, with the woodwinds having a "chromatic rip ('shriek')" marked and the strings playing a cluster glissando. The terror of the Red Death, now fully ready to attack and destroy, is on display. As it rises into the air, a variation on the opening of the *Dragon Tune* is heard in the low brass and low strings. The violins and violas continue their cluster glissando, and the woodwinds play a different scale every other measure in 8–14, first D Aeolian, then E Phrygian, F Lydian, and finally G Dorian. These rapid scalar passages are indicative of the action music and the immediate chaos of the battle throughout the entire orchestra.

As the Red Death chases Hiccup and Toothless, the Vikings watch the aerial battle from below. The heroic harmonization of the *Warring Vikings* theme is heard, leading into a full harmonic cycle of a whole-tone scale in measures 30–31—GM-FM-E♭M-D♭M-BM-AM. The whole-tone scale is symmetrical, meaning that it doesn't necessarily have a clear tonic, which is how it is used here, making the action music more exciting as we don't know when the passage will end. As Hiccup declares, "It's time to disappear," the music transforms into the *Heroic Dragon* version of the *Dragon Tune*. This variation tells us that Hiccup and Toothless will be successful in their fight, and it leads directly into final heroic harmonization of the *Warring Vikings* theme, the Vikings still watching with anxiety.

As both dragons ascend above the clouds, the Red Death arbitrarily chomps at Toothless, unable to find him. The orchestra sustains a mysterious-sounding EmM^7 chord while the gong player bows the instrument. The Vikings are anxious from not knowing how Toothless and Hiccup are faring in the battle, which also makes the audience anxious, the cue sliding directly into the next cue.

5M39—Counter Attack (1:21:43–1:23:29)

2–5—Flying Ostinato (E Aeolian)
27–29—Dragon Tune variation (D doubly harmonic minor)
33–39—Dragon Tune variation (D doubly harmonic minor)
43–44—Vikings (B-flat major)

A fireball is shot at the Red Death from behind, and now we know where Hiccup and Toothless are. The shot hits the dragon, and a variation on the *Flying Ostinato* is played in the violins and violas. It's not happy flying; it's fighting-for-their-lives flying. The Vikings can only watch the sky light up through blasts from the two dragons and hope that things are going well.

As the Red Death breathes fire everywhere it can, a three-measure pattern of Cm-Cm-Cm-A♭M is used, as seen in Figure 4.18. The three-measure pattern is unexpected, as four-measure patterns are far more familiar and expected in music. The effect is that the pattern only increases anxiety because of its shortened length, not giving

Figure 4.18. 5M39, measures 12–14, three-measure ostinato pattern.

away how the battle will end. Toothless's prosthetic tail catches on fire, so he and Hiccup go all in on a final attack. They loop around to get the Red Death to chase them, and a brief, rhythmically diminished opening of the *Dragon Tune* is played by the trumpets and horns. It is exciting, visually and musically, and the speed at which the opening of the theme is played emphasizes the size of the Red Death. This varied opening is heard multiple times throughout the brass. Meanwhile, the choir and string harmonies consist of hexachords, septachords, and octachords, all connected through the basses, who are playing the notes of the varied *Dragon Tune*.

The Red Death closes in on Hiccup and Toothless, preparing to chomp them out of existence, and they take their final shot, turning around and firing a fireball into the Alpha's mouth, accompanied by the opening of the *Vikings* theme. Victory is imminent, but Toothless's tail continues to burn, and both the Red Death and Toothless fall from the sky. The Red Death crashes in a huge fireball, and Toothless tries to avoid the flames, but in doing so, is hit by the Alpha's tail, knocking Hiccup off Toothless's back, and the cue ends with a B♭ minor triad (037), which shifts to a B♭-D-E trichord (026). The fate of Hiccup and Toothless is unclear, both visually and musically.

5M40—Where's Hiccup (1:24:13–1:26:56)

22–31—Flying Ostinato variation (D major)
37–44—Flying A (C major)
45–55—Flying B (C major)
56–66—Flying A (C major)
64–66—Flying Ostinato (C major)

Stoick searches for Hiccup among the ash and fog. He finds Toothless, unclear if the dragon is alive, and sees the broken harness and destroyed tail. The music at the start of the cue is ambiguous, using triads and seventh chords non-functionally, not giving any information to the audience. When Toothless opens his wings and reveals Hiccup inside, the music changes, foregrounding B minor, then shifting to D major when Stoick exclaims, "You brought him back alive!" At that moment, the triple-meter version of the *Flying Ostinato* is played by the full orchestra, somewhat harmonized with the *Flying B* theme harmonies, as the *Flying Ostinato* appeared in "Romantic Flight." Stoick personally thanks Toothless for saving Hiccup, and the orchestral texture drops to only strings. It's a very gentle passage that alternates between D major and C major triads, before ending on both chords—C-D-E-F♯. The scene then shifts back to Berk, with Hiccup convalescing in bed in his home.

Toothless waits for Hiccup to awaken after the battle. Much like a dog would, Toothless licks Hiccup's face when he sits up, and bounds around the house excitedly. This tender moment is scored with solo piano playing the complete *Flying* theme in C major (at least, until the final couple of measures). The music is not as intimate as the solo voice, but the piano is the only instrument that can be played by a single performer and can play in both treble and bass clef simultaneously. The choice of solo piano represents a level of intimacy; Hiccup and Toothless are indoors as Hiccup convalesces from his injuries, his best friend waiting for him to awaken. The *Flying* theme remains incomplete because Hiccup is now *incomplete*, as he lost part of his leg in the battle. The music pauses on the penultimate harmony, then restarts as Toothless sniffs at Hiccup's new prosthetic limb.

Hiccup attempts to walk on his own but cannot. Toothless is there to catch him when he falls, then be his support to help him get to the door. We hear the *Flying A* theme on piano, accompanied by the strings. The music is still quite intimate, two timbres, two best friends. As they approach the door, and the *Flying A* theme ends, we hear a ii^7-V-I PAC in C major. They continue to approach the door, and the opening of the *Flying Ostinato* is used as a codetta to the cue, reaffirming the love between the two friends. A lesser film would have ended here, completing the journey between the boy and his dragon. All is well, even though Hiccup doesn't know that Stoick and the entire village have embraced Hiccup's ideas of keeping and training dragons.

5M41—Coming Back Around (1:26:57–1:29:01)

    3–16—Love theme (A major)
    18–26—Flying Ostinato (F-sharp major)
    26–39—Love theme (E major)
    43–46—Flying Ostinato (E major)
    47–54—Flying A (E major)
    55–64—Flying B (E major)
    65–67—Flying Ostinato (E major)
    68–75—Flying A (A major) *not in film*
    76–85—Flying B (A major) *not in film*

As Hiccup opens the door, he sees a dragon, and quickly slams the door shut. As he reopens it, the cue begins, and he sees his friends riding dragons. The trills in the woodwinds and strings increase in volume and Hiccup looks around Berk to see dragons everywhere. The magical feeling of the lengthy harp glissando leads into a statement of the *Love* theme; Hiccup's dream has come true. Hiccup doesn't believe this could be real, and thinks he's dead, but Stoick comes over to reassure him he is very much alive, and asks him, "What d'ya think?" The *Love* theme ends and turns into the *Flying Ostinato* in triple meter as the whole village of Berk comes over to greet Hiccup. The *Flying Ostinato* links back with the *Love* theme as Gobber announces how proud he is of building Hiccup's new prosthetic leg. Astrid comes over and punches Hiccup, again, and the *Love* theme shifts to a solo violin. She then kisses him in front of the entire village, Hiccup standing stupidly in love. Toothless joins the fun, jumping on Vikings before the scene changes.

The final bit of the film forms a bookend with the opening of the film, as both have

Hiccup's voice-over narration explaining the village of Berk. This section opens with the *Flying Ostinato* on dulcimer and bagpipes in the key of E major, the key of adventure. Hiccup locks into the stirrups on Toothless's harness, a new tail piece in place, and the complete *Flying* theme enters as Hiccup's narration does. The film ends with a final statement of the *Flying Ostinato* over the title card, and as the End Credits begin, the song "Sticks and Stones," sung by Jónsi, begins. Measures 68–87, the end of the cue as written, do not appear here, but are used in the End Titles.

"Sticks and Stones" (1:29:01–1:31:02)

Jónsi's lyrics are in both English and Icelandic, but with the quickness of the English lyrics, combined with the lack of clear enunciation, understanding many of the lyrics is difficult. The titles words never actually appear in the song. Instead, the lyrics reference "broken bones," part of the rhyme with "sticks and stones." In general, the lyrics refer to a strong friendship between two individuals, with lines referring to being in close proximity to each other.

The song doesn't follow typical popular song structure, as it comes to a complete stop just before the verse that is sung in Icelandic. The song itself is far less memorable than any of the themes used throughout the film, and because of its placement in the End Credits, feels more like an afterthought than anything. Even though it may feel like an extraneous song, the connection between the singer and the music in the film runs deep, and the relationship continues into the other two films as well.

End Credits (1:31:03–1:37:39)

The remaining music for the End Credits are culled from existing cues and stitched together.

5M41—"Coming Back Around," measures 67–87
1M2—"This is Berk," measures 1–36
2M14—"Forbidden Friendship," measures 56–134
3M24—"Astrid Goes for a Spin," complete cue
3M25—"Romantic Flight," complete cue

The End Credits begin with the portion of cue 5M41 that was cut from the film. The use of 1M2 is the original opening to "This is Berk" that was unused in the film. These are the two most prominent portions of music written for the film that were not included, which makes sense to include them here in the End Credits.

5M50—The Vikings Have Their Tea

1–8—Vikings A (G major)
8–16—Vikings A (G major)
17–20—Vikings B
21–24—Vikings C
25–28—Vikings D
28–38—Vikings A
||: 1–8 :|| 17–28 || 28–38||—Small Ternary/Rounded Binary

In his cue description, Rodier writes, "Powell thought it would be fun to imagine a scene where Vikings are sitting around doing something completely out of character. He wrote the Viking tune in the style of a minuet to accompany the cheeky tableau. Solo violin and sopilka take turns playing the tune in G major while the other strings pluck notes quietly in the background amidst gently rolling harp chords."[4] The form of a Classical minuet is a rounded binary, with an opening eight-measure segment that is repeated, moving on to contrasting material, and ends with a return of the opening material in the home key. Powell's dainty reimagining of the *Vikings* theme fits that formal description. In fact, the contrasting section even ends on the dominant of the home key, exactly as would be expected in the Classical minuet. It is a wonderful exercise in stylistic appropriation but has nowhere to live within the context of the film, and is lovely that the cue is included both in the published edition of the score as well as on the deluxe edition of the soundtrack recording.

5

How to Train Your Dragon 2 Cue Analysis

1M1—Dragon Racing (0:00:29–0:05:00)

4–15—Flying A (C major)
16–23—Hiccup/Vikings (C Aeolian)
24–31—Flying B (C Aeolian)
44–51—Hiccup/Vikings (A-flat Aeolian)
62–66—Hiccup/Vikings (D Aeolian)
66–75—Vikings A (G major)
75–76—Flying Ostinato (D Phrygian with ♯3)
77–81—Fate theme (F-sharp Dorian)
103–110—Warring Vikings (reharmonized) (D Aeolian)
115–118—Hiccup/Vikings (G Aeolian)
123–126—Warring Vikings (D Aeolian)
127–130—Warring Vikings (G Aeolian)
132–140—Love theme (B-flat major)
140–141—Warring Vikings (D Aeolian)
143–146—Hiccup/Vikings (G Aeolian)

The parallel music between the opening of the initial cues in the first two films in the trilogy is quite remarkable. The order of thematic statements is fundamentally identical. However, in the second film, the music begins in C, a perfect fifth higher than F, where it began in the first film. The location of Berk has not changed, but the ideology of the village has, accounting for the different tonal center. Additionally, C major, where the *Flying A* theme begins, is often considered to be the key of perfection, and Berk is now idealized in Hiccup's mind, a utopia of human-dragon symbiosis. Nothing could possibly make it better. Of course, all of these thoughts will be proven wrong over the course of the film, but the idea must be presented before it can be rejected.

Following an interlude that accompanies Hiccup's voice-over narration explaining that Berk has something that makes it unique—dragon racing—the *Hiccup* theme begins in A♭ Aeolian as we fully see the competition occurring. We hear three four-measure statements of the theme with an interlude between the second and third statement that resembles both the *Hiccup* theme and the *Warring Vikings* theme, as seen in Figure 5.1. When the third statement enters, it is in D Aeolian, a tritone away from the previous statements. The tritone relationship signals something special is at work in Berk, something that does not happen anywhere else.

Figure 5.1. 1M1, measures 48–55. The *Hiccup* theme and interlude.

The opening of the *Warring Vikings* theme leaps from *Do* down to *Sol* before climbing back up to *Do*. In the music derived from the theme, measures 52–55, the opening *Do* leaps up to *Fa* before stepping up to *Sol* and returning back down to *Do* at the start of the next measure. The opening gesture is inverted. The initial leap of an ascending fourth—*Do* down to *Sol* and *Do* up to *Fa*—move in opposite directions, and the opening gesture of *Do* to *Sol* also occurs in opposite directions. In the third measure, the *Warring Vikings* theme moves *Do-Fa-Me*, and descends back down to *Do*, while the variation ascends *Do-Me-Fa* before continuing to climb up to *Sol*, the second most stable pitch behind *Do*. Once again, the direction of the line is inverted, and the order of the notes *Me* and *Fa* determines if the music will ascend or descend. Additionally, the *Warring Vikings* theme is played by low brass, woodwinds, and strings in the first film. This interlude is played by violins and flutes, opposite registers and the timbres are inverted. The playful nature of the *Hiccup* theme is present in the interlude, and these additional notes act as melodic embellishment of the *Warring Vikings* theme. The melodic inversions can be seen with more clarity when the embellishments are removed from the interlude. Powell's clever technique of inverting and embellishing the *Warring Vikings* theme neutralizes the fighting nature of the Vikings and turns it into something much more playful, and more closely resembling Hiccup, as he was the one who convinced Berk to accept dragons as friends and not adversaries.

In the first film's opening cue, the *Warring Vikings* theme was played in the low brass between the second and third statements of the *Hiccup* theme, as the village is fighting off the attacking dragons. The "interlude" in this film is in E major, and is played by upper woodwinds and strings, with brass melodically absent. The contrast in timbre gives this interlude a much lighter feel, as dragons are not attacking the village, but are instead incorporated into a game.

As Stoick announces the scores by naming each player, the *Vikings A* theme begins in G major, since all the Vikings are present and cheering the competition. When he reaches Hiccup's name, he notices that Hiccup is absent; the minor mode version of the *Flying Ostinato* sounds once, then leads into a statement of the *Fate* theme in F♯ minor as we return to the competition, Hiccup still conspicuously absent.

Hiccup's voice-over narration returns, as he describes the dragon problem that used to be present, "but that was five years ago," clearly stating how much time has passed since the first film. The music in this portion of the cue was heard in the first film in cue 3M18, "See You Tomorrow." The combination of the *Fate* theme as well as this other material in measures 77–97 can be traced in measures 45–65 of 3M18. We see all the "amenities" now available to the dragons, concluding with "fire prevention." In this cue, the music goes into the octatonic cycle after eight measures, but the (0,1) cycle, unlike the (1,2) cycle of the first film. The chords here are F♯M-E♭M-CM-AM, with the cycle ending on C major. This leads into the final stages of the Dragon Racing match. The music in measures 98–101 is in D minor, derived from 2M9, "Dragon Training," from the first film. It is exactly the same music and serves a similar function, repeating in order to increase the tension and stakes of the match.

As Astrid goes after the black sheep to win the match, the *Warring Vikings* theme is used in D Aeolian. Gobber speaks to the black sheep, comedically telling it to have a nice flight. As he does this, the musical texture drops in measures 108–110, leaving pizzicato strings and choir, making the moment more silly than serious. Once the sheep is caught by Fishlegs' dragon Meatlug, the *Hiccup* theme returns in G Aeolian. The sheep is tossed to Ruffnut, who smacks Fishlegs away, causing him to crash into Snotlout, and provoking the Vikings into wild cheering. This smack is accompanied by the *Warring Vikings* theme in D Aeolian, as it looks like the match may end. The Nut twins fight over the glory of victory, and Astrid swoops in and steals the sheep, breaking away to win the match. As she secures the black sheep, the *Love* theme is sounded in B♭ major. In this instance, the *Love* theme is used in a highly non-traditional way, although this scene doesn't feature Astrid walking away from an explosion as in the first film. On her way to winning, she is intercepted and the *Warring Vikings* theme in D sounds again, as the other team attempts to steal the sheep back from Astrid. Snotlout tries to take out Astrid with a hammer, but she ducks and he hits Fishlegs instead, another instance of visual comedy in this opening cue, highlighting the difference between the opening of the two films. Astrid flies low, accompanied by the *Hiccup* theme, deposits the sheep in the basket, and the match and the cue conclude at the end of the thematic statement.

Rather than introduce one or more new themes in this opening cue, Powell exclusively uses themes from the first film. The only theme used in the opening cue from the first film not present here is the *Dragon Tune*, as the Berkians are not fighting dragons, but living and playing with them. The *Fate* theme is present here, which was not present in the first film's opening cue. Using familiar themes in the opening cue of a sequel film serves multiple functions. First, it allows those familiar with the first film to reengage with the themes that they already know. Second, it allows those who did not see the first film to hear the themes from the first while hearing Hiccup's narration, catching them up on the events of the first film. One does not have to see the first film to be caught up at the start of the second film. Third, it confirms that the sound world of the first film will be similar to the sound world of the second film. The presence of all these themes means that the music cannot stray too far, regardless of the new themes introduced in the second film. It is a masterful cue that recapitulates the music from the first film, while providing underscore for a completely new scenario at the start of the second, in particular, repurposing the *Warring Vikings* theme from a fighting theme to music supporting the participation in a sport.

1M2S—Where No One Goes (0:05:17–0:07:39)

    4–31—Flying Ostinato (E major)
    32–42—Flying B
    43–62—Flying Ostinato
    63–73—Flying B
    74–77—Flying Ostinato

This is the only time in the three films where a song is used during the film's narrative, and the only one where Jónsi and Powell collaborated. Unlike "Sticks and Stones" for the first film, "Where No One Goes" features a full orchestral accompaniment and uses both the *Flying Ostinato* and *Flying B* themes. Hiccup declares Berk "pretty much perfect," thanks to his hard work, and because they can ride dragons, the world has expanded and can be explored. The action then cuts to Hiccup and Toothless flying over the ocean.

While the action isn't a montage like 3M18's "See You Tomorrow" from the first film, it is definitely meant to show how far Hiccup and Toothless have come in the five years since the first film, as Hiccup now has "wings" on his suit that he can use to glide through the air. One consistent element between this song and "See You Tomorrow" is that each has a section of dissonance where things go wrong. In the "See You Tomorrow," Hiccup loses his cheat sheet. In this song, Hiccup is about to glide into rocks as the song nears its end. Toothless prevents this by shooting a fireball at the rocks and removing them, but both of them crash onto a forested island, as the music comes to an immediate halt, a deformed version of the *Flying Ostinato* sounding in measures 78–84. Once again, the action ends with a fireball from Toothless and a comedic aftereffect.

Powell spoke about working with Jónsi across the films in our conversation.

> The first film starts with the relationship between Dean and Jónsi. Dean knew Jónsi very well, asked him to write something, and Jónsi wrote that very wonderful song for the End Credits. It was puzzling to Jeffrey; he didn't really understand it, but it had this strange and wonderful feeling that felt happiest, very unlike the usual stuff [with Sigur rós]. Jónsi just done this album of very happy music [titled Go] and then I think we temped something from that album in there. And Dean and Chris loved the feeling of it, and asked him to write something original, so he did.
>
> Then, on the second film, they asked him to write something original, and it was suggested that because the first song is actually in a flying scene, why not use some of the *Flying* theme from the first film. That was after the first thing we did together, which was the "Courting Song" for Stoick and Valka. That needed to get written first. While we were doing that is when we talked about this other moment, the flying scene early in the film, Dean said to us both, "There's this flying moment, and I'd like you to write something, but maybe it could be a bit of a co-write." Rather than try and jump in on Jónsi's style, I said, "Why don't I give you some material from the first movie, and you can try that out. If it doesn't work I can try something else." But he liked it so he used it. It was a couple of afternoon playdates that we had together, and it was a collaboration that went very well. Jónsi sent me a rough groove that he wanted to try and write to, and I set some of my material going that he could cut around and use, some orchestral things. He finished off the song using those bits, and then he sent it back. It was an interactive process.

On the third movie, he wrote another song, but I also got him in to do his vocals for an idea that I really had no idea what he was going to do. I just loved the idea of getting to do something. I set him up with Logic (a digital audio workstation), alone, with a microphone, and he just went into the studio and laid down loads of vocals. We talked about it a few times. He was basically in there for an afternoon and laid all those vocals. Then I started to piece it together, took all the tracks, and integrated it into the cue I was doing. We had fun doing those kinds of things. He's very easy to work with.

1M3-4—Together, We Map the World (0:07:55-0:10:29)

3–15—Map the World (C Aeolian)
17–23—Map the World variation (G Mixolydian/Aeolian)
26–33—Heroic Dragon (D major)
33–36—Flying Ostinato (6/8 version) (A major)
37–51—Map the World (F-sharp Aeolian)
52–53—Hiccup/Vikings (B Aeolian)
54–57—Love theme (E major)
55–57—Hiccup/Vikings (E Aeolian)

As Hiccup gets up from the crash and collects himself, he begins looking around. The first new theme for the film is introduced here, *Map the World*. As Hiccup stands on the edge of the island and looks around, he tells Toothless that they appear to have found another new location. He then taunts Toothless about his flying and tries to put him into a bear hug. A varied statement of *Map the World* is used, shown in Figure 5.2, this one much more lighthearted. At the end of this statement, Toothless carries Hiccup to the edge of the island, ready to drop him into the ocean 1000 feet below, and the cue pauses.

Hiccup and Toothless playfully wrestle, and Toothless signals his win by licking (or slobbering) all over Hiccup, laughing at the situation. The music re-enters at this point,

Figure 5.2. 1M3–4, measures 17–24, lighthearted variation of *Map the World*.

with the harp playing a version of the *Flying Ostinato* in A major. Hiccup then pulls out a small book and adds the current location to his map of his known world, from where the theme derives its name. The theme begins again as Hiccup spreads the map on the ground, and they add their location to the map, sarcastically naming it "Itchy Armpit." Hiccup asks Toothless what they might find there, and begins naming dragons. He then says, "Maybe we'll finally track down another Night Fury." As Hiccup reaches the words "Night Fury," the music shifts from an E minor triad in measure 48 to an E♭ major triad in measures 49–51, a Neo-Riemannian operation known as **SLIDE** (or **S**). In the **SLIDE** operation, the third of the first chord remains the same, and the root and fifth "slide" down a half step to create a different harmony. The SLIDE function did not appear in the first film, but appears in the second and third films, connecting to the third film through the Light Fury and the Hidden World.

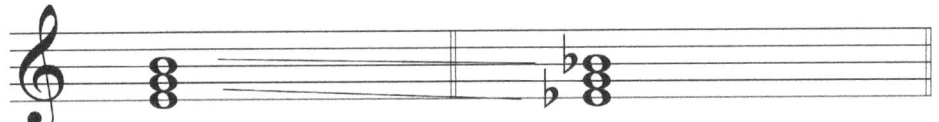

Figure 5.3. A Neo-riemannian *SLIDE* from E minor to E-flat major.

As Hiccup asks what they should do next, Astrid and her dragon, Stormfly, appear on the island with a flourish in the horns of the opening two measures of the *Love* theme, followed by a pizzicato statement of the opening of the *Hiccup* theme, Stormfly and Toothless playing. This is the first time that the *Hiccup* theme and the *Love* theme have musically interacted. In the opening cue, Stoick proclaimed Astrid as his "future daughter-in-law," even though Hiccup and Astrid are not engaged and are only dating. This brief moment foreshadows the long-term trajectory of their relationship.

1M5—Hiccup's Gonna Be Chief (0:11:33–0:14:34)

2–10—Hiccup the Chief (D major)
10–18—Flying Ostinato (B major)
20–34—Love theme (E major)
36–44—Love theme (D-flat major)
47–49—Map the World (B-flat Aeolian)
67–70—Flying Ostinato (D Phrygian with ♯3)
75–80—Good Alpha variation (D Phrygian with ♯3)
81–86—Good Alpha variation (D Phrygian with ♯3)
95–96—Flying Ostinato (B-flat Phrygian)

Also looking into the future is the cue 1M5, as one day Hiccup will assume the role of chief of Berk. Stoick is actively looking for the right opportunity to have the discussion with Hiccup about taking over, but Hiccup consistently manages to deflect and avoid it. The conversation is the classic "What are you going to do with your life, son," conversation that fathers often have with their sons. In this instance, though, Hiccup's future is preordained, as the son of the chief will ultimately succeed the father. Hiccup is not yet ready for the responsibility, nor does he truly want it, preferring to spend his time with Toothless.

The cue opens with the new theme *Hiccup the Chief*, a melody that is passed around the orchestra, with solos for the horn and bassoon, and melodic segments for strings and woodwinds. The entrance of the music corresponds to when Hiccup, imitating his father, says, "You're all grown up," and Astrid interrupts, excitedly exclaiming that Stoick wants to make Hiccup the new chief. The theme is somewhat hymn-like, using almost exclusively major triads in its harmonization, and is much more mature than the *Hiccup* theme in its stately tempo and rhythms. The conclusion of the theme leads directly into a triple-meter statement of the *Flying Ostinato*, a statement sometimes paired with the *Love* theme. Here, it is used because of Astrid's support. She encourages Hiccup to take the job, and as she does, the *Love* theme enters. Hiccup says to her, "I'm not like you. You know exactly who you are." Hiccup feels lost in the world, not having the same personality as his father and having never met his mother (deep foreshadowing), but Astrid has been by his side for years now, encouraging him to be the best version of himself. Hiccup says that "there's something out there," as he longingly looks into the distance. The opening notes of the *Map the World* theme, harmonized by an ominous-sounding B♭ minor triad, are played by the solo horn, and the scene changes as Astrid and Toothless fly into a darker part of the archipelago. As they discover a location that has been unnaturally covered in ice, the minor-mode version of the *Flying Ostinato* sounds, still in triple meter in measures 67–70, as Astrid and Hiccup are together.

As they fly around the fort and inspect it, the harmonies in measures 75–87 are wondrously chromatic, as illustrated in Figure 5.4. The melody feels as though it should be in G minor, based on the contour and relationship to the *Map the World* theme. However, this melody is harmonized in D major with DM-E♭M-Cm-A^{M}m7-DM, or I-♭II-♭vii (or iv/iv)-V7-I in D major. A short codetta is attached to the end of the idea, alternating between D major and A major, or I and V in D. The harmonic progression is also similar to the progression of the *Calming Motif* (I-♭II-♭VII-I), except this situation is anything but calm. On the restatement, beginning in measure 81, we hear DM-E♭M-Cm-A^{o7}-F♯m-C♯M-F♯m-BM-D♭M (C♯M). The statement clearly begins in D, but ends in F♯ minor, the last five chords as i-V-i-IV-V in F♯ minor. The A^{o7} chord

Figure 5.4. 1M5, measures 75–87, varied statement of *Good Alpha* theme.

occupies the same position in the harmonic progression as the AMm^7 did in the first statement, so the connection between the two chords is clear. Additionally, in order to create the A^{o7} chord, Powell simply adds a third below the C minor triad. The melody is able to remain intact because the root motion remains the same, and the harmonic change is minimally disruptive, allowing for the modulation from D major to F♯ minor, closely related keys, but a harmonic relationship that is rarely heard in tonal music, modulating from the major tonic to the minor mediant. Additionally, the modulation occurs quite abruptly, so the minimally disruptive harmony stabilizes the connection between the two keys.[1]

The full version of this theme is not heard until later in the film, but this music is a variation of the *Good Alpha* theme. It is heard as Hiccup and Astrid inspect the mysteriously ice-covered location, unsure of what kind of creature could have done that. Only later does the audience learn that Valka's Bewilderbeest, a good dragon, breathed ice at the home of dragon trappers, forcing the bad guys to find a new base of operations. Since none of this information is known yet, Powell takes the extraordinary step of presenting a variation of a theme long before the actual theme is introduced. Powell's choice works into the long history of Leitmotifs and thematic transformation in film, connecting these films with some of the great film scores of the past, most notably with John Williams's scores for the original *Star Wars* trilogy and his introduction of the Force Theme in the binary sun scene.

The pair come across dragon trappers, and as they recognize their perilous situation, a dissonant (01268) pentachord is sounded in the brass. Stormfly is caught in a net and the minor-mode version of the *Flying Ostinato* is played in the strings. As the trappers try to secure the dragon, Toothless lands with Hiccup and Astrid. The conclusion of the cue, measures 107–109, contains similar music to what was heard in measures 10–13 of 5M39, "Counter Attack," from the first film (Cm-Cm-Cm-A♭M), where the Alpha breathes fire everywhere in a flailing attempt to attack Toothless. Here (F♯m-F♯m-F♯m-DM), the trappers flail to secure Astrid's dragon under the net. The music between the two cues is a tritone apart; the instance from the first film was high in the sky, above the clouds while this moment is tethered to the ground. The cue ends without fanfare or rescue.

Powell spoke about the need to have themes to always fit the situation rather than specific naming themes. Concerning Hiccup's music, Powell had this to say:

> I try not to put a theme with one particular character. I always try to associate a theme with a character arc, or a common trait. So, in the first film, the theme with the [Scotch] snap is more about being a Viking. When Hiccup is trying to be a Viking, I would use that. But later on, as he develops and grows through the movies, I needed different themes to represent what he was going to have to face, so the idea in *How to Train Your Dragon 2* is that his father is going to die and he's going to become chief. The idea of a theme to set his fate as growing up; it was a maturing theme. I can interpret any of the themes in slightly different ways, depending on what they need to do for the story, but I try to focus on an arc that I might have to follow and when I'm writing it, will that theme do the various things I need it to do. Can it sound forlorn but then be heroic but then be noble? Hopefully there's lots of variation on each theme that would show that. It's not really this character, so why's it got that theme on it? Well, he's leading them, so maybe I would use it. Or, this sense of flying in the movie needing themes. Is it freedom or is it flying or is it friendship? The themes can be a bit vaguer, certainly not Wagnerian as when Tristan shows up on stage and you hear his tune. It's never that. That often happens, but it's always trying to base it on who's Hiccup at this moment. We have to start something that we can then finish. So that the threads of the story are then followed.

Although Hiccup will one day transition into the chief of Berk, he is not yet at that point in his journey.

1M6—Eret Educates Hiccup (0:15:23–0:17:02)

1–22—Pulsing 16th notes
1–4—Valka's Tune
30–33—Map the World Swashbuckling version (C-sharp minor)
34–37—Map the World Swashbuckling version (E minor)
38–43—Flying Ostinato (E Aeolian)

This cue opens with a sound unheard in the film series to this point: pulsing sixteenth notes in the strings, creating a sound not unlike John Adams's composition *Harmonielehre* or perhaps something by Steve Reich. The harmony, a (01368) pentachord, which can be arranged as a C♯^{o7} chord with an 11th, avoids a clear triadic root association due to B, the chordal seventh, sounding as the lowest note, adding to the mystery of what the lead trapper, Eret, tells Hiccup—there are (other) "do-gooder dragon riders" out there. When Hiccup asks the question, "There are other dragon riders," the Celtic Harp plays the faintest hint of *Valka's Tune*, a melodic fragment we have not yet heard, and have no association with, yet. This is a further example of Powell's musical foreshadowing, carrying on from the previous cue. Of course, we know the meaning of the melodic fragment because we have seen the film, but on a first viewing, the meaning and

Figure 5.5. 1M6, measures 30–37, swashbuckling version of *Map the World*.

association are unclear. Perhaps it has something to do with the "other dragon riders," or perhaps it means more.

Eret discusses needing a quota for Drago Bludvist's Dragon Army, and the pulsing continues. Toothless is clearly agitated by Eret, who shows a scar from the last time he returned to Drago without a catch, a moment accompanied by a tritone drop in the basses in measures 11–12 from E♭ to A. Eret introduces himself, and the pulsing stops, landing on a G♯^sus4 chord. Hiccup responds by introducing Toothless, the harmony changing to BM. The strings resume, now playing moving triplets, and a sign that they are about to leave the trappers' fort. The harmony shifts back to a G♯M triad, forming a Hero chromatic mediant pair with the BM triad, as Hiccup's heroics will be necessary in a moment. The G♯M triad also serves as the dominant harmony for the swashbuckling-style statement of the *Map the World* theme in C♯ Aeolian, then quickly repeated up a third in E Aeolian, presented in Figure 5.5. The use of the *Map the World* theme here is to highlight the many dangers to which Hiccup is oblivious in the larger world. The swashbuckling style of the theme represents the good guys fighting against, essentially, pirates. While this fight doesn't occur on a boat, it doesn't need to because the dragon trappers are stealing what doesn't belong to them. While they might not be pirates in name, their actions are quite similar.

Hiccup and Astrid escape with both of their respective dragons. As they fly away, we hear the minor-mode version of the *Flying Ostinato*, with Eret yelling, "You will never hold on to those dragons. You hear me? Drago is coming for them all!" Eret speaks a foreboding statement that necessitates foreboding music, hence the minor-mode version of flying music.

2M7—Drago's Coming (0:19:42–0:21:29)

10–17—Hiccup/Viking (D Dorian)
22–25—Hiccup/Viking (C-sharp Dorian)
25–30—Warring Vikings (C-sharp Aeolian)
29–33—Warring Vikings (G Aeolian) *tritone apart*
34–39—Hiccup the Chief (B-flat minor)
45–54—Hiccup the Chief (D doubly harmonic minor)

Stoick corrects Hiccup when he mentions the name of "Dargo Bloodyfist," by solemnly stating, "Drago Bludvist." At the mention of his name, the violins sustain long notes, and with recognition in his eyes, Stoick orders Berk to protect the dragons, the music finally moving. A variation on the *Hiccup* theme is used, but played in the violas and cellos, assuming Stoick's timbral role rather than Hiccup's. This is "real" Viking work, and as Hiccup is not the chief of Berk, Stoick's timbres take over the theme. The syncopated accompaniment is reminiscent of something from the *Pirates of the Caribbean* series, another reference to pirates, or in this case, dragon trappers.

Hiccup sees and hears the fear in his father and offers a radical idea: he will fly to Drago and "talk some sense into him." As Hiccup says this, we hear the *Warring Vikings* theme in C♯ Aeolian, beginning in measure 25, but only in the bassoons and cello, a very unemphatic statement. All brass and percussion are tacet. It is a thematic statement meant to sound unimposing, much like Hiccup would in front of Drago. A second statement of the *Warring Vikings* theme follows, shown in Figure 5.6, but this one is in G Aeolian, up a tritone rather than the expected perfect fourth. Trying to "talk it out" with Drago will lead to failure, the tritone signaling the wrong interval.

Figure 5.6. 2M7, measures 29–34, octatonic version of *Warring Vikings*.

Stoick even says, "Peace is over. I must prepare you for war." An additional measure of music is attached to the end of the second statement of the *Warring Vikings* theme to reset the music. Powell uses the (2,3) octatonic cycle in measures 33–34 for the chords DM-A♭M-DM-BM-FM, with the bass line ascending F♯-G♯-A-B-C, and the melodic line descending D-C-D-B-F. This cycle is heard as Hiccup says, "Let's find him and change his mind." Octatonic cycles were used in the first film to denote plans not working, or to see something unexpected. Here, Hiccup's plan will not work, no matter how much he believes in it.

Stoick instructs Hiccup that he must protect his people above all else because that is what a chief does for his village. We hear a highly modified version of the *Hiccup the Chief* theme in B♭ minor. Stoick is trying to instill the values of a leader to his son. The music, however, seems to inspire Hiccup to take action and seek out Drago instead of staying home to protect his village. Beginning in measure 45, the horns play a melody that is a variation even further afield of the *Hiccup the Chief* theme. This variation shares a scale with the *Dragon Tune* from the first film, D doubly harmonic minor. The *Dragon Tune* was the musical representation of the villain from the first film. Since we have not yet seen Drago, we don't know anything about him, other than he has an army of dragons he uses to conquer others, but connecting the villain of the second film to the villain of the first film through the use of common scales and thematic variation and development is brilliant.

2M8—Eret Has Visitors (0:21:41–0:22:38)

5–8—Map the World Swashbuckling version (C Mixolydian)
9–12—Map the World Swashbuckling version (E Mixolydian)
14–15—Map the World Swashbuckling version (A Mixolydian)
16–17—Hiccup/Viking Theme ending only (C Mixolydian)
20–39—Hiccup the Chief variation (C major)

The action cuts to Eret's ship, as they continue their hunt for dragons to deliver to Drago. One of the crew sees something approaching, and we hear a C Mixolydian melodic statement of the *Map the World* theme, again in a swashbuckling style. When Eret sees who the dragons (and riders) are, his eyes widen, and the music modulates up from C Mixolydian to E Mixolydian, and finally to A Mixolydian. As Hiccup and Astrid land on the ship, an ending similar to how the *Hiccup* theme ends is used; Hiccup is quite confident in his plan.

Of course, Hiccup hasn't told Astrid the plan, which is to surrender both themselves and their dragons. As he gives himself up, the *Hiccup the Chief* theme is played in the woodwinds and strings, still with an absence of brass and percussion. However, this statement is not noble like the first time it is heard in the film. Instead, it is a bit silly and goofy, as is Hiccup's plan. Hiccup is very clearly not prepared to be the chief of Berk because he is still placing his desires ahead of the needs of the village, and the style of the thematic statement illustrates that Hiccup is continues to make rash and foolish decisions, much like a child would.

2M9—Me Likey (0:23:38–0:24:36)

1–4—Hiccup the Chief (G-flat major)
9–12—Warring Vikings (C Aeolian)
13–16—Warring Vikings (F Aeolian)
18–29—Love theme (B major)
33–36—Vikings A (D-flat major)

Hiccup says that he can change Eret's mind about dragons and the cue begins. A melodically and harmonically modified opening statement of the *Hiccup the Chief* theme is used at the opening, and while it *is* possible to change some minds, it certainly won't be as easy as Hiccup expects. The musical transformation and comparison are shown in Figure 5.7.

Suddenly, Eret announces that Dragon Riders are attacking the ship, but a few seconds later, it turns out to be Hiccup's friends, as the *Warring Vikings* theme is used. It appears in its expected two-statement form, first in C, then in F, but at the end of the second statement, the music shifts, and Ruffnut sees Eret, love at first sight. Her slowed-down words, "Oh, my," are mimicked by a trombone glissando. The *Love* theme is sung by wordless choir and the action is in slow motion, Eret's bulging muscles on display. This is the first time that the *Love* theme has been used for characters other than Astrid and Hiccup. Although it often doubles as the "*Astrid* theme," Powell uses it more generally as a *Love* theme, and its meaning is quite clear in this cue. Ruffnut offers herself up as a bigger target for Eret's net, a willing captive. Hiccup escapes, leaping through the air, back down onto the ship, and the cue ends with a swashbuckling statement of the opening of the *Vikings* theme, coupled with a variation of the famous "Hollywood

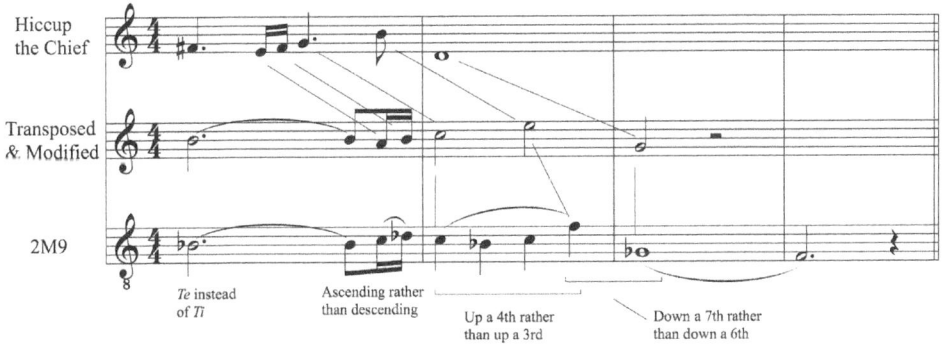

Figure 5.7. 2M9, measures 1–4, transformation of *Hiccup the Chief* theme.

Cadence," a progression that ends IV-ii⁰⁶/⁵-I, or G♭M-E♭⁰⁶/⁵-D♭M. In the final cadence here, we get E♭m⁷/G♭-E♭⁰⁷/A-D♭M, or ii⁶/⁵-ii⁰⁴/³-I. The B♭-A♮-A♭ line, synonymous with the Hollywood Cadence, is present in this cue in the trumpets. However, we keep wondering about the mysterious other "Dragon Riders," as well as who Drago Bludvist is. Both entities will be revealed soon.

The music in measures 30–33 is closely derived from the end of Igor Stravinsky's ballet, *The Firebird*. The work closes with the following harmonic progression: BM-CM-C♯M-FM-C♯M-CM-BM. In measures 30–33 of "Me Likey," the harmonic progression is: BM-Cmaj7-Em-A♭M. The A♭ major triad then serves as the dominant to lead into the varied Hollywood Cadence and statement of the *Vikings A* theme. The enharmonic major third root motion from C♯ to F in Stravinsky's piece is present here, from E to A♭. Powell has a deep appreciation for Stravinsky's piece, and this is one particular way it manifests in the trilogy.

2M10—War is What He Wants (0:25:25–0:27:06)

3–12—Drago's Tune (A doubly harmonic minor)
13–15—Drago riff
18–22—Warring Vikings (B-flat Aeolian)
22–29—Hiccup the Chief (B major)
29–34—Flying Ostinato (E Aeolian)

As it turns out, it's not just Hiccup's friends who have come to the rescue, but Gobber and Stoick, as well. Stoick then tells Hiccup (and the audience) about Drago through a flashback, which is when the cue begins. Stoick describes Drago as a cloaked stranger, using additional mysterious terms. This is the first time we hear *Drago's Tune*, played here by the English horn, a timbre often associated with mystery. Stoick paints Drago as believing in himself a Messiah, claiming that Drago said only he could tame the dragons and save mankind. Drago lusts for power, and in return, wanted the chieftains to bow down to him. When they rebuffed his offer, Drago unleashed his dragons on the council, accompanied by the *Drago* riff; only Stoick escaped alive. In the aftermath of the tale, we hear the *Warring Vikings* theme played as an elegy, its harmonization nearly unrecognizable through the use of half-diminished seventh chords.

Despite everything that Stoick has told him about Drago, Hiccup will still try to reason with him, eschewing his duty to Berk. A solo horn plays a modified opening of the *Hiccup the Chief* theme, with Hiccup believing that if he could change Stoick's mind about dragons, he can change anyone's mind, his youthful naïveté winning the battle. The cue concludes with a rhythmically augmented ending to the *Flying Ostinato*, concluding with a Picardy third and an E major triad. Although the scene is extremely serious, its ending adds a bit of comedy, as Ruffnut continues to be infatuated with Eret, and touches him while he lays underfoot of a dragon, unable to move, a pizzicato note on harp and contrabass to conclude the cue.

2M11—Hiccup and Toothless Attacked (0:27:37–0:30:03)

2–10—Pulsing 16th notes
3–9—Good Alpha (C Phrygian)
18–38—Lost and Found (B-flat Aeolian)
50–67—Lost and Found (C Aeolian)

68–72—Good Alpha (C minor)
74–79—Good Alpha (E Aeolian)

Hiccup tells Toothless that he'll never let anything happen to him, which guarantees something bad is about to happen. As they soar above the clouds, we see something that looks like a shark fin sticking out of the water, but flying through the air, sticking out of a cloud. This *Jaws* reference is not played humorously or for laughs, but ominously, as the *Good Alpha* theme sounds in Phrygian mode, as it did earlier in the cue "Hiccup's Gonna Be Chief," and significantly rhythmically augmented in this instance. The cue opens with the pulsing sixteenth notes heard in "Eret Educates Hiccup," and uses the same prime form of the pentachord (01368). Here, the music is transposed up six half-steps from earlier, but the harmony and texture easily recall the earlier location, when Eret spoke of "other dragon riders." The tritone distance maintains its meaning from earlier in the film, the two locations representing earth and sky. It appears that Hiccup has now come face-to-face with the other dragon riders. A masked rider pulls ahead of them, disappears, and re-emerges from beneath, with action music sounding. As the masked rider stands atop (presumably) his dragon, the *Lost and Found* theme is heard for the first time. Like so many of the themes in this film, the immediate association is unclear, but the melodic prominence indicates its importance to the film.

Hiccup and Toothless are fully focused on the rider and the dragon, and they don't see a second dragon flying in from the side, one that snatches Hiccup and knocks Toothless out of the air, sending him crashing through the ice-covered ocean and into the water, the trumpets rapidly playing through 9 of the 12 possible major triads, as well as a single minor triad in measures 42–43, seen in Figure 5.8.

Toothless struggles to get out of the icy water, and he and Hiccup are now separated. As Toothless watches Hiccup carried away, a wordless female choir initiates the *Lost and Found* theme again. Powell again uses the intimacy of the human voice in this portion of the cue, with the theme adapted to sound like an elegy. The sadness inherent in the theme clearly represents Hiccup being taken away from Toothless, but what we don't know is that Hiccup is with his mother, the maternal voice that has been absent from his life since shortly after his birth. While this moment does not parallel the gentle intimacy of "Forbidden Friendship" from the first film, it does contain shades of that level of closeness. We then see Toothless bobbing on a piece of ice, then a large water dragon approaches in the water, and Toothless is gone. All that remains is Hiccup's helmet, floating on the water. The possibility that Toothless has been eaten by this dragon is real.

The musical style changes as the dragons are shown flying Hiccup somewhere, beginning in measure 68. They do not turn around, even as Hiccup begs them to go back and get Toothless. The harmonies in this passage are fascinating, in that they are fully non-functional, but they work as a progression; the melody is the driver of the music in

Figure 5.8. 2M11, measures 42–43, trumpet triads as Toothless crashes.

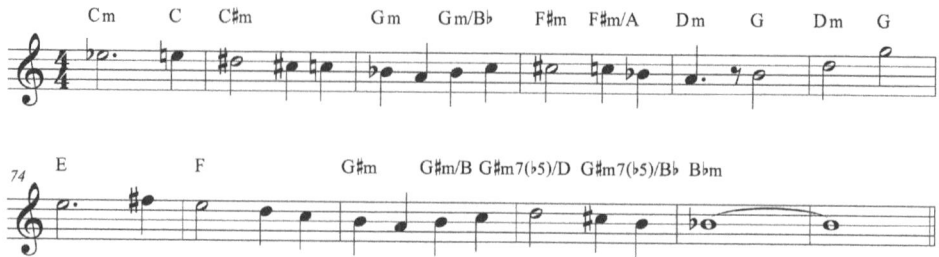

Figure 5.9. 2M11, measures 68–79, highly modified statements of *Good Alpha* theme.

this instance, but the harmony is strange, uncanny, and confusing, certainly expressing how Hiccup is feeling at this moment. Two statements of the *Good Alpha* theme are used here, and while I have tried to discern tonal centers and scales, the chromaticism present, particularly at the end of each statement, combined with the harmonies, makes identifying a tonal center challenging at best. These *Good Alpha* thematic variations are shown in Figure 5.9. As the cue ends, Hiccup finds himself inside a cave that has been frozen over like the dragon trappers' fort, face-to-face with unfamiliar dragons. In its use here, it is anything but majestic. Quite the opposite, the tonal center fluctuates, the harmonies don't belong to a single mode, and the final chord, B♭m, doesn't belong to any of the tonal centers previously heard in the passage. Hiccup is in for the surprise of his life.

2M12—Dragons' Lair (unused in film)

3–8—Calming Motif (starts on F-sharp)
9–13—Calming Motif (starts on E)
18–21—Good Alpha (D major)
22–25—Good Alpha (C major)

This cue was unused in the film, but was clearly intended to be used as Hiccup attempts to calm the dragons inside the cave, and interacts with the mysterious masked "dragon thief." The wordless choir, strings, and brass move almost completely in unison, creating a nearly homophonic texture. The most interesting part of this cue is its second half, where modified statements of the *Good Alpha* theme are presented in D, then in C. It is unclear how these thematic statements work narratively had they been used in the film.

2M13—Should I Know You? (0:31:52–0:33:42)

2–22—Valka's Tune (G Dorian-C Dorian-F Dorian)
26–35—Hiccup/Vikings (with interruptions) (C Aeolian)
37–44—Flying B variation (D Aeolian)
37–40—Warring Vikings (D Aeolian)
41–44—Warring Vikings (F major)
59–62—Hiccup/Vikings (F-sharp Aeolian)

The masked dragon rider calms Toothless and gets him to roll onto his back, far more easily and quickly than Hiccup has ever done, and then the rider tries reaching for Hiccup's face. As the rider sees the scar on Hiccup's chin, she gasps, and the music immediately begins, serving as a point of recognition for the masked person. The wordless choir sings *Valka's Tune* four times in a row, as she is about to be made known to us. The theme rises by fourths, from G to C to F, an atypical gesture for the themes in these films. Although the *Warring Vikings* theme is often stated twice, up a fourth the second time, this is an unusual instance of sounding consecutive perfect fourths higher, as this is the most unusual instance of character interaction in the film trilogy. Male and female voices are used here, representing both Valka and Hiccup, and the tenderness between a mother and child. The interaction between the two leads Valka to reveal herself as Hiccup's mother, and as she does, the music arrives on a GMm^7 sus4 chord in measures 21–22, a harmony that not only needs to resolve due to its dominant seventh quality, but also needs to resolve the suspended fourth above the bass. It is a moment where Hiccup has to take in that his mother is not only alive but standing directly in front of him after missing her his entire life. She then asks him to follow her; the music still needs resolution from earlier.

The music accelerates, but the harmony remains, now over a pedal C. As the scene shifts to Stoick and Gobber looking for Hiccup, the *Hiccup* theme is played, but accompanied and interrupted by swashbuckling music within the phrase. The "real" Vikings are searching for Hiccup, whose actions, via music, interrupt the theme. Stoick comments on how Hiccup's traits are like his mother's, the interruption of the theme also serving as an indicator of the absence of his mother in his life. Stoick then comments on Hiccup's persistence, and Powell inserts a variation on the *Flying B* theme in the oboe beginning in measure 37, the connection between Hiccup taming dragons and Stoick and Gobber flying dragons quite evident. Underneath the varied melody, the *Warring Vikings* theme is stated twice in a row in the solo horn, Stoick and Gobber ready to fight anyone as they search for Hiccup. Gobber says that nothing can hurt Hiccup as long as his Night Fury is around. Stoick then looks down and sees the broken ice in the ocean and Hiccup's helmet floating, an ominous sign. The chords used in measures 45–49 are all minor triads, Dm-G♯m-Em-B♭m-F♯m. Nothing is hopeful about this progression, derived from the whole-tone scale. The connections between both Dm-G♯m and Em-B♭m contain root motion separated by a tritone, an aural marker of antagonism and danger, while the connections between G♯m-Em and B♭m-F♯m, as well as Dm-F♯m, the first and last chords in the progression, are all chromatic mediants with roots separated by a major third, indicative of evil. A horrible fate has befallen Hiccup, or so Stoick and Gobber are led to believe through their eyes, and their belief is reinforced by the harmonic progression used by Powell.

The final section of the cue begins in measure 51 with a C♯ pedal in the timpani, low woodwinds, and low brass. The music is imbued with anxiety as to Hiccup's fate and whereabouts. Even the major triads hold no repose. Stoick holds the helmet to his dragon Skullcrusher's nose, and orders him to find Hiccup based on the scent. The cue concludes with a final statement of the *Hiccup* theme in F♯ Aeolian. The lengthy pedal C♯ serves as the dominant, holding tension, and resolves to F♯ when Stoick takes action. While Hiccup's location is unknown, a plan is in place, and rescue is coming.

2M14—Valka's Dragon Sanctuary (0:34:10–0:35:00)

 3–10—Valka's Tune (E Dorian)
 11–25—Derived from Valka's Tune
 25–28—Valka's Tune (B Dorian)

When we last saw Hiccup and his mother, she wanted him to come with her so she could show him something. The action cuts back to Valka leading him through the cave, not pausing to wait. Hiccup is completely floored by the knowledge that she is his mother, and begins asking questions to which he receives no answers. As Hiccup keeps talking, he emerges from the cave into a lush opening, where hundreds of dragons are flying. Valka saw how Hiccup behaved and treated the dragons, and wanted to share a common bond with him.

The cue opens with *Valka's Tune* played by the full orchestra, followed by variations on that theme. The harmonies instill wonder and awe in both Hiccup and the audience. Neither has ever seen a dragon sanctuary like this. The music uses significantly meaningful triadic relationships. Beginning in measure 12, the pair of triads F♯M-C♯m is used, I-v in F♯, a harmonic relationship that often indicates wonder and transcendence and will be used as the opening harmonic relationship in the *Good Alpha* theme. Following that, we get pairs of B♭m-E♭M, Gm-CM, and Bm-EM, with all three pairs indicating exotic geography, sounds befitting a secret dragon sanctuary.

Additionally, the harmonic progression in measures 15–19 is as follows: B♭m-E♭M-Gm-CM-E♭m. The way that Powell constructed these harmonies is fascinating, in that he used a progression that nearly fits basic Neo-Riemannian Theory functions. If the two major triads were replaced, the progression could be: B♭m-B♭M-Gm-E♭M-E♭m, which would yield a P-R-L-P progression, indicating minimal movement from one triad to the next, but defying a specific pattern or chain. However, the ideas of wonder and transcendence supersede the idea of NRT functions, and by using those harmonies in the cue, Powell created a far more interesting and deep progression.

The cue ends on a Bm-F♯M combination, i-V in B, a half cadence, leaving the cue open to allow Valka to explain her whereabouts for the last 20 years. Although this cue is extremely short, it is one of the most triadically colorful and rich in the film.

2M15-16—Hiccup and Valka Bond (0:35:02–0:37:29)

1–16—Map the World (B Aeolian)
21–40—Map the World (D Aeolian)
41–44—Drago's Tune (C Dorian)
44–48—Map the World variation (C Aeolian)
49–53—Flying A reharmonized (C major)
60–65—Warring Vikings (D Aeolian)

Valka asks Hiccup if he's upset that she's been rescuing dragons; the cue opens with the *Map the World* theme in B Aeolian, here used to denote her previously unknown location. Valka has not been around people for 20 years, so she is quite awkward around Hiccup. She asks him if he likes the sanctuary, and the music pauses from its thematic music, replacing it with harp and slate marimba arpeggios. The slate marimba was first used in "Forbidden Friendship" in the first film to highlight the unusual nature of the relationship between Hiccup and Toothless. Here, it acts as an aural signifier that the sanctuary is unusual, perhaps unique in the world. The *Map the World* theme begins again, this time up a minor third in D Aeolian.

During this statement of the *Map the World* theme, Valka plays with Toothless, inspecting him, noticing his teeth, his age, and basically playing with him as though he was a dog. Valka then speaks of the injuries to her dragons caused by Drago, and the opening of *Drago's Tune* is played by the alto flute, a timbre not typically associated with villains. Because Valka tells the story and the dragons are not in any current danger, this timbral shift makes sense in the film's narrative context.

Hiccup then tells Valka how he came to be with Toothless. First, we hear the reharmonized *Flying A* theme, which segues into to a somber statement of the *Warring Vikings* theme. Valka asked how Stoick took to Hiccup's approach to dragons. Hiccup says that at first he didn't like it, but he changed, and the whole village changed with him. Valka is amazed at this development, thinking that Stoick could never change. The lack of the second half of the *Warring Vikings* theme indicates this shift, as does the strings-only texture of the thematic statement, sounding like a lament, perhaps a nod to the old ways of Berk having passed.

3M17–18—Valka's Flash / Good Alpha (0:37:38–0:40:57)
6–15—Dragon Tune (A-flat doubly harmonic minor)
23–39—Lost and Found (C Aeolian)
42–62—Lost and Found (C Aeolian)
63–75—Good Alpha (E-flat Mixolydian)
76–89—Good Alpha (G Mixolydian)
102–117—Good Alpha (G Mixolydian)

Valka's flashback to the night that she disappeared initiates this cue. Dragons are attacking Berk; the *Dragon Tune* sounds. Valka recalls that she didn't think it needed to be a kill-or-be-killed situation between the Vikings and dragons. Valka then tells of a dragon that broke into the house and approached baby Hiccup in the cradle. The dragon, instead of attacking baby Hiccup, played with him, confirming Valka's suspicions concerning the nature of dragons as sentient sensitive creatures. As she recalls this incident, the wordless female choir sings the *Lost and Found* theme, the dragon playing with the baby, in a type of mother-child dyad.

In the flashback, Stoick tries to protect her by attacking the dragon, but the dragon, seeing that Valka understood the nature of dragons, grabbed her and flew off. This portion of the cue features another statement of the *Lost and Found* theme, but with full orchestra. Valka was devastated to leave and Stoick's life was immediately changed; Hiccup asks how she stayed alive, and the second half of the cue begins.

The *Good Alpha* theme is properly used for the first time in the film, in E♭ Mixolydian. The dragon that abducted Valka, Cloudjumper, brought her to be with the Bewilderbeast, the Alpha species of dragon, and the one that breathes ice. The theme repeats, up a major third in G Mixolydian, continuing to sound majestic. The use of the minor dominant and major tonic triads invoke wonder and transcendence, as the Bewilderbeast is a dragon larger than any other, with only a few remaining in the world. He is regal, rare, and the king of the dragons.

The Bewilderbeast comes over to check out Hiccup, and even Toothless drops his head and eyes in deference to the Alpha. As he does, a wonderful flute solo begins in measure 90, providing a musical sound for the Bewilderbeast's assessment of Hiccup, itself a variation of the *Heroic Dragon* theme. The *Good Alpha* theme is played once more, again in G Mixolydian, but with only strings, harp, and female choir, the timbres emphasizing the mystical nature of the dragon, the first iteration at a dynamic of *piano* and the second at *mezzo-forte*. When the theme concludes, the cue ends.

3M19—I Grew Facial Hair for You (0:41:01–0:42:16)

> 4–10—Dragon Tune (E minor)
> 22–34—Love theme (A major)
> 37–44—Love theme (D major)

Hiccup's friends are resting on an ice floe. Ruffnut discusses Eret, while Snotlout and Fishlegs both declare they grew facial hair for her in attempts to woo her, seeing Eret as a romantic rival. Astrid, not wanting to sit and wait, leads the gang into action. The *Dragon Tune*, reharmonized in E minor to not sound as scary, is used to underscore Ruffnut's description of Eret as the perfect man. Eret is a dragon trapper, not a dragon, and as a love interest, cannot be as scary as a dragon trying to kill Vikings. As the gang flies to kidnap Eret, the *Love* theme sounds; Astrid grabs Eret in her dragon's talons, but Ruffnut is in love with him, giving the theme dual meanings in this context. The harmonization of this theme is also new, again, emphasizing the dual and changing context of this theme, seen in Figure 5.10.

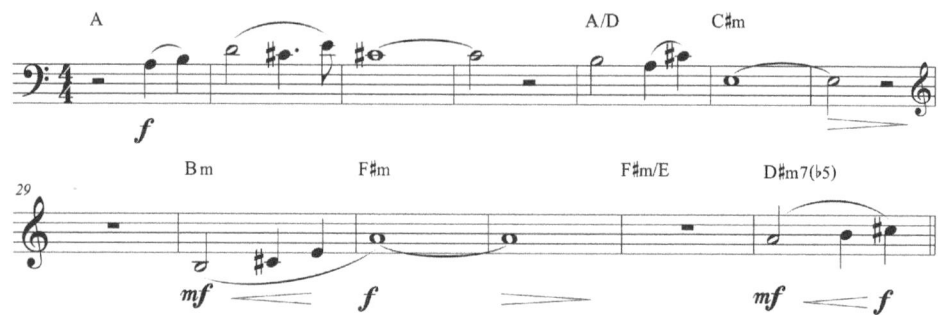

Figure 5.10. 3M19, measures 22–34, *Love* theme for Ruffnut.

When Eret says he'd rather die than show the way to Drago's, he is dropped by Stormfly and falls from the sky. Powell scores this moment, measures 35–37, using chords belonging to the Octatonic (0,1) scale as the scale has been used before. Eret is caught by Stormfly before landing on the ground, and a final statement of the opening of the *Love* theme sounds, with yet another reharmonization. Eret agrees to take the gang to Drago's, and the cue abruptly ends with a perfect authentic cadence, bringing that action to a close.

3M20—Flying with Mother (0:42:18–0:45:01)

> 4–17—Lost and Found (G Aeolian)
> 7–20—Lost and Found (piccolo) (G Aeolian)
> 29–50—Lost and Found (G Aeolian)
> 51–66—Map the World (C Aeolian)
> 67–87—Map the World (A Aeolian)
> 91–119—Lost and Found (A Aeolian)
> 120–144—Map the World (A Aeolian)
> 145–164—Lost and Found (C-sharp Aeolian)

If there is such a thing as a "single" from a soundtrack, this would be that cue for this film. The cue features the primary and secondary themes from this film, *Lost and*

Found and *Map the World*, along with an exciting percussive accompaniment. As a testament to its popularity and quality, this cue won the 2015 International Film Music Critics Award (IFMCA) for Film Music Composition of the Year, essentially meaning "Best Cue of the Year."

The cue opens with drums and the *Lost and Found* theme played by the Uilleann pipes. As Hiccup and Valka pause in mid-air, he turns and sees the entire group of dragons behind them. The music thematically pauses as well, introducing bagpipes, horns, and strings in measure 17 while the big eating "reveal" is prepared. The Bewilderbeast appears from the ocean, and launches thousands of fish into the air for feeding time. As he does this, the *Lost and Found* theme restarts in measure 29. As added comedy, Toothless's eyes are huge, his tongue waggles, and he's salivating, basically asking Hiccup for permission to engage in the feast. They take off, snatching fish out of the air. Eventually, Toothless has a mouthful of fish that he can barely handle.

As the *Lost and Found* theme reaches its conclusion, the scene changes to Hiccup showing his handmade map to Valka, and the *Map the World* theme sounds, played on the Celtic Harp. Hiccup and Valka are on an ice floe, and much like Hiccup drawing Toothless in the dirt with a stick, she draws the map of the world she knows in the snow and ice with her staff, and not that dissimilar from Toothless's "drawing" of Hiccup, either. When the *Map the World* theme begins again, it is in the cellos, with light accompaniment, notably sleigh bells, as Toothless "draws" with an icicle.

The scene changes back to flying and the soprano voices sing the *Lost and Found* theme, accompanied by the alto voices singing a variation on the opening of the *Map the World* theme. The *Map* theme brought Hiccup and Valka back together, and the *Lost and Found* theme represents their missing time that they now catch up on, measures 91–119. The use of the voices also allows the music to function as another layer of intimacy, now between a mother and son. This is the first time where two themes specific to this film are layered on top of each other as the electric bass propels the music forward in an exciting fashion. Eventually Valka rejoins Hiccup in the air and describes the joy she feels soaring in the air on the back of dragons. The oboe plays the *Map the World* theme, ending on the dominant chord rather than finishing. Hiccup, like any child, is about to show off to his mother; here, he shows that he can "fly." The music comes to a complete halt, then restarts, sounding the *Lost and Found* theme in C♯ with nearly the full orchestra. The beginning of the theme is synchronized to the moment when Hiccup puts out his "wings." But like earlier in the film, Hiccup gets lost in the moment, is about to crash into a rock, and Toothless has to save him. The theme is abruptly interrupted, but upon safely emerging from the snow where Toothless has pushed him, we hear an authentic cadence in E major, with Toothless appearing when the dominant is sounded, and Hiccup emerging with the tonic.

This cue serves as the parallel music and scene to 3M18's "See You Tomorrow" in the first film. The sequence in this film is a montage, but one where little time appears to elapse, and we see moments of mother and son bonding, which is what makes this cue so special. The montages in both films feature Hiccup. "See You Tomorrow" highlights Hiccup learning techniques from Toothless and applying them in the training arena while "Flying with Mother" shows Valka teaching Hiccup what she knows about dragons and geography, and helping Hiccup find his way. Powell felt that the *Lost and Found* theme was originally significant, but perhaps not the film's primary theme. His words concerning the theme and how it was specifically developed into "Flying with Mother" appear below:

In *How to Train Your Dragon 2*, it was going to be a song, when Hiccup flies with his mother, until the last minute. Then this theme that I had was the *Lost and Found* theme, which was for losing the father, finding the mother, losing innocence, finding maturity, all of these kinds of things. The one glitch in that was that I then had to, at the last minute, write that cue. Dean said to me, "I think it would be better if you wrote something for 'Flying with Mother.'" I never thought of it being such a joyous theme, and so it took me quite a while to figure out how to make that cue work with that theme. These are the moments when you say, "Forget it, I'll write something else." But by that time, everything was structured in a certain way, and I didn't feel as though I could put in a "random" bit of music that doesn't mean anything, so I struggled with it until I found the right rhythm and the right way of doing it and the female voices. It was just a lucky accident after about four or five days of just fiddling about with it. Then it clicked for me about the way to do it. It's always about, "Can you vary your themes to do everything you need to in the movie?" You have to have a plan to do it, and if somebody says, "No, you're never going to have to score that scene," and you are, suddenly, at the last minute, that can really throw it off.

I've done things where I've had a theme that works in a certain way in a movie, and near the end, I've gone back and completely changed it all because I just cannot get the material to do all the things I realize by the end of the movie when I'm finishing scoring. That theme isn't working well enough for this moment, and it's the important moment for that theme. I will either adapt another theme or realize that theme I'm using for the most important moment, I then go back and I rebuild the sections using that theme rather than the one that had been building to this moment. Some things just work better than others and you're looking for an overall success rate with the same theme, and if it doesn't have the percentage of success rate for the moments it needs, and especially those certain moments where it has to shine, then strip it out and try something else through that thread. The *Lost and Found* theme is very much like that. It was not intended for certain things, but in the end, it worked. I liked it. I couldn't lose it with the things it was doing earlier. I think the first cue it was written for was the flashback of the mother being taken, and it worked so well for that, I thought, that it would work very well for the film, not thinking I'd have to do a bloody cheerful dance version of it.

3M21—Can We Start Over (0:45:08–0:46:57)
2–14—Valka's Tune (A Aeolian)
16–23—Flying A (F major)
24–32—Flying B (F major)
33–43—Lost and Found (A Aeolian)

Valka inspects Hiccup's "wings," saying "incredible," and her theme begins in the solo clarinet and Celtic harp, a very gentle and tender thematic statement, with a very light string accompaniment. Valka speaks to Hiccup, excited that he took after her rather than his father. As she continues talking about being absent for his life, a minor-mode harmonization of her theme is used, suggesting sadness at having missed out on his childhood. She asks him if they can start their relationship over, asking for another chance to be his mother. The response comes in the form of music. The solo piano plays the complete *Flying* theme, much like it did near the end of the first film when Hiccup needed to relearn how to walk and Toothless was there to assist in the cue 5M39, "Where's Hiccup." Like Hiccup's new start with a prosthetic leg at the end of the first film, the solo piano represents another new start, a renewal of the relationship between mother and son. The end of the *Flying* theme is immediately followed by the *Lost and Found* theme, as Valka tells Hiccup of all the things they can accomplish together. This theme is reharmonized; their relationship is rekindled (or found), but the suggestion about the future is neither lost nor found, explaining the reharmonization.

The entire cue is soft and intimate. Brass and percussion are completely absent, and solo instruments play the themes, with light string accompaniment. The intimacy between mother and son, renewing their relationship and bonding over a common idea drives this cue. It is, perhaps, the gentlest cue in the trilogy.

3M22—Meet Drago (0:47:33–0:51:54)

1–3—Drago's Tune (B-flat doubly harmonic minor)
4–11—Drago's Tune (B-flat doubly harmonic minor)
26–43—Drago's Tune (B-flat doubly harmonic minor)
43–46—Drago riff
47–56—Drago's Tune (B-flat doubly harmonic minor)
56–59—Flying A (starts on D)
60–67—Drago riff (rhythmically augmented)
68–76—Vikings A (B-flat melodic minor)
78–81—Warring Vikings (G Aeolian)
85–88—Drago riff
89–98—Drago's Tune (E-flat doubly harmonic minor)
99–101—Drago riff
102–106—Heroic Dragon variation (E-flat Aeolian)

After forty-seven minutes of the film, we finally get to see the villain, Drago. His music is the antithesis to what was just heard in the previous cue. Everything that Valka is—kind, thoughtful, gentle, generous—Drago is the opposite: evil, mean, harsh, violent.

Astrid climbs a snow-covered mountain and the cue begins with the opening three notes of *Drago's Tune* in canon, from the slate marimba to the harp to the first violins to the second violins. As she reaches the top and looks down at all the ships in port, *Drago's Tune* begins in earnest in measure 4 in the low woodwinds, low brass, and low strings. As the teens are inspecting the ships, Drago's men sneak up behind them, starting in measure 12 and tranquilize the dragons, hauling them, and the team in for Drago. The action of the tranquilizer darts is scored with rapid sixteenth notes, all belonging to the Octatonic (1,2) scale, defying a clear tonal center and contributing to the chaos of the moment. Eret and the teens are taken prisoner, and the action shifts to the ships in port. Tenor voices and the cello initiate *Drago's Tune* again in measure 26, but still at a *piano* dynamic. By now, we know what this theme represents, but without seeing the villain, the dynamic remains soft with a thinly scored texture. During this statement, Drago appears on screen, but we still don't see him fully revealed. He begins walking toward the dragons and the prisoners.

One of the teens' dragons breathes fire at Drago, and he simply puts up his dragonskin cloak to protect himself, continuing to walk forward, in measures 43–46, as the *Drago* riff is heard, his evil nature on display. The music grows in intensity, and as the dragon roars at him, Drago roars back, his theme played in measures 47–56 by the full woodwind and string families, with full choral support, all at a dynamic of *fortissimo*. This is the nature of Drago: to rule by fear and violence. Instead of putting his hand on the newly subservient dragon's nose, he puts his foot on it, a startling shift in respect from the Berkians treatment of dragons. The tempo of the theme is slow and methodical, like Drago. As Eret tells Drago he also caught the dragons' riders, the first violins play a reharmonized version of the opening of the *Flying A* theme. It is soft, and somewhat difficult to hear because of the dialogue, but it is certainly present. The gang is in trouble, so naturally, the *Flying A* theme, representing dragon riders, should be modified to reflect their current situation.

Drago interrogates Eret, asking how many more dragon riders are out there, his anger on display, the *Drago* riff broken into a single sixteenth-note triplet per measure. Astrid interrupts and answers, telling him, "Hundreds! A whole island full!" As she does, the minor-mode version of the *Vikings A* theme is played by the horns. Astrid then threatens Drago with Hiccup, the greatest dragon master in the world, to which Drago takes offense. She tells him that Hiccup will come in with his Night Fury and "blast your ships to smithereens." The *Warring Vikings* theme sounds in the brass beneath her statement, indicating that Hiccup has the capacity for battle, should it be required. We have not seen that side of him, as he still wants to talk Drago down from battle, but the music gives Hiccup a sense of duty that he may not yet possess. Drago takes out his anger on Eret for leading the Berkians to him, again accompanied by the *Drago* riff. Drago announces the change in plans, as they will now go to attack Berk.

Drago also orders the death of Eret, but Stormfly leaps in front of him to protect him. As this happens, Drago's men shoot tranquilizer darts at him, and Eret begins to realize that the dragons should not be part of an army. Even without Hiccup's help, he begins to come around to see things the way the rest of Berk does. As he has this realization the strings play an elegiac variation of the opening of the *Heroic Dragon* theme, no other part of the orchestra sounding. It is the death of Eret's old way of thinking about dragons as his life has been saved. The cue ends abruptly as the scene changes back to Valka's sanctuary.

3M25–26—Stoick Finds Beauty (0:52:14–0:54:36)

17–23—Warring Vikings (G Aeolian)
26–33—Warring Vikings (D Aeolian)
34–41—Warring Vikings (G Aeolian)
75–93—Lost and Found (D Aeolian)
96–102—Lost and Found (G Aeolian)

While in the sanctuary, Hiccup decides he needs to find Drago before Drago finds him, unaware of the happenings in the world. As he's getting ready to embark, he is grabbed from behind by Stoick, who, with Gobber, announces he's being rescued. The cue enters in the film in measure 17 as Stoick grabs Hiccup; the opening 16 measures are cut from the film. No thematic material was cut, but a lovely melodic line in English horn and clarinet did not find its way into the film. The cue, as used in the film, opens with a rhythmically augmented statement of the *Warring Vikings* theme; Stoick will save Hiccup from his kidnapper. As they make their way from the sanctuary through the caves, Hiccup tries to tell his father about new information—his mother is alive and here!—but Stoick is uninterested. The *Warring Vikings* theme is sung twice by a male choir, with the expected second statement up a perfect fourth from the first. This pair of thematic statements is rhythmically augmented and finds its dotted rhythms mostly normalized, slightly more romantic than its original version.

The surprise Hiccup attempts to tells is certainly not one that Stoick expects. As they approach an opening in the passageway, the music continues, changing chords every beat, and working functionally in D minor. When Gobber, who is in the lead, reaches the opening, the music arrives on a deceptive cadence, a DMm^7 chord rather

5. How to Train Your Dragon 2 *Cue Analysis*

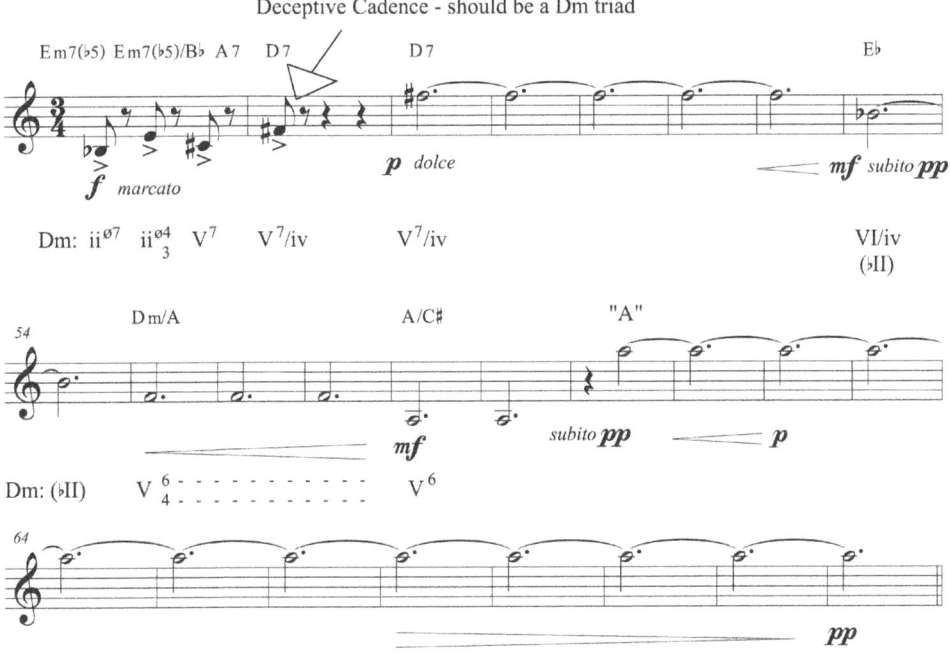

Figure 5.11. 3M25, measures 46–71, Stoick sees Valka.

than a DM triad. This deceptive cadence works in tandem with the surprise reveal of Valka to Stoick, coming momentarily. As Gobber says, "You might want to take this one," Stoick picks up his sword, preparing to fight a dragon. The harmonic progression of DMm^7-E♭M-Dm/A-AM/C♯, also works functionally in Dm, then all that remains is a single A5 in the violins, as Stoick sees Valka from afar and removes his helmet. He is so stunned that the music is unable to even sound a chord, only a single note. The cadence in this progression is not reached; it is left dangling and unresolved on the dominant. Figure 5.11 illustrates this musical passage.

Valka gives a long monologue about being absent, while Stoick approaches her, almost in a trance, Hiccup and Gobber watching as Valka assumes all Stoick's thoughts. The *Lost and Found* theme is rhythmically augmented and sung by female choir, with a *pianissimo* string accompaniment. She expects him to yell and be upset, and instead, he touches her cheek. Once again, the intimacy of the voice is used to perfection by Powell. Instead of the mother-child relationship, this is the relationship between a married couple, a different type of love. This moment is similar to Drago approaching the dragon, highlighting the differences between the heroes and villain. Drago yelled at the dragon, forcing it into submission. Stoick caresses his wife, overjoyed that she is alive, saying, "You're as beautiful as the day I lost you." The solo violin restarts the *Lost and Found* theme, with a slightly larger and louder orchestral accompaniment than before. The couple kiss, Valka's dragons lie down, contented, and the cue fades out, ending on a half cadence in G. Stoick has just found his wife after 20 years, so although they are together, there is certainly time and space between them. The cue cannot end with an authentic cadence.

3M27—Get 'Em You Son of an Eret (0:55:02–0:56:17)
- 13–23—Map the World (C major)
- 25–28—Warring Vikings (F Aeolian)
- 41–46—Heroic Dragon (F-sharp major)

Eret's allegiance changes in this cue from Drago to the Vikings of Berk, having personally experienced the kindness of dragons. As he and the others are about to be forced to jump from Drago's ship into icy waters, he fights back. The cue, which omits the first 11 measures in the film, begins with an F Aeolian ascending run, but instead of arriving on F, the music arrives on E, initiating a major-mode swashbuckling-style statement of the *Map the World* theme. Ordinarily, this would be an example of a CMCR, but since no tonal center has been clearly established, the music cannot function that way, particularly as used in context in the film. The swashbuckling style of the theme from earlier with Eret is again used, but this time, he's on the same side as the Berkians. Eret takes out Drago's men, hitting the final one with a tranquilizer dart, the music sustaining a G-D open fifth until he falls, where the music resolves to a C major triad, measures 23–24. The escape is under way.

An idealized statement of the *Warring Vikings* theme is sung by the choir, fully harmonized by major triads; Eret is becoming one of them through his actions, the Magic chromatic mediant relationship of FM-D♭M serving as an aural indicator. The next task is to release the dragons without attracting attention. As the teens search the ship, a pedal A♭ sounds, often against a D major triad, creating a tritone. The pedal moves up to B, and the harmony shifts to a prominent C♯ major triad, creating a major second between the bass and root, which can be heard as a signifier of protagonism. The C♯ major triad resolves to F♯ major, in a dominant-tonic relationship as Eret enters the cage of the dragon that saved him. As Eret tells the dragon, "Thank you for saving my life," the *Heroic Dragon* theme is used, but with a *piano* dynamic and sparse orchestration—only alto flute and strings. It is quite an extraordinary event, and harmonically fascinating. The scene cuts back to Valka's sanctuary, and the music fades out.

3M28S—Courting Song (0:57:20–0:59:48)

Hiccup thinks that his mom and her dragons will move back into Berk, and everything will be fine. Stoick pumps the brakes, saying, "Slow down, son. It's a lot to take in." He then begins to whistle the Courting Song tune. Valka's eyes show immediate recognition of the melody. Stoick then begins singing to Valka in the anacrusis to measure 12. When Stoick reaches the third eight-measure phrase, the Celtic Harp enters in measure 25, as idealized accompaniment (no one is present to play the harp in the scene). Gobber tries to sing along, interrupting and interjecting humor as the sidekick, but quickly quiets and sits down, as he recognizes the significance of the situation. Stoick cannot bring himself to sing the final two measures of the verse, but Valka, after a pause, sings it for him, accompanied by the harmonium, an instrument used when Astrid was falling in love with Hiccup in the first film.

Valka continues singing, now accompanied by a violin, and as the tempo increases, they begin to dance together. The accompaniment grows, and they exchange lines. When the song modulates up a step from C major to D major in measure 66, they sing in unison rather than in alternation, the duet fully realized. The song serves to facilitate their full reconciliation, as their song from their early years brings them back together. The dance is somewhat reminiscent of Jack and Rose's dance in *Titanic* when they visit the Irish musicians, the connection here with the pennywhistle and Uilleann pipes rather than through drums.

4M29—Courting Song Instrumental (0:59:42–1:00:34)

Stoick asks Valka to come home and be a family again, to which she agrees, and a fragment of the Courting Song plays instrumentally beneath the dialogue. This is the last upbeat moment for some time in the film.

4M30—Battle of the Bewilderbeast (1:00:46–1:06:57)

4–8—Good Alpha (D Phrygian)
10–14—Good Alpha (D Phrygian)
20–33—Heroic Dragon (D Mixolydian)
40–45—Drago riff
48–49—Warring Vikings
50–58—Vikings A (C major)
60–69—Vikings B/C/D (B = G Aeolian despite harmonization;
    C = B-flat major; D = A-flat Dorian)
71–75—Love theme (B-flat major)
76–79—Action Motif (starts on E)
80–87—Flying A (F-sharp major)
80–87—Flying Ostinato (F-sharp major)
88–90—Flying Ostinato (F-sharp minor)
91–94—Action Motif (starts on A-flat)
95–100—Flying B (D major)
102–109—Good Alpha (E major)
125–132—Flying B (E-flat major)
142–144—Drago's Tune (in G-sharp Aeolian)
146–155—Drago's Tune (E-flat doubly harmonic minor)
162–163—Courting Song (G major)
164–169—Warring Vikings (D Aeolian)
172–175—Warring Vikings (G Aeolian)
176–178—Good Alpha (C-sharp Mixolydian)
180–182—Warring Vikings (A Aeolian)
184–190—Drago riff

Moments after the happy family momentarily reconciles, the dragons begin to flee the sanctuary. Something large is attacking the ice-encrusted refuge, large enough to break off gigantic pieces of ice. The cue opens with polyrhythms between the woodwinds and strings; sixteenth notes play in the woodwinds while triplet sixteenth notes sound in the strings, and these polyrhythms continue through the first thirty seconds of the cue. Additionally, the initial harmony in measures 2–5 is D minor with an added B♭, a sixth above the bass. As Valka runs to the top of the refuge, we hear a D Phrygian statement of the *Good Alpha* theme with a new harmonization, Powell perhaps foreshadowing to the emergence of Drago's Bewilderbeast. Valka sees Drago's fleet, and we can only assume that one of Drago's dragons has attacked the refuge. Stoick asks Valka what to do over the Dm^{add6} harmony. Her response is to save the dragons, over an AM triad in measures 18–19. This A major triad functions as the dominant to the theme about to sound. The *Heroic Dragon* theme sounds in D major, as Valka and others take flight against Drago's fleet and army.

We see Drago order his men to keep attacking the mountain in order to draw out Valka's Alpha. As they continue their volleys, the music turns dissonant and athematic, again emphasizing the 6:4 polyrhythm. Drago orders the traps to be opened, and a sustained DMM$^{7\text{-}\sharp5}$ sounds in measures 42–45, amplifying the tension. As dragons begin to be caught, the brass play chords synchronously with the closing of the traps. We then hear the last two measures of the *Warring Vikings* theme in the brass, Drago's army confused. The team arrives to fight, having escaped imminent death, and a nearly complete statement of all four parts of the *Vikings* theme is played, beginning in C major in measure 50. Only the last two measures are absent and replaced because Ruffnut falls off her dragon, with Snotlout and Fishlegs catching her, each grabbing a hand, the opening of the *Love* theme played by violins and sung by female choir as a momentary break in the action of the battle. Perhaps the local Berk boys aren't so bad after all.

The cue continues with the *Action Motif* in the strings and brass, and with Astrid in trouble, Hiccup, Stoick, and Valka all appear, supported by the *Flying A* theme and the *Flying Ostinato* in F♯ major. Instead of progressing beyond the opening two measures, this variation of the *Flying A* theme features the same two-measure unit four times, each one harmonized differently, shown in Figure 5.12. It is a triumphant statement, as the family that fights together, stays together.

Gobber knocks over most of Drago's army while flying his dragon during a variation of the *Flying Ostinato* statement, and Drago sees Hiccup, the "Dragon Master," over an inverted form of the *Action Motif*. Hiccup catches up to Astrid and Eret on her dragon, and the *Flying B* theme sounds, serving as a momentary point of repose before the *Good Alpha* theme interrupts it, and Valka's Bewilderbeast appears from inside the mountain.

Following this single statement of the *Good Alpha* theme, the music alternates between B♭M and DM triads in measures 110–115, the exact same triads heard in 4M35–37, "Over/Less Okay" from the first film, a cue used during the battle at the dragons' island, and an obvious connection between the two battle scenes. After a passage with a

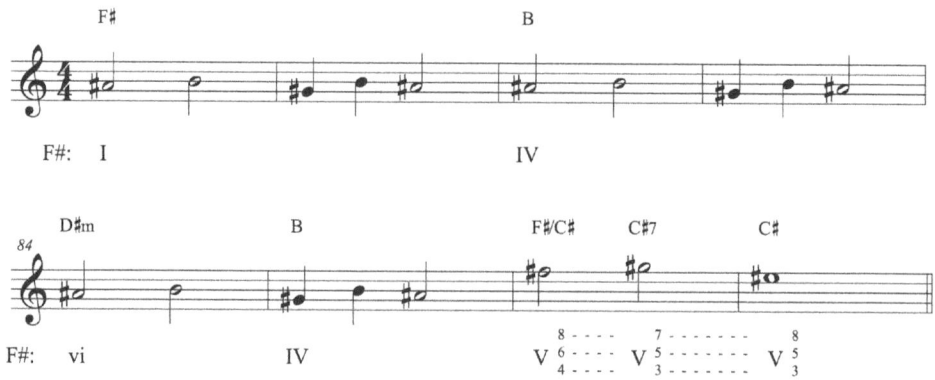

Figure 5.12. 4M30, measures 80–87, modified *Flying A* theme.

Figure 5.13. 4M30, measures 123–126, CMCR leading to *Flying B* theme.

pedal D, the music forms an outwardly shaped wedge in measures 120–123, expanding with each harmony. Toothless becomes involved in the battle, and as the bass reaches its destination of C♯ in measure 123, Powell shifts from a wedge to a cadential progression, and the bass line rises by fourths, C♯-F♯-B, with the BM triad sounding like the dominant, and wanting to resolve to EM. This resolution never happens, as the music shifts to E♭ major and begins the *Flying B* theme. The D♯ leading tone from the B major triad resolves to E♭, the tonic note of the new key. It is an elegant and efficient CMCR. This passage is seen in Figure 5.13.

At the end of the *Flying B* theme, in measures 132–134, Valka is caught in a net and she and her dragon go down. The same rhythmic gesture that concluded "Over/Less Okay" in the first film is used here. In the previous film, it coincided with the moment that Toothless hits the Alpha with a fireball. Here, it coincides with Valka going down. The rhythm continues as Valka and Drago battle with their staffs, and Drago announces he's brought a challenger to her light-skinned Bewilderbeast, a dragon we still have not yet seen. Drago calls for it, and it emerges from the water, a dark-skinned Bewilderbeast to ensure the visual battle is unsubtle. As Drago's Bewilderbeast emerges, we hear the opening three notes of *Drago's Tune* in stretto in the trombones, horns, and trumpets, then a full statement of his theme in the strings and choir.

Drago unmasks Valka and tries to smash her face with his staff but is prevented from doing so by Stoick over sparse orchestration. A two-measure fragment of the *Courting Song*, played in unison by the full orchestra, highlights the love Stoick has for Valka, and as he prepares to fight Drago, the *Warring Vikings* theme sounds in the brass in D. The battle between Stoick and Drago mirrors the battle between the Bewilderbeasts; Valka tries to intervene and stop them from fighting. Two whole-tone fragments are used here: BM-AM-GM and CM-B♭M-A♭M, before the *Warring Vikings* theme sounds again, now in G, up the expected perfect fourth from D. Both battles rage on, and the *Good Alpha* theme sounds, not entirely convincingly, indicating that Drago's Bewilderbeast may have the advantage. The *Warring Vikings* theme sounds in A, but stops halfway through, as Drago knocks Stoick off his feet, with Gobber coming to his aid. The *Drago* riff is used as the Bewilderbeasts battle; Drago's Alpha delivers the fatal blow to Valka's. The cue fades out under dialogue, sound effects, and disbelief on the faces of the Berkians.

The big battle cue in this film occurs far earlier than in the first film, due to the events that transpire and necessitate Hiccup's maturation. Figure 5.14 below provides the breakdown of this cue.

Measure	1	20	30	34	38	40	46	48	49
Marking	Tempestoso					Slightly Slower			
Tempo	q = 135					q = 128			
Meter	4/4								
Tonal Center	D minor	D major	A major	A major	D minor	Unclear	G♯ minor	WT$_1$	WT$_0$

50	59	63	71	76	80	91	95	100	110	116
			Amoroso					A hair faster		
			q = 136					q = 137		
C major	G major	B♭ major	B♭ major	E major	F♯ major	A♭ major	D major	D major	D major	"D"

120	121	123	125	140	146	150	151	152	153	155
Slightly faster			A little faster	Much slower						
q = 142			q = 147	q = 89						
WT$_0$	WT$_1$	E major	E♭ major	"E"	E♭ minor	B♭ minor	A major	C♯ minor	E minor	E minor

159	170	171	172	176	180	182	187	191	196
Triumphant			Slightly faster					Faster	End Cue
q = 102			q = 109					q = 125	
"D"	WT$_1$	WT$_0$	G minor	C♯ minor	A minor	E♭ major	C♯ minor	Unclear	

Figure 5.14. Breakdown of 4M30 by measure, marking, tempo, meter, and tonal center.

In this battle cue, the meter remains relatively consistent in 4/4. While a handful of measures exist of 5/4, 2/4, and 3/4, they are only single measures, and the expansion or contraction of the measure serves a narrative purpose for the succeeding measure to begin in an appropriate location.

The adjacent tempo changes are extremely slight, but by taking a step back, we can see that the tempo accelerates from q = 135 to 147, despite slowing a bit, before significantly slowing down to q = 89 approximately 75 percent of the way through the cue. From there, the tempo accelerates to q = 109 through an incremental step. The large-scale acceleration through the majority of the cue is atypical for Powell, but the pivot to slowing then speeding up is quite typical.

Since meter and tempo are not the most enlightening parameters through which to observe this cue, tonal centers must be the primary focus. The opening 25 percent of the cue features tonal centers that shift from D to A, back to D and then up a tritone to G♯. The shifts from D to A are extremely standard, according to common-practice styles, but the move from D to G♯ is extremely uncommon. Another ascending fifth motion, from C to G, occurs, but the tritone motion is more common, with shifts from B♭ to E, A♭ to D, and G to C♯ throughout the cue. Additionally, the whole-tone scale plays a small part in the tonal scheme, momentarily, breaking up the diatonic tonal centers, and helping the music transition from "D," a tonal center without a clear third to distinguish major from minor, to the subsequent tonal center. A short section early in the cue features music that is tonally ambiguous, as it rapidly shifts through triads without preferencing a tonal center, and the final portion of the cue features a trichord, certainly avoiding a tonal center. Over the course of the cue, the music changes tonal centers over 30 times, making that the primary means of change in this action cue.

4M31—Hiccup Confronts Drago (1:07:32–1:11:35)

2–8—Courting Song (G Dorian)
10–15—Courting Song (B Dorian)
16–19—Good Alpha variation (E major)
26–34—Dragon Tune (B doubly harmonic minor)
39–56—Drago's Tune (C doubly harmonic minor)
56–62—Warring Vikings (C Aeolian)
71–95—Dragon Tune (G doubly harmonic minor)
96–112—Flying Ostinato (G Dorian)

Drago orders his Alpha to kill Valka and her dragon, Cloudjumper. Stoick, obviously upset, jumps into action, flying his dragon, Skullcrusher, into the air. Exciting rhythmic string music is most prominently heard, but underneath that, the *Courting Song* is played by the horns as Stoick is desperate not to lose his wife again. As she falls from Cloudjumper, he leaps from Skullcrusher to catch her in mid-air, and the *Courting Song* leaps up to B Dorian.

Hiccup then flies down to Drago on Toothless, and a rhythmic and melodic variation of the *Good Alpha* theme is played by the violins and trumpets, the theme nearly modified beyond recognition. This quick thematic statement reminds the audience of the positive power of dragons and foreshadows the film's conclusion. As Hiccup tells Drago of all of the good things that dragons can bring to humanity, the contrabasses, bassoons, and tubas play a rhythmically augmented and slightly melodically varied opening of the *Dragon Tune*. Drago is wholly unconvinced by Hiccup's argument, shows his false left arm, then tells Hiccup what dragons "really are," that he's known it since he was a boy. This monologue is underscored by *Drago's Tune* in C Aeolian, with a timbre similar to what was heard earlier in "Meet Drago," an air of mysticism still surrounding the villain.

Hiccup figures out Drago's endgame, and once more, tries to convince him that peace, not war, between people and dragons is the path forward. As Hiccup gives his final plea, the *Warring Vikings* theme sounds in C Aeolian as an immediate response to *Drago's Tune* in C Aeolian, the two thematic statements vying for supremacy. Drago will hear none of it. The bagpipes sound the call to war as Drago's Alpha is summoned. Drago plans to use Toothless against Hiccup by forcing him to be under the Alpha's command. The *Dragon Tune*, heavily rhythmically augmented, is played by the brass alongside the bagpipe call, and the Uilleann pipes add additional dissonance and anxiety as Toothless rejects the Alpha's control but finally succumbs to its command, as shown in the constriction of his pupils. Stoick, still with Valka on the mountainside, sees what is happening, and runs down to the base of the mountain to try to save Hiccup from certain death. A rhythmically augmented statement of the *Flying Ostinato* in G Aeolian sounds as Stoick gets closer, beginning in measure 96. Toothless, fully under the command of the Alpha, is no longer able to recognize Hiccup. Toothless is ordered to kill Hiccup with a fireball, and Stoick arrives just in time to push Hiccup out of the way. However, Stoick is hit; all that remains in the score is a sustained D7 pitch in the violins. Is Stoick simply injured, or it is worse? By ending the cue on the dominant, the music does not answer the question, much like the question regarding Hiccup's safety near the end of the first film.

4M32—Stoick Saves Hiccup (1:11:40–1:13:53)

1–22—Lost and Found (C Aeolian)
23–43—Map the World (C Aeolian)
43–48—Good Alpha variation (A Aeolian)
49–64—Good Alpha variation (C Aeolian)

A solo harmonium opens the cue with the *Lost and Found* theme in C Aeolian, while Hiccup sees his father, unmoving on the ground. Toothless continues panting, still under the Alpha's control, pupils still constricted. Valka and Hiccup both race to Stoick, trying to revive him and listen for a heartbeat. As they reach him, two solo violins enter with a countermelody. This is brilliant musical writing: the imposing physical figure of Stoick the Vast represented by the harmonium, which can play in two clefs, and which represents love, based on its use associated with the *Love* theme in 3M26C, "Let's Find Dad" from the first film, and Valka and Hiccup, each represented by their own respective violin, the two countermelody lines to Stoick's melody. Figure 5.15 shows the opening measures of the cue.

The Alpha leaves and Toothless regains self-control while the other dragons come to Stoick's side. The *Lost and Found* theme is now played by a string ensemble, a small portion of the full orchestra, like the small portion

Figure 5.15. 4M32, measures 1–21, *Lost and Found* as lament for Stoick.

of Berk now surrounding him. Toothless, back to himself, looks perplexed at what has happened. He walks over to the deceased Stoick and a solo flute is added to the melody, an octave higher than the violins; Toothless can soar in the air as the flute soars over the strings. In his grief, Hiccup yells at Toothless to get away. Toothless is stunned, having never been pushed away by Hiccup before. Valka tries to soothe Hiccup, telling him that it wasn't Toothless's fault, that he could not stop himself from his actions.

A new melody enters that enhances the emotional impact of Stoick's death, which is derived from the *Good Alpha* theme. The music modulates up to A Aeolian in measure 43 and is now in the highest range it has been in for this cue. Valka speaks of good dragons under control by bad dragons. The melody is a distortion of the *Good Alpha* theme, but fulfills a dual meaning as Stoick, the "Alpha" of Berk, is now dead, and as a result, the theme cannot be in its original form. Toothless tries to fly away on his own but is snared by Drago's staff. The music continues to shift higher and moves up to C Aeolian in measure 49, where it will remain for the remainder of the cue. Drago will ride the Night Fury and use him for destruction. The music conveys the emotion of heartbreak, with Toothless turning on his human, taking a life, and ultimately rejected by his best friend. Both Toothless and Hiccup are feeling the heartbreak. Nobody wins. Everyone loses. Everyone except Drago.

4M33—Off to Valhalla (1:14:00–1:17:41)
    3–19—Courting Song (E-flat major)
    20–35—Courting Song (C major)
    38–46—Flying Ostinato (A major)
    38–47—Flying B variation (A major)

Stoick's funeral occurs with the small group of Berkians at Valka's sanctuary. Gobber delivers the service, and Hiccup shoots the first flaming arrow onto the ship that will take Stoick's body to Valhalla, as per the Viking tradition. The cue opens with the *Courting Song* played on Celtic Harp, violins, and choir, and is in E♭ major, the heroic key, as Stoick sacrificed himself to save his son from certain death. The third section of the song adds both bagpipes and Uilleann pipes to the melody, instruments that are often played at the funerals of those who lost their lives in the line of duty. Instead of reaching an authentic cadence and closing the song, the music modulates and begins anew, now in C major, as Hiccup apologizes to his father for not being the person his father wanted him to be. Valka tells Hiccup that he was born prematurely, and that his father said Hiccup would become the strongest Viking of them all. Valka says to her son, "You have the heart of a chief, and the soul of a dragon. Only you can bring our worlds together." Hiccup is unique among Vikings, and the orchestration proves it.

Hiccup laments about the fear of becoming his father, saying, "How do you become that great, that brave, that selfless?" Powell's use of music here is outstanding. Again, the *Courting Song* fails to reach an authentic cadence. Instead, Powell connects the C major and E major triads, related by chromatic mediant, through a gesture similar to Ralph Vaughan Williams' style: with an inverted D^{o7} chord, a fully functional ii^{o7} in C major, but rather than resolving to the expected G major dominant, it resolves to an E major triad, the enharmonically-spelled A♭ as G♯ serving as the common tone between the D^{o7} and EM chords, the E major triad serving as the dominant to the new key of A major. Figures 5.16 and 5.17 show Powell's and Vaughan Williams's respective musical gestures.

128   The Music of the *How to Train Your Dragon* Trilogy

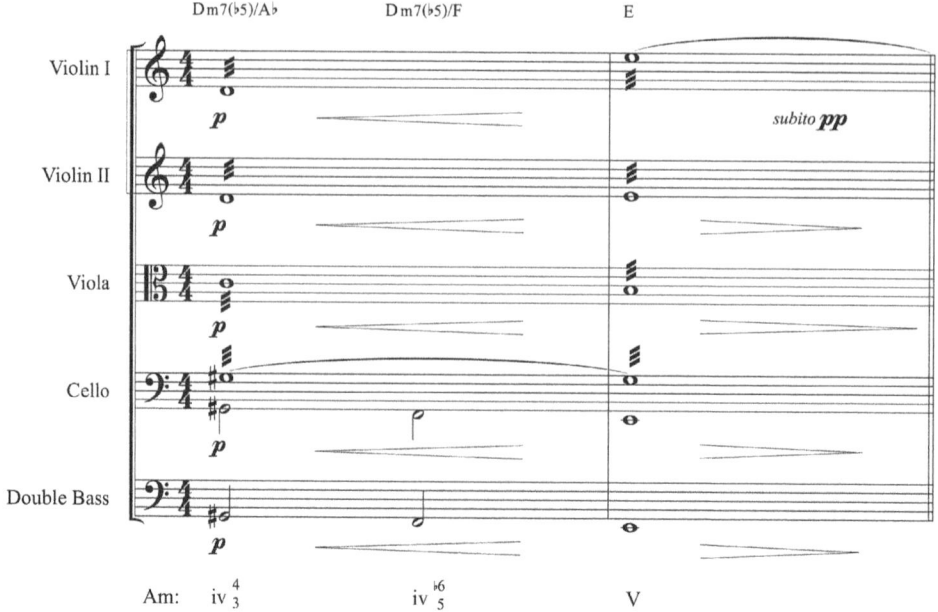

Figure 5.16. 4M33, measures 35–36, reaching a half cadence.

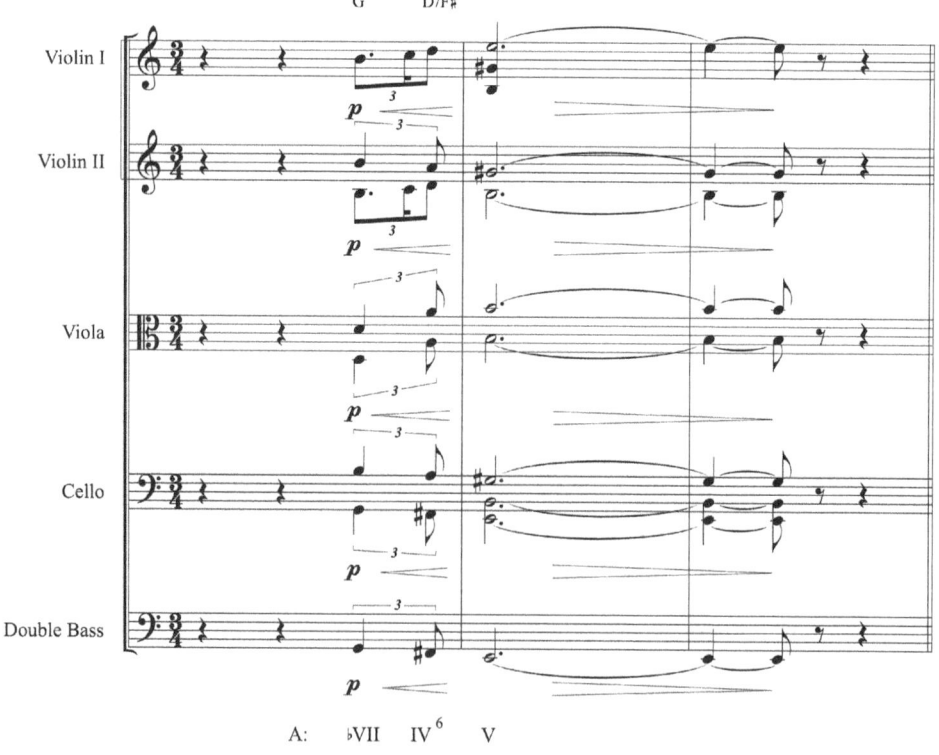

Figure 5.17. Vaughan Williams, *Fantasia on a Theme by Thomas Tallis*, measures 88–90, reaching a half cadence.

Hiccup's answer to his question comes in the form of the music, which plays both the *Flying Ostinato* and the *Flying B* theme in A major. Hiccup is not his father. As he gains confidence in his new role, the tempo accelerates, and uses chromaticism within the phrase, particularly when it is no longer expected. Based on nearly two films worth of music, the *Flying B* theme, in A major, should end BM-DM-BM. In this instance, it ends BM-FM-DM in measures 43–45, subverting the expected chromatic mediant alternation and replacing it with tritone root motion, another example of a *Durchbruch*. Hiccup, who has been unwilling to change his position on talking to Drago, is changing and willing to do what is necessary to protect the people of Berk. Hiccup now has a dynamic element to his leadership.

4M35—Riding to Drago's (1:17:42–1:18:34)

2–22—Vikings (D-flat major)
22–29—Vikings A (D major)

The team wonders how they'll return to Berk since Drago took all the dragons. Hiccup reminds them that not *all* the dragons are gone. They return to the sanctuary and ride the baby dragons to Berk. A line earlier in the film that was thought to be a throw-away is now significant: "They are babies. They don't listen to anyone." Because they don't listen to anyone, they cannot be controlled by the Alpha, so the team will be able to attack. They begin flying out of the cave, accompanied by a statement of the complete *Vikings* theme. As the theme nears its end, it modulates up a half-step, and starts again. Hiccup announces the plan: get Toothless back and kick Drago's [ass]. The cue ends with an alternation of DM and B♭M triads, the magic chromatic mediant relationship. The magician this instance is that the baby dragons cannot be controlled by the Alpha, giving the team an unexpected advantage. These are also the exact same triads that were heard in 4M35–37, "Over/Less Okay" in the first film in measures 242–247, another connection between the two films. In the first film, it was the initial time the team had flown dragons. In this film, it's the initial time the babies have been flown.

4M36-37—Alpha Comes to Berk (1:18:43–1:20:52)

10–14—Heroic Dragon (D Phrygian)
14–24—Heroic Dragon (D Phrygian)
27–30—Flying A (F major)
34–37—Flying A (F major)
41–43—Flying A (D major)
43–52—Flying B (D major)
53–56—Hiccup/Vikings (E Aeolian)

As Berk sleeps, Drago comes to attack. The cue begins softly, but with a curious harmonic progression: DM/F♯-D°7/A♭-Dmm7/A-B split-third (both D♮ and D♯). The progression is clearly non-functional, but works musically and narratively because it is mysterious and unexpected. The one constant note between all the chords is D. Both F♮ and F♯ are used, both A♭ and A♮ are used; half-step manipulations of harmonies to create tension can be very effective, as they are here.

A solo oboe plays the opening of the *Heroic Dragon* theme with an entirely new harmonization, as a prelude to the impending attack on Berk. The Berkian dragons are all under the control of the Alpha now, and the musical confusion contributes to the confusion of the villagers. Drago flies up with his Bewilderbeast, and the Berkians gasp at the sight of the creature. Drago announces Stoick's death to the people, and says, "No one can protect you now." Fear shows in their eyes. The Bewilderbeast blows ice at Berk and the action cuts to the team flying back as the sun prepares to rise, accompanied by the *Flying A* theme in a solo horn and over a tonic F major triad. Hiccup orders the team to distract the Alpha, while the *Flying A* theme is reharmonized, since Hiccup needs to bring Toothless back from the Alpha's control. This new harmonization presents four chords over a pedal A—AM, B♭M, E♭M, AM. The pedal tone is indicative of the standard version of the theme, while the reharmonization indicates something amiss. Hiccup must reconcile the loss of his father with renewing his relationship with Toothless.

The town recognizes Hiccup's return with the other dragon riders and cheers as a triumphant statement of the *Flying B* theme in D major sounds in the brass. Drago cannot believe that the team is back, again, having flown the baby dragons to Berk. The music turns playful, with Irish rhythms, and a four-measure musical unit that highlights baby dragons and catapulted sheep, all of which distracts the Alpha, and this portion of the cue concludes with the same gesture as the end of the *Hiccup* theme. The cue ends playfully, with the choir singing "ba-ba-ba-bum bum," as it did in the opening cue of the film when the sheep is catapulted by Gobber, a visual device transformed from a portion of a game to a distraction technique in order to save the village.

5M38—Toothless Comes Back (1:21:10–1:24:44)
5–41—Pulsing 16th notes
8–14—Good Alpha (G Phrygian)
18–25—Lost and Found (E-flat Aeolian)
29–46—Lost and Found (C Aeolian)
48–58—Lost and Found (C Aeolian)
67–76—Flying Ostinato (D Phrygian)
78–83—Lost and Found (D Aeolian)
84–86—Flying Ostinato (D Phrygian → B major)
87–100—Lost and Found (E Aeolian)
101–105—Flying A (E major)
101–102—Flying Ostinato (E major)

Hiccup, flying a baby dragon, approaches Drago, flying Toothless. The pulsing sixteenth notes in the strings return for the third and final time, connecting this cue with 1M6, "Eret Educates Hiccup" and 2M11, "Hiccup and Toothless Attacked." In the former, the sixteenth notes referred to the unseen Drago, the villain. In the latter, it is still possible that Drago is the masked non-speaking attacker. Here, there is no question that Drago is directly in front of Hiccup, and as a result, the harmony used in the pulsing chord is different, now a $G^{ø7}$ chord over a C pedal, an (01368) pentachord. As Hiccup tries to get Toothless back by speaking to him, a variation on the *Good Alpha* theme is played in the horns that alters the rhythm and places it in the minor-mode. Toothless is in a fog, unable to recognize Hiccup. The solo horn then plays the opening of the *Lost and Found* theme, but rhythmically augmented and with a radical reharmonization, representing Toothless's state of mind. Hiccup tries explaining to Toothless that he understands what happened, but to no avail. Toothless's fog is shown in Figure 5.18.

Hiccup tries moving even closer to Toothless, approaching a distance where he can touch the dragon. Toothless's pupils begin to dilate, showing him fighting the effect of the Alpha, and the *Lost and Found* theme begins in C Aeolian in the choir. By the end of the theme, Hiccup has brought Toothless all the way back from the Alpha's control,

5. How to Train Your Dragon 2 *Cue Analysis*

Figure 5.18. 5M38, measures 8–25, variations of *Good Alpha* and *Lost and Found* themes.

much to Drago's disbelief. Toothless was lost, but now is found, was (kind of) blind, but now he sees. The pulsing sixteenth notes fade as Toothless returns to Hiccup.

Toothless bucks Drago off his back, and a triumphant statement of *Lost and Found* begins again in measure 48. But, without a rider, Toothless falls from the sky. The theme continues, unaltered, and as Hiccup reaches Toothless, he saddles the dragon and they pull up before hitting the water, another parallel moment with the first film. The music also pulls up, resolving unexpectedly higher at the synchronous moment, measure 58. They zip past the Alpha and take momentary refuge on the other side of the rocks. The harp plays a minor-mode version of the *Flying Ostinato* in eighth notes, while the rest of the orchestra plays a consistent rhythm of triplets as the danger is not yet resolved, the polyrhythm highlighting the chaos.

With the bond between Hiccup and Toothless back, the *Lost and Found* theme sounds in the strings and brass as they attack Drago and the Alpha. As the Alpha shoots its ice at them, Toothless pulls straight up into the air, Drago laughing that Hiccup has fallen off. The *Lost and Found* theme begins anew as Hiccup soars through the air and sprays gas above the Alpha's head, which Toothless ignites, causing an explosion. The second part of the *Lost and Found* theme, beginning in measure 93, is in a swashbuckling style, with a short-short-long rhythm occurring throughout the entire section.

The first two films have several parallel locations, and this is yet another instance. In the first film, Hiccup and Toothless were hit by the Red Death's tail and spectacularly crashed to the ground. It looks like it will happen again, but Toothless spreads his back fins, a trick taught by Valka, and is able to negotiate his way through the Alpha's tail without crashing. Their success is marked with a statement of the opening of the *Flying A* theme *in* E major. The cue comes to a quick and unexpected halt as Hiccup throws his sword at Drago's hand, thinking he's won the fight. The harmonies in measures 101–107 are: EM-AM-C♯m-F♯M, or I-IV in E and v-I in F♯. The Roman numerals create a logical progression, but because of the tonal shift, they don't work together. However, the two tonal areas can be connected through the AM and C♯m triads, linked through the

Leading Tone (*L*) NRT operation. Once again, Powell uses NRT relationships when it best suits the needs of the film. In this case, the cue ends quite unexpectedly and segues directly into the succeeding cue, with no cadence necessary.

5M39A—Challenging the Alpha (1:24:45–1:27:30)

  3–6—Drago's Tune (C-sharp Aeolian)
  28–35—Lost and Found (G Aeolian)
  36–41—Lost and Found (G Aeolian)
  42–46—Lost and Found (C Aeolian)
  49–57—Lost and Found (C Aeolian)
  61–69—Lost and Found (D Aeolian)
  70–77—Lost and Found (D Aeolian)
  88–120—Heroic Dragon (G major)

Drago has one last card to play; the opening three notes of his theme initiate the cue. The Alpha breathes ice onto Hiccup, Toothless darting in front to protect him. Drago turns and laughs at the ice-encased heroes, and the music lands on a G♯Mm^7 chord, sustained for an almost-unbearable amount of time, begging for resolution, in measures 17–23.

Toothless uses his powers to heat and explode the ice, as both he and Hiccup are revealed to be fine. The G♯Mm^7 chord resolves down by half-step to Gm, by way of a timpani roll, as the *Lost and Found* theme begins in rhythmic augmentation. The resolution of G♯Mm^7 to Gm is unusual, to say the least. Typically, a V^7 chord would not resolve to ♯iv, but it does here, as a sort of downward moving "breakthrough," figuratively and literally on screen. Toothless roars at the Alpha, blinks tenderly at Hiccup, and goes back to roaring at the Alpha, challenging him for supremacy. The *Lost and Found* theme restarts in measure 36, still in rhythmic augmentation. Toothless lost Hiccup once. He won't do it again.

Toothless fires at the Alpha, hitting him in the face, and the dragons snap out of its control. During this second part of the *Lost and Found* theme, beginning in measure 49, the dragons flock to Toothless's side of the battle, with Drago losing them and Berk finding them. Drago refuses to walk away from the fight, choosing to battle to the death. The music shifts to a style similar to the "Dragon Training" cue from the first film in measure 80, the lead-in to the first day of dragon training in the arena. The music here serves a similar prelude-like function here, but it is the prelude to Drago's demise.

The *Heroic Dragon* variation is used, as Toothless has the dragons cast an all-out assault on the Alpha, shooting fireballs and everything else at it, Toothless observing like a field general. The Alpha roars in defiance, and Toothless takes the last shot, severing one of the Alpha's tusks. The Alpha concedes, leaving Toothless as the new Alpha dragon.

5M39B—The Chief Has Come Home (1:27:44–1:30:59)

  7–19—Good Alpha (E-flat Mixolydian)
  20–33—Good Alpha (G Mixolydian)
  33–41—Vikings (D major)
  53–70—Vikings A (D major)
  72–81—Love theme (G major)
  82–90—Hiccup the Chief (D major)
  92–98—Flying A (E major)
  92–98—Flying Ostinato (E major)

Contrary motion between the bass and melody along with a sense of tonal ambiguity initiate this cue as Drago's Bewilderbeast retreats. The tonic and mode are unclear until the final three chords of the introduction, leading into the half cadence in measure 5: A♭-M-Fm-B♭M, or IV-ii-V in E♭ major (or Mixolydian once the next theme begins). To exert his dominance once more, Toothless roars, the people of Berk cheer, and the *Good Alpha* theme sounds in E♭ Mixolydian twice. This is the most majestic statement of that theme in the film, as Toothless has earned the role of Alpha through his actions, not his size. Drago's Bewilderbeast leaves Berk with Drago still on its back, but submerges back into the ocean. Drago is never seen again, which is good enough for Hiccup to presume Drago to be dead.

The *Good Alpha* theme is heard again twice, up a major third, in G Mixolydian, with Cloudjumper and all the other dragons bowing to Toothless. This leads directly into a complete statement of the *Vikings* theme, a much more playful tune, as the dragons have returned home and all is well in Berk. As the *Vikings D* theme leads back into the *Vikings A* theme, the orchestration thins and the dynamics drop to *piano* everywhere except the solo flute, playing the melody. Eret approaches Hiccup and tells him he'd be a good trapper. Hiccup offers Eret the job of taking care of Skullcrusher, Stoick's dragon, and Eret accepts, fully joining the Berkian way of life. As the tune winds down, Valka tells Hiccup she'll stay in Berk.

Like the first film, Astrid approaches Hiccup during the "happy ending," but instead of punching him, she touches him on his chest, while a solo violin plays the *Love* theme, and they kiss, but their celebration is cut short as the village elder taps Hiccup on the shoulder. It is time for his coronation as the chief of Berk. The *Hiccup the Chief* theme sounds, at first quietly, but grows in volume and orchestration as it continues, reaching a sustained B major triad, measures 90–91, with Gobber announcing, "The chief has come home!" Hiccup has grown and will continue to grow into his role as chief.

The sustained B major triad serves as the dominant to the conclusion of the cue in E major, first playing the *Flying Ostinato* with the opening two measures of the *Flying A* theme, followed by the final three measures of the *Flying B* theme. Hiccup is now fully the chief of Berk. Fireworks explode over the village, and the music segues into the final cue of the film.

5M40—Where No One Goes Reprise (1:30:59–1:34:38)

To keep with the parallels between the two films, Hiccup delivers voice-over narration at the film's conclusion. The vocals of the song are omitted to avoid overlap with Hiccup's narration until measure 40, when the sheep is catapulted into the air and the *Flying B* theme is used as the interlude between verses of the song. Hiccup delivers the final line, "We have our dragons," and after a slight pause, the song resumes, complete with Jónsi's vocals. The song continues into the End Credits, through the artwork portion, and spilling into the rolling credits.

End Credits (1:34:39–1:41:45)

The End Credit music is culled together from two cues in the film:
3M20 "Flying with Mother"—complete
1M1 "Dragon Racing"—complete, excluding measures 67, 78, and 94–98

6

How to Train Your Dragon: The Hidden World Cue Analysis

1M1—Rescue Mission (0:00:59–0:05:00)

4–12—March of the Warlords
20–22—Fighting riff (D doubly harmonic minor)
31–33—Fighting riff (F-sharp doubly harmonic minor)
62–66—Heroes A (F Dorian)
68–76—Heroes B (F-sharp minor)
76–78—Fighting riff (C-sharp minor)
90–95—Fighting riff (D doubly harmonic minor, then B doubly harmonic minor)
99–107—Fighting riff (D doubly harmonic minor)
108–111—Fighting riff (F-sharp doubly harmonic minor)
125–128—Fighting riff (E-flat doubly harmonic minor)
130–137—Heroes A variation (D Dorian)
138–145—Heroes A variation (F Dorian)
147–150—Light Fury Motif (E-flat major)

The opening of *The Hidden World* stands in sharp contrast to the opening of the first two films, signaling how different this story will be. Rather than beginning in Berk with voice-over narration from Hiccup, this film opens with a rescue mission in progress, as the Avengers of Berk attempt to free several dragons from trappers.

The cue begins after the opening credits—the Universal logo and theme and the Dreamworks logo and theme, an element consistent between the second and third films—drums sounding before any pitched instruments. The scene occurs on the foggy ocean at night. The musical timbres are ominous, quite the opposite of the beginnings of the first two films. Once the low woodwinds, brass, and strings enter, they play *March of the Warlords*, thematically based on an ascending half-step. Through its title, we know that the music does not refer to the film's primary antagonist, but it still signals a strong level of villainy. A figure stands in the darkness. His sword becomes fire. He and his electrified dragon can walk through flames (likely a trick learned from Drago), and he begins fighting with the man on the ship. Curiously, when they begin fighting, the music switches to triple meter in measure 14. The meter transforms the battle into a dance to free the dragons, while inflicting pain on the dragon trappers through the loss of their cargo and transportation.

The horns then play the opening of the *Fighting* riff, a melody not all that dissimilar

6. How to Train Your Dragon: The Hidden World *Cue Analysis* 135

Figure 6.1. 1M1, measures 99–107, complete statement of *Fighting* riff.

from the *Dragon Tune*. Although the *Fighting* riff is not one of the themes and motifs provided by Powell, it occurs repeatedly throughout this film, so I have given the music its label. The riff appears below as Figure 6.1.

The *Fighting* riff is a musical accompaniment to the Avengers of Berk in their quest to keep dragons out of the hands of their enemies. It is loosely based on the doubly harmonic minor scale, particularly at its outset, but later seems to operate more as a minor scale, with scale-degrees 6 and 7 fluctuating between *Le* and *La*, as well as *Te* and *Ti*, respectively.

Another theme that seems to favor the sentence structure, the *Fighting* riff opens with a two-measure statement confirming tonic function, followed by a related two-measure repeated statement confirming dominant function. The second half of the structure rhythmically accelerates the opening gesture and fragments it into a one-beat unit by its conclusion. The final chord creates a modified half cadence as the dominant chord is inverted, but not a half cadence in the original key of D minor, a highly unusual trait for a standard sentence. The fighting is not static, as the Avengers of Berk physically move during the fight, but the situation and circumstances are continually shifting. With this in mind, ending the *Fighting* riff in a different key than where it started makes perfect sense.

The trapper believes Hiccup to be a "demon," and is terrified of him. Snotlout and the Nut twins arrive in succession, with the music largely beneath the dialogue and sound effects. Fishlegs appears, a baby dragon in tow. Finally, Astrid appears and knocks out the man on the ship, not to the *Love* theme, but to a melody in English horn and clarinet at measure 62, an early preview of the *Heroes B* theme, shown in Figure 6.2. However, the team has not grown into their role as heroes yet, and the dynamics remain

Figure 6.2. 1M1, measures 62–66, early statement of *Heroes B* theme.

piano and *mezzo-forte*, the tune played by solo woodwinds, not brass. They begin to unlock the dragon cages.

A new melody, the *Heroes A* theme, is introduced in measure 68. In the score, it is marked as "Lovely Dragons," played by the flute. This is an example of extreme foreshadowing, as the full *Heroes* theme will not be revealed for some time and in this instance, the B section appears before the A section. The team is excited by all the different types of dragons they're releasing, except Ruffnut, who looks at the "Bug Dragon" and expects it to be "super dumb." The opening notes of the *Fighting* riff are played by the bass clarinet, a timbre implying silliness and foolishness on the part of Ruffnut. She can't get the cage open despite pulling on it, so Astrid walks over and slides the gate open; Ruffnut, not the dragon, is "super dumb."

The team has been spotted, and the music immediately becomes *forte* and active. Once again, the opening of the *Fighting* riff sounds in the horns and middle strings as Snotlout defeats another bad guy on the ship. Finally, the full *Fighting* riff is heard, beginning in measure 99 in the trombones and violin I, played in D doubly harmonic minor. It's not quite the swashbuckling style the second film, as this is a bit more serious and with higher stakes, but dotted rhythms are present. The *Fighting* riff is restated, up a major third in F♯ doubly harmonic minor, and broken between various part of the orchestra as the fighting continues. At the conclusion of the thematic statement, an Octatonic (0,1) scalar run propels the music into the next section of the cue.

In the first two films, the doubly harmonic minor scale was used to represent the villains, the Red Death and Drago. In this instance, the scale is used to accompany our heroes battling to save and free dragons. This means that the villain's music will likely be derived from some other scale, or if his music does come from the same scale, it will be used in a dramatically different fashion.

Valka sits atop the ship's mast, surveying the action from above. The music features continuous eighth-note triplets for eight measures, four measures of E minor and four measures of C♯°7, the tension growing to Snotlout's attack, which he unintentionally self-sabotages by getting caught on a cage. Hiccup calls for the team to "move out," and we hear another tune in the flute and strings.

Derived from *Valka's Tune*, the melody seen in Figure 6.3, in D Dorian, rallies the team to their dragons to leave. This is an early variation of the *Heroes A* theme, which is normally in 4/4 meter rather than the 3/4 meter here. The presence of Valka in the scene is why I suggest that the melody is a variation on her theme, even though it is really its own theme, particularly because we don't have the clear association with the new theme

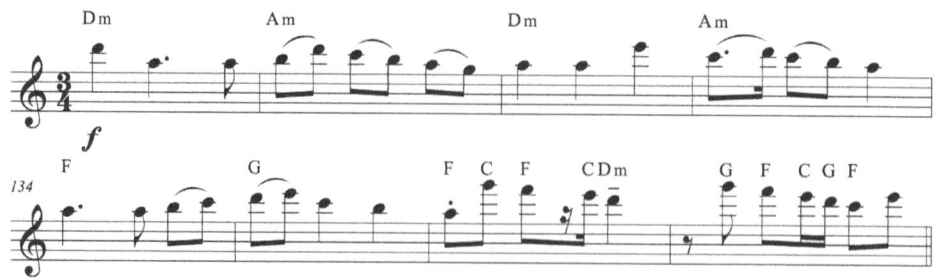

Figure 6.3. 1M1, measures 130–137, early statement of *Heroes A* theme.

as yet. Hiccup may be the leader of the operation, but Valka is still the overseer as a mother and as someone who conducted raids for 20 years. The melody is repeated, up a minor third in F Dorian, as we see Fishlegs escape on his dragon. The only ones still on the ship are Hiccup and Toothless, who catches a scent of something ... familiar? This is the first statement of the *Light Fury Motif*, an ascending arpeggio of a major triad, here an E♭ major triad resolving to a D♭ minor triad, quite a distant and uncommon relationship, I and ♭vii in E♭M, but the Light Fury is quite an uncommon dragon in this world. The music fades and segues into the next cue.

1M2A-B—Busy Busy Berk (0:05:01–0:06:25, 0:07:20–0:08:19)

13–21—Hiccup/Vikings (B Aeolian)
21–29—Hiccup/Vikings (F-sharp Aeolian)
30–37—Flying B (A major)
38–41—Flying Ostinato (F-sharp major)
41–50—Heroic Dragon (A major)
59–71—Lost and Found (C-sharp Aeolian) *not in film*
71–86—Heroes A and B (B-flat major) *not in film*
98–106—Warring Vikings (E-flat Aeolian)

Hiccup and Toothless are the only team members still on the ship. Hiccup turns off his fire sword and whirls around, revealing the dozen or so members of the trapping crew still on board. The music is immediately tense, thanks to the continuous sixteenth notes and their syncopated accent pattern. To enhance this tension, the bass line plays an ascending G major scale from G2 to B3, and B becomes the new tonic. During this scalar run, the rest of the orchestra implies E Aeolian, a mode which uses the same seven notes as G major, so while there's not a harmonic clash, like in a polychord, this music is functioning as polymodal. Toothless plows through the trappers, knocking them all down, Hiccup jumps on, and they fly away.

The action shifts to Berk at daytime at measure 9 and the mode is B Aeolian. The *Hiccup* theme is played in rhythmic augmentation beginning in measure 13, and rather than voice-over narration for the audience, Hiccup speaks directly to the newly acquired dragons, telling them about the village (even though it is narration for the audience). For the repeated statement of the *Hiccup* theme, the music jumps up a fifth to F♯ Aeolian as Hiccup continues to describe the amenities to the new dragons. Hiccup's music leads directly into a statement of the *Flying B* theme in A major followed by a brief interlude of the *Flying Ostinato* in F♯ major, as Hiccup declares the thing that makes Berk unique to be dragons, "Lots and lots of dragons."

As the new and very large dragon, the Crimson Goregutter, lands, we hear the *Heroic Dragon* theme, here marked as "Dragon Tune on Drugs." While the theme is the heroic version, the orchestration is not, as hardly any woodwinds or brass are playing this theme and the sparseness of the orchestra enhances the goofy sound. The music fades out at the conclusion of the thematic statement, omitting measures 51–86 from the film.

Although it was not used in the film, the omitted portion of the cue used both the *Heroes A* and *Heroes B* themes. It may have been omitted because the team is not yet ready to be heroes. The team returns, only for Astrid to chastise them for being sloppy, and Valka commenting that she believes they rely too much on their dragons, and not enough on each other, a line that foreshadows the entire arc of the film.

The cue returns in the film in measure 87 as Fishlegs' little dragon, Fishmeat, scampers over to the Crimson Goregutter who attempts to play with it, knocking down multiple buildings in the process. Gobber asks Hiccup to ask Toothless to keep the dragons in line, while the *Warring Vikings* theme sounds, but a version that, again, sounds lighthearted and playful since the Vikings are not actively fighting an enemy. It is clear to everyone except Hiccup that Berk has too many dragons for its size. Rather than the expected repeated statement of the *Warring Vikings* theme, the music shifts into a whole-tone scale of major triads—E♭M-C♯M-BM-AM-GM-FM-E♭M—and Gobber shrieks at the sight of the "Bug Dragon," which he calls a Hobgoblin and a bad omen. The cue ends on an E♭^{o7} chord, dissonant, worried and without resolution.

1M2C-3—Marry Her / Grimmel's Terms (0:09:42–0:11:18, 0:012:32–0:13:32)

    1–10—Village Hymn (F Dorian)
    12–16—Warring Vikings (F Aeolian)
    17–24—March of the Warlords
    24–36—Grimmel's Tune A (F Aeolian)
    45–49—Grimmel's Tune A (B-flat Aeolian) *not in film*
    53–56—Grimmel's Tune B *not in film*
    56–73—Grimmel's Tune (A-flat Aeolian)
    64–67—Flying Ostinato (F-sharp Aeolian)

Inside the dining hall, Gobber says what everyone is thinking: Hiccup and Astrid should get married. Everyone in the hall stops, and a momentary silence ensues. The cue begins with a new theme, the *Village Hymn*, here played by the strings in F Dorian. It is a modal tune that sounds like an old folk tune because of the varied use of accidentals on scale-degrees 6 and 7, here, the play between D♭ and D♮ and E♭ and E♮. Following a turn of comic relief from Tuffnut and his "full beard," Eret enters the hall to give Hiccup the update on the location of the trapping ships. His entrance coincides with a statement of the *Warring Vikings* theme in F Aeolian in the cellos, with minimal accompaniment in celeste and harps. Eret is now truly a Viking of Berk.

The action shifts from Berk to the trapping fleet and fort in measure 17, where the *March of the Warlords* is once again heard. The texture here is thicker than in the opening cue, and the addition of male choir, marked "Wotan men," gives extra gravitas to the motif. In Wagner's four-opera cycle *Der Ring des Nibelungen* (The Ring of the Niebelungen, or in the vernacular, "The Ring Cycle,"), Wotan (aka Odin, King of the Gods) is performed by a bass-baritone, hence the meaning of the marking in the score. As a further Wagnerian connection, the harmonization of March of the Warlords, Cm-G♯m, is a chromatic mediant relationship that represents antagonism and evil and is used as the harmonic foundation of the "Tarnhelm" motive from *Der Ring des Nibelung*. The "Tarnhelm" is a magic helmet that can turn its wearer invisible or into any creature of any size. The harmonic relationship is the same as "Darth Vader's motive" from "The Imperial March" in the *Star Wars* films.

March of the Warlords leads into the initial statement of *Grimmel's Tune*. Grimmel is the primary villain in the film, accounting for the alternate title of *March of the Warlords, The Other Bad Guys*. Like *Drago's Tune* from the previous film, *Grimmel's Tune* has two sections, uses chromaticism, features rhythms that feel "out of time," and sounds nasty and evil. Only the first part of his theme sounds here. In the film, the cue cuts out from measures 37–63 as the warlords explain their predicament to Grimmel. Only when they mention that Berk is protected by a Night Fury does Grimmel become interested in their proposal, which is when the cue resumes. As it does, the second half of *Grimmel's Tune B* is played softly in the cellos and basses, with the minor-mode version of the *Flying Ostinato* atop the theme. Grimmel agrees to capture the Night Fury, even though it is against his entire being because he kills dragons rather than capture them. The warlords show Grimmel "his favorite bait," and when they say, "a female," we hear a G minor arpeggio in unison in the celeste and harps, but not harmonized as the *Light Fury Motif* typically is.

A dragon escapes its chains, charges, and Grimmel lives up to his statement that he "kills dragons," rather than trapping them. As the dragon falls to its death, the contrabassoon and tuba play the opening three notes of *Grimmel's Tune*, but the leap from *sol* to *do* here is inverted and is descending, since Grimmel has just murdered a dragon. The audience needs to see how evil Grimmel is, and the seriousness of the threat he poses to Berk. His last words in the scene mention that Hiccup will hand over the Night Fury. When the words "Night Fury" are spoken, a descending line in the celeste is played in measures 79–81, the opposite direction of the *Light Fury Motif*, ending on an A. Powell's music, working with the narrative, is both subtle and telling. It is elegant and shows just how attuned he is to both the current scene and the overall story of the film.

1M4—Legend Has It (0:13:33–0:17:59)

1–15—Fate Tune (D centric)
16–25—Village Hymn (D Aeolian)
27–41—Map the World (G Aeolian)
42–45—Village Hymn (D Aeolian) *not in film*
50–54—The Hidden World (D Aeolian)
58–67—Love theme (G major)
79–81—Furies in Love (G Aeolian)

The cue opens with a sustained A4, almost sounding like the A in the celeste at the end of the previous cue has continued into this one. This scene is clearly a memory because of Stoick's presence. The first melodic material in the cue presents the *Fate Tune*. Unlike the *Fate* theme from the first and second films, this tune refers to Toothless and the Light Fury coupling and leading the dragons away from Berk to their own safe haven. The ultimate fate of Berk is to be dragonless. The *Fate Tune* is in D, but the use of both F♯ and F♮, as well as other chromatic notes, make the theme impossible to classify in a single mode. The texture is light, with solo woodwinds and sopilka playing the tune, and the full choir providing accompaniment. It is intended to sound mysterious, as Stoick, in a flashback, describes the location of The Hidden World to a very young Hiccup, a place "at the edge of the world." As a result, no brass or strings are used in this portion of the cue after the opening continuation of the A4.

As the scene dissolves into present-day Berk, just the strings, without contrabass, play the *Village Hymn*, Hiccup surveying his village. The *Village Hymn* is also in D, here D Aeolian, so the flashback and the present-day both use the same tonic, avoiding a strange modulation during the dissolve. Toothless wants to play fetch with Hiccup's prosthetic leg, and as Toothless retrieves it, Hiccup pulls out his map of the known world, searching for the Hidden World. As he begins looking it over, the Celtic Harp begins playing the *Map the World* theme, an obvious choice of Leitmotifs in this instance. As in the second film, Astrid finds Hiccup with his map, and comes to talk. After a brief pause, the cue resumes, omitting measures 42–46.

Hiccup believes the solution to the overcrowded Berk to be to find the Hidden World and move all of Berk there, dragons and humans. As he mentions this, a solo flute and clarinet play the opening four measures of *The Hidden World* theme, alluding to the fact that this legendary place exists. Astrid, always the skeptic, wants something more tangible.

Hiccup mentions marriage to Astrid, and the *Love* theme sounds, initially on the sopilka before moving to flute. However, neither Hiccup nor Astrid is ready to marry the other yet. As the *Love* theme comes to a close, Toothless hears a sound and goes chasing after it, following a descending arpeggio in the celeste, essentially the same thing heard in the previous cue. The opening gesture of the *Furies in Love Tune* is played in E♭ major, and the music fades out on the last note.

2M5—Mysterious Creature (0:18:26–0:20:53)

 3–7—Light Fury Motif (C-sharp major)
 14–21—Furies in Love (C-sharp Aeolian)
 23–26—Flying A (G major)
 28–35—Furies in Love (C Aeolian)

Following Toothless's search in the night, he comes across the Light Fury in an open field, and the cue begins with a high C♯ in the violins, and a mark tree glissando, leading into the *Light Fury Motif*. This theme is now in C♯ major, and in its full form, beyond just the arpeggio since Toothless has finally found her. She looks at him and the music continues with magical textures in measures 10–14—celeste and harp—for Toothless's natural mate. This music serves as the introduction to the *Furies in Love* theme. She initially growls at him, but gradually allows him to approach. As she does, the first threads of the *Furies in Love* theme are heard. The Light Fury hears a branch break, growls, and the theme is halted. She shoots a fireball into the forest, destroying a hole in the trees. Both Hiccup and Astrid emerge from different sides, and the reharmonized *Flying A* theme is heard, all over a pedal G. This harmonization contains elements of the standard *Flying A* theme (tonic pedal) and the variation (harmonizing each melodic note), as Hiccup and Astrid cannot believe that there's another Fury, Hiccup whispering, "Oh my gods!" This type of harmonization was used in the second film in the cue 4M36–37 "Alpha Comes to Berk," where something is not quite right. Here, it's the presence of the Light Fury, who sends another fireball their way, Astrid diving and pushing them both out of the path of it. In response, Toothless growls at the Light Fury, protecting Hiccup.

She flies away, accompanied by the *Furies in Love* theme, beginning in the cello, then moving up to the flute, the timbres representing Toothless on the ground and the Light Fury high in the air. She disappears in a ball of fire as the *Furies in Love* theme slightly progresses into its second part. Astrid coins the name "Light Fury," for this new dragon, due to her white color and the cue fades out as Toothless stares longingly into the night sky.

2M6A-B—In Love / Dart Trap (0:21:02–0:24:44)

 2–5—Sex riff (D Aeolian)
 4–10—Furies in Love (D Aeolian)
 10–17—Sex riff (D Aeolian)
 26–30—Village Hymn (E-flat Aeolian)

6. How to Train Your Dragon: The Hidden World *Cue Analysis*

> 33–38—Village Hymn (A Dorian)
> 41–44—Grimmel's Tune A (F-sharp Aeolian)
> 50–58—Grimmel's Tune A (F Aeolian)

Back at the stables, Toothless is in love, slobbering and panting. He sees other dragons performing a mating dance, set to the *Sex* riff before the *Furies in Love* theme enters in the first violins in measure 4. immediately progresses into the second part of the theme in the flute and clarinet. The theme doesn't reach its conclusion, since the Light Fury is absent from the scene. Instead, the music shifts back to the *Sex* riff in measure 10, as Toothless practices dancing on his own, playing with his shadow on a rock, like a person might practice kissing in the mirror. The *Sex* riff is the foundation of the wooing scene later in the film.

Tuffnut takes Hiccup out into the forest to give him love "advice," coinciding with the musical change in measure 18. As he does, a variation on the first phrase of the *Village Hymn* is played by bass clarinet and bassoon. This variation is neither serious nor reverent like the original theme, since Tuffnut has no idea what he is talking about. The *Village Hymn* is interrupted, yet Tuffnut continues, saying Astrid is looking for something more than Hiccup, and the trombones play a descending glissando twice, the second one larger than the first, music speaking for Hiccup, saying "Yeah, right." The *Village Hymn* then restarts in the strings, with a lovely countermelody in the flute and Tuffnut continues backhandedly complimenting Hiccup. The flute countermelody represents Hiccup, with a marking in the score that asks, "Is this going to stop," in measure 33. As they come to the clearing where Toothless saw the Light Fury the previous night, the *Village Hymn* abruptly ends, replaced with dissonant ascending lines in the harps in measure 40. The silliness must immediately end because Hiccup finds a tranquilizer dart, yells at Toothless to be still, and the opening of *Grimmel's Tune*, with an additional pause between the opening gestures, enters in the low strings and woodwinds. Hiccup activates a trap by throwing a stick into it; no music plays.

The music resumes when the action returns to the village. Hiccup brings the dart to Gobber's smith shop, and *Grimmel's Tune* starts again, broken between various instruments of the orchestra. Eret sees the dart, inspects it, and tells Hiccup not to take Toothless anywhere because the dart belongs to Grimmel. We learn a bit more about the villain, that everything he does is intentional, but Hiccup is unimpressed. The cue concludes with a PAC in C minor, Hiccup "prepared" for Grimmel to return to the area. Perfect Authentic Cadences are rare in the trilogy, so when they *do* occur, they bring more meaning and more finality to the on-screen action. Hiccup thinks he knows all he needs to about Grimmel, explaining the PAC, but he knows absolutely nothing about his enemy, completely underestimating Grimmel.

2M7A-B—Grimmel Visits / First Fight (0:25:17–0:28:45)

> 10–21—Grimmel's Tune (F Aeolian)
> 28–43—Grimmel's Tune (B-flat Aeolian)
> 68–73—Fighting riff
> 75–83—Grimmel's Tune (B-flat Aeolian)
> 91–94—Grimmel's Tune (E Aeolian)

Hiccup, inside his house, hears steps on his roof and creaking from within. When another person is revealed to be inside, the cue begins. The music initially focuses on creating a mysterious atmosphere through a bowed waterphone, a (0134) cluster in the celeste, and a glissando through the overtone series, via harmonics, in the cellos. The mysterious figure is quickly revealed to be Grimmel through his voice. Without warning, Grimmel hits Toothless with a tranquilizer dart to a (0124589) septachord that grows in volume from *pianissimo* to *forte* before descrescendoing and introducing *Grimmel's Tune* in the bassoon.

Grimmel takes the opportunity to introduce himself to Hiccup and treats his "host" quite rudely. He tells Hiccup that Stoick had it right, wanting to kill all the dragons, and by changing his mind, look where that got him. In this portion of the cue, the B section of *Grimmel's Tune* sounds, completing the thematic statement of Grimmel's music. Without giving his name, he tells Hiccup, "I am the Night Fury hunter." This

Figure 6.4. 2M7, measures 25–26, Grimmel the Hunter ostinato.

Figure 6.5. 2M7, measures 28–40, fully harmonized *Grimmel's Tune*.

immediate rise in tension is accompanied by a sixteenth note pulse in the violas, shown in Figure 6.4. This pulse becomes an ostinato figure through measures 25–42.

Grimmel's laughs at Hiccup's naïveté, and his theme begins again, this time each melodic note harmonized with triads, illustrated in Figure 6.5. As the theme continues, a complete cycle derived from the Octatonic (1,2) scale is used to harmonize the theme—Gm-B♭m-Em-C♯m. The standoff progresses as Gobber rushes in, but Grimmel is unimpressed, the second portion of his theme sounding. Hiccup threatens Grimmel, and triplet eighth notes begin in the strings, primarily sounding an F minor triad. As Grimmel says, "You've never seen anything like me," the harmonies move from Fm to CMm^7, i-V^7 in F minor, but the dominant fails to resolve to its tonic in measures 64–68. Instead, everything slides down by half-step to BMm^7, which serves as the dominant to E minor, the key where the dragon attack occurs, a melody that is somewhat related to the *Fighting* riff, in terms of contour and intervallic relationships.

As the dragons begin to destroy Hiccup's home, the opening gestures of *Grimmel's Tune* are played by the full orchestra. Hints of the theme continue during the battle, which shows acid-spitting dragons for the first time in the trilogy. The action music in measures 85–88, derived from the second part of *Grimmel's Tune*, is not meant to be heard above the sound effects. The opening of *Grimmel's Tune* is stated one final time, now in rhythmic diminution, as he yells his terms at Hiccup regarding Toothless. As the crossbeam falls from the roof, the full orchestra plays an E Aeolian line in octaves, with no harmonization before settling on an E minor triad to conclude the cue. The unison melody in measures 97–101 is very much in line with the orchestral writing of Ralph Vaughan Williams, continuing the influence of the composer on Powell's music across the trilogy. The music fades out under lightning with the assembled crowd now present in the dining hall for an all-village emergency meeting.

2M8A-B—Townhall / Exodus (0:30:08–0:34:37)
 3–17—Fate Tune (C Aeolian)
 19–26—Village Hymn (F Dorian)
 27–38—Heroes A (C Dorian)
 38–44—Grimmel's Tune (C-sharp Aeolian)
 45–50—Heroes B (B Aeolian)
 51–55—Grimmel's Tune (F Aeolian)
 56–58—Fate riff (G Aeolian)
 59–70—Furies in Love (C Dorian)
 76–82—Furies in Love (F Dorian)
 83–88—Grimmel's Tune B
 89–97—Village Hymn (F Dorian)
 102–108—Grimmel's Tune (C-sharp Aeolian)

Hiccup convenes an all-village meeting to discuss what to do about their new foe: stay and fight, or find a better place to settle. Hiccup announces his decision to leave in search of a new place to settle, much to the initial dismay of the town. Hiccup says that they need to take their dragons where no one can find them, "off the map." The cue enters at this point, strings alone, with the violas playing the *Fate Tune*. Astrid supports Hiccup, telling the village he's looking for "The Hidden World." Hiccup continues his speech, the dynamics of the orchestra growing to *fortissimo*, followed by a grand pause in measure 18.

The scene changes from the hall to the sky, as the Berkians and all their belongs fly in search of a new place to settle. The horns play the *Village Hymn*, but this setting is much more in line with traveling music, as the snare drum plays a march-like pattern. Following the *Village Hymn*, we hear the full statements of the *Heroes A* and *B* themes in the strings and woodwinds. Gobber asks Hiccup about a plan, Hiccup responding that they'll keep flying until they reach the end of the world. The *Heroes A* theme dovetails into a statement of *Grimmel's Tune*, as the action cuts to him and the other warlords at Berk. Grimmel proudly informs them that he has Hiccup on the run. As the action returns to the travelers, the *Heroes B* theme is heard, as the Nut Twins laugh at "stupid" things, something that is not particularly heroic. The *Heroes B* theme then dovetails into another statement of *Grimmel's Tune*.

Grimmel begins telling the others that the Night Fury is distracted, and we see Toothless become aware of the Light Fury's scent. We also hear the *Fate* riff for the first time in the film, played by the upper woodwinds and strings, beginning in measure 56. As the Light Fury comes into sight, the *Furies in Love* theme sounds, quite excitedly. Even Astrid and Hiccup are excited that she has followed them. The theme is played in full, and just as it ends, in measure 68, the Light Fury "attacks" and snatches Hiccup off Toothless's back and tries to throw him into the ocean, the score marked "Get off my boyfriend." Even though triadic harmony is used in this dissonant passage, measures 71–74, the harmony is non-functional: Bm-B♭M-E♭Mm^7-D♭Mm^7. None of those chords are diatonic with the other three, and the resolution from the E♭Mm^7 chord should be to A♭M, not down a whole step to D♭Mm^7. When the triadic harmonies resume, the first chord heard is F minor, a logical chord to follow E♭Mm^7, but a deceptive resolution. The two Furies have different goals. The Light Fury thinks she is saving Toothless from a human. The score even indicates "Saved you, love!" in measure 76. Conversely, Toothless is with Hiccup, searching for a new home, looks ashamed at the Light Fury, and dives to rescue Hiccup from certain death. The Light Fury is acting out of love so that she and Toothless can be together, without people, explaining the presence of the *Furies in Love* theme. The theme almost reaches its conclusion, but is interrupted, as has happened so many times in this montage, by Grimmel's music. This time, the second part of his theme initiates the statement as he explains to the dimwitted warlords to where the Berkians have traveled.

We then see Hiccup looking through a telescope, the clouds disappear, and an island comes into sight. The *Village Hymn* is played by the full orchestra in F Aeolian, and we know this will be not just their camp for the evening, but the location of New Berk, despite Hiccup's calls for a temporary rest. We cut back to Grimmel excitedly showing the warlords where they have gone, set to his theme played by alto and bass flute and tuba, an unusual orchestrational combination. The first part of *Grimmel's Tune* ends, the music fades out, and the cue ends. A significant amount of action occurs in this cue, and rather than the passage of time, this montage cuts back and forth between the opposing forces in the film.

2M9A-B—Setting Up Camp / Valka's Warning (0:36:42–0:37-39)

1–3—Fate Tune (D-flat Dorian) *not in film*
3–6—Warring Vikings (G-sharp Aeolian) *not in film*
9–12—Warring Vikings (C Aeolian) *not in film*
13–16—Warring Vikings (F Aeolian) *not in film*

6. How to Train Your Dragon: The Hidden World *Cue Analysis*

18–22—Vikings (B-flat Aeolian) *not in film*
23–25—Fate theme (D Aeolian) *not in film*
39–41—Flying A reharmonized (starts on B-sharp)
42–53—Fate Tune (F-sharp Aeolian)

The opening 38 measures of this cue were not used in the film. According to the score indications, the music would have started as Snotlout fantasized about his tower-house. The deletion of the measures results in a deletion of the *Fate* theme from the first film, the presence of which is narratively unnecessary in this film. As the cue is used in the film, the music enters when Valka tells Snotlout to stay at New Berk and not fly with her because he's "too important." The reharmonized opening to the *Flying A* theme at the cue enters is used as a sort of goofy signaling of Valka's sarcasm.

Valka warns Hiccup that they'll never be able to truly hide from the world, and Astrid does the same in quick succession. This section is all underscored by the *Fate Tune*, melodically modified and broken between instruments, shown in Figure 6.6. The cue concludes with a functional half cadence in F♯, with GM/B leading into C♯M/E♯, or ♭II⁶-V⁶ in F♯. This open-ended cadence implies that Hiccup's plan of taking *everyone* to The Hidden World will not work. Only half will go, and it is clear which half will ultimately end up in The Hidden World.

Figure 6.6. 2M9A-B, measures 42–53, modified *Fate Tune*.

3M10—Toothless Goes a Courtin' (0:37:52–0:44:34)

2–11—Light Fury Motif (D major)
12–15—Light Fury Motif (D major)
16–19—Sex riff (D Aeolian)
20–23—Sex riff (D Aeolian)
24–27—Sex riff (D Aeolian)
28–31—Sex riff (D Aeolian)
32–35—Sex riff (D Aeolian)
36–39—Sex riff (E Aeolian)
61–63—Sex riff (E Aeolian)
64–70—Sex riff (F-sharp Aeolian)

71–73—Sex riff (A Aeolian)
108–113—Furies in Love (C Dorian)
128–131—Sex riff (D Aeolian)
132–135—Sex riff (D Aeolian)
136–139—Sex riff (D Aeolian)
140–143—Sex riff (D Aeolian)
144–147—Sex riff (F Aeolian)
148–153—Furies in Love (B-flat Dorian)
154–157—Sex riff (F Aeolian)
168–179—Furies in Love (F Dorian)

Toothless is awakened from sleep and once again picks up the scent of the Light Fury. The cue begins with the *Light Fury Motif*, an ascending D major arpeggio, and the full version beyond the arpeggio is used here. We even get a restatement of the arpeggio, to "round off" the *Light Fury Motif*. During the motif, Toothless is searching for the Light Fury, following her scent into the forest on New Berk.

Once he finds her, the courting ritual begins. The *Sex* riff, a four-measure gesture, is the foundation of this cue. The first four-measure phrase, measures 16–19, doesn't have the melodic portion of the *Sex* riff, but it does have the same pizzicato harmony and rhythm in the strings as would be expected for the theme in D minor. The complete *Sex* riff begins in the second four-measure phrase in the woodwinds and glockenspiel. As this music is restated again and again, Toothless and the Light Fury play a sort of "hide-and-seek" around the tents, taking care to not wake up the Vikings.

An ascending E minor pentatonic flourish in measure 35 leads the music into a modulation up to E minor, as the Light Fury flies into the sky. Like the initial statement in D, the initial statement in E does not contain the actual *Sex* riff, but contains the harmony and

Figure 6.7. 3M10, measures 43–55, Toothless falls and rolls in the sand.

6. How to Train Your Dragon: The Hidden World *Cue Analysis*   147

rhythm, and a countermelody broken between the Uilleann pipes and sopilka. Just as the *Sex* riff begins, Toothless comes to a hole, and has lost track of the Light Fury. The *Sex* riff stops, replaced by a descending string gesture completely outside of E minor. The meter shifts to 3/4 as the Light Fury lands on the edge of a cliff, Toothless watching from afar. The music is elegant, lyrical, and soft to represent the female Fury. Toothless, however, is none of those things. He attempts to casually approach her, slips, and the music immediately shifts into 4/8, feeling like the tempo has greatly accelerated. He falls, rolls through the sand, but sticks the landing at the cliff's edge. In this very short section, seen in Figure 6.7, Powell has written brilliantly funny cartoon music for Toothless's lack of refinement.

She sits, waiting for him to make the first move. They blink at each other as the harmonies oscillate between C major and A major in measures 56–59, the Hero chromatic mediant relationship. Hiccup has awakened and found the pair, and watches silently from the trees. She begins her dance, with chords and rhythms that belong to the *Sex* riff in E minor, where it was interrupted earlier in the cue, and looks at Toothless expectantly, waiting for him to dance. Toothless, realizing Hiccup is present, looks up at him for support, and starts "dancing." Both the slate and glass marimbas are introduced at this point in the cue, as the "forbidden friendship" is an essential part of Toothless's self-confidence. But because Toothless's dance is unattractive to the Light Fury, the *Sex* riff is absent. She is so unimpressed that she begins giving herself a bath. Hiccup stands and tries to mimic a dance to further encourage Toothless, flapping his "wings," but steps on a branch and the Light Fury looks in his direction.

Figure 6.8. 3M10, measures 74–85, Toothless creates a whirlwind.

The *Sex* riff begins anew, now in A minor, as Toothless begins flapping his wings, blowing sand in the air, and gets caught up in his own self-made whirlwind, leading to dumping sand on her. The fourth measure of the *Sex* riff contains significant syncopation, and Powell seizes on this by turning that fourth measure, measure 74, into a self-sustaining whirlwind that results in the Light Fury covered in sand, and concludes on an A♭ major triad, shown in Figure 6.8. She sneezes, and the music almost completely stops, a lovely oboe line preventing silence.

Hiccup has another idea and mimes to Toothless again. As he does, the music begins anew in G♯ minor, preparing the *Sex* riff after a four-measure introduction. Toothless still has no idea how to behave around a female dragon, and tries walking on his hind legs, looking like a human pretending to be a chicken. It's no surprise that this attempt also fails to impress her, and the *Sex* riff remains absent. In its place, a new melody in the flutes, piccolo, and bassoon is played in octaves, as shown in Figure 6.9.

Some of the melodic notes, notably the notes sounding in the melody over the G♯m⁷ chords, are not part of the harmony. Toothless is out of sync, both with what Hiccup suggests he try to win the Light Fury's heart, and with the Light Fury herself. These melodic chord tones are quite logical in the overall design of the melody, but sound dissonant with the harmony. Toothless wants to impress the Light Fury, has tried twice, but has not yet succeeded. The nuance and level of detail given to the melodic and harmonic design here is exceptional.

Toothless tries a new technique where he covers his body with his wings and jumps around. The musical style becomes louder and more intense, all of which works to put fear into the Light Fury. She has no idea what Toothless is doing, and neither does he! Border pipes and Irish flute, and combined with boobams and other percussion, makes the music sounds obviously incorrect for the task at hand, beginning in measure 101. She finally "slaps" him in the face to get him to stop and flies to a nearby tree branch above the sand. Toothless follows, the music rising by a half-step from C to C♯. He begins bouncing on the end of the branch, to an A major triad. The bouncing becomes more intense and the harmony changes to an E♭Mm⁷ chord, a root motion of a tritone, but

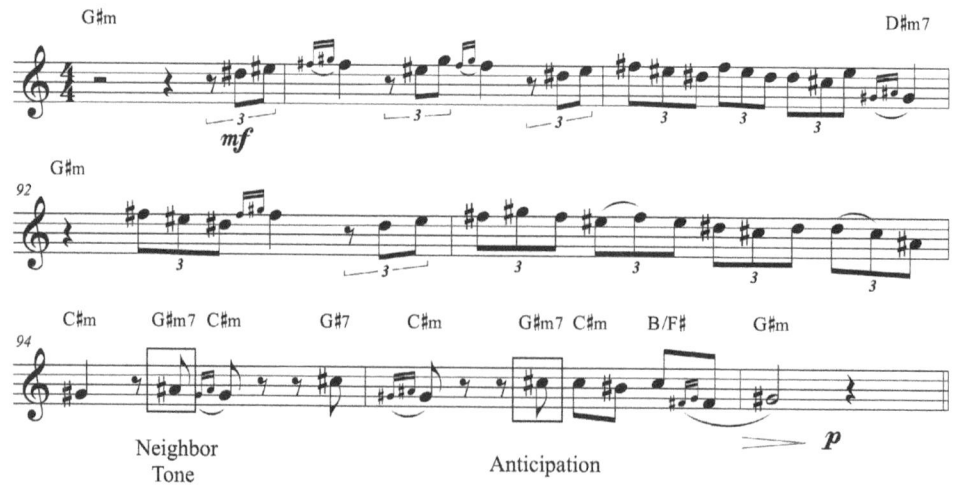

Figure 6.9. 3M10, measures 89–96, Toothless is not in sync.

6. How to Train Your Dragon: The Hidden World *Cue Analysis*   149

with a common tone in the bass: C♯, which is enharmonically D♭. The resolution to A♭ never comes.

Instead, the branch breaks and the *Sex* riff in D minor begins at measure 128 as Toothless hits the ground, the Light Fury still hanging on the branch, arms crossed, wings closed over her very angry face. Instead of the harmonic resolution from E♭Mm⁷ to A♭, the C♯ in the bass resolves up to D, the A major triad resolves to D minor. Toothless has one final chance, and musically gets to start over in the key in which the cue began. He is still trying to figure out how to impress the Light Fury, sees a smaller branch on the ground, and decides to draw in the sand, much like he did in the first film with Hiccup. The *Sex* riff continues in the glockenspiel while the countermelody is broken between the Uilleann pipes, sopilka, and Irish flute. As Toothless's drawing begins to take form, and he grows in confidence, the music modulates up to F minor—he may yet succeed in winning her affections! She comes down from the branch and barks in appreciation to Toothless at his portrait of her. As we see the full drawing, we hear the *Furies in Love* tune in B♭ Aeolian, but harmonized with F minor and D♭ major triads. She steps on the line of his drawing and he growls at her, like he growled at Hiccup in the first film. She growls back and he drops his drawing branch in a comedic moment, and the familiar four-measure pattern resumes. It is clear who is the dominant force in this relationship!

This four-measure phrase, measures 154–157, does not contain the *Sex* riff. Instead, it contains the glass and slate marimba, again referencing 2M14, "Forbidden Friendship" from the first film. Here, it's applied to the burgeoning relationship between the Furies; Hiccup doesn't realize he's sending his "child" out into the world. He thinks they will live *with* him. Instead, they will be together, living away from Hiccup. She comes around to Toothless, and the *Furies in Love* theme is played by the solo flute above the slate and glass marimbas. They look to be about to kiss, but she pulls away and begins to fly, trying to get Toothless to come with her. After waiting for him, she growls and takes off. Toothless tries to follow, but crashes in the water, with the cue ending on a half cadence in A♭, their relationship burgeoning, but not complete.

The music in this final section of the cue sounds very similar in style and orchestration to renowned French composer Maurice Ravel. The harmonies, containing sevenths and ninths, and orchestral colors are what can be found in such works of his as *Daphnis et Chloe*, and also foreshadows the big cue when the Furies reach The Hidden World. The style change, one that has not been heard before in the trilogy, is significant because it exclusively belongs to the Furies and their romance and relationship.

Even though this cue is not a battle or action cue, it is one of the longest cues in the film, so an investigation of the ways in which Powell propels the music forward is necessary. Figure 6.10 outlines the typical musical parameters for a cue of this length.

Measure	1	15	36	43	49	55	61	64	71
Marking									
Tempo	♩ = 94								
Meter	3/4	4/4		3/4	4/8	4/4			
Tonal Center	D major	D minor	E minor	D minor	D minor	Ambiguous	E minor	F♯ minor	A minor

74	82	85	86	101	108	114	127	128	144	148
							q = 101			q = 99
	3/8	4/8	3/4	4/4				2/4	4/4	
A minor to D minor	E minor	A♭ major	G♯ minor	G minor	C minor	C♯ minor	C♯ minor	D minor	F minor	F minor

152	164	166	168	169	172	176	177
q = 100	q = 101	q = 102	q = 103	q = 104		q = 100	q = 88
F minor	B♭ major	E♭ major	E♭ major	E major	F♯ major	B♭ major	B♭ major

Figure 6.10. Breakdown of 3M10 by measure, marking, tempo, meter, and tonal center.

As the table in Figure 6.10 demonstrates, changes in tonal center are most common in this cue, followed by meter changes, then tempo changes. The tempo hardly moves, and when it does, it happens mostly in small increments, barely noticeable, if at all, by an audience. The primary meter of the cue is 4/4, as the *Sex* riff is a four-measure 4/4 groove. The locations where the meter changes, particularly the 4/8 and 3/8 sections, are where Toothless's actions spiral out of control, the music mimicking his physical gestures. The longer stretches of D minor music are made more interesting through the addition of layers in every four-measure iteration. The G♯ minor section features a new pattern and use of the piano, while the music from measures 154–169 uses both glass and slate marimba, new textures to the cue. Since the cue does not accompany a battle scene, it is easier for the visuals of the film to take the lead, and we are happy to watch Toothless repeatedly fail in his efforts to impress the Light Fury, all supported by the score.

3M11—Toothless Flies Alone (0:45:48–0:47:06)

> 3–14—Sex riff (C Dorian)
> 8–14—Furies in Love (C Dorian)
> 15–19—The Hidden World (A Aeolian)
> 20–23—Hiccup/Vikings (D Aeolian)
> 25–26—Flying Ostinato (D minor)
> 28–31—Hiccup/Vikings (G Aeolian)
> 32–38—Flying B (B-flat major)

Upon seeing Toothless's distress at not being able to fly along with the Light Fury, Hiccup decides to fashion Toothless's tail so that he can fly without a rider. As he begins affixing the "new new tail" to Toothless, the *Sex* riff, modified rhythmically, begins in the violins, a statement that feels more frantic and urgent than before. This is the same rhythmic modification that was present at the start of the cue "In Love" earlier in the film. The *Furies in Love* theme enters in the piccolo during the second and third statements of the *Sex* riff, as all of the music is working to allow Toothless to be alone with the Light Fury. Not ready to give up on his big plan, Hiccup thinks he'll bring her back and then take everyone to the Hidden World, and the opening of *The Hidden World* theme is heard as Hiccup imitates Stoick and gives dating instructions. Toothless gives Hiccup

6. How to Train Your Dragon: The Hidden World *Cue Analysis* 151

a slobbery lick/kiss, and Hiccup exclaims, "Save it for your girlfriend!" Toothless is so happy that Hiccup has given him freedom, but it is the *Hiccup* theme that sounds, not the *Furies in Love* theme, as Hiccup has performed the action of setting Toothless free, albeit without wholly realizing it. Hiccup is behaving as a Viking should, and as he ultimately will near the conclusion of the film.

Toothless runs, but pauses and turns, afraid to leave without Hiccup. The minor-mode *Flying Ostinato* sounds as Hiccup gives reassurance to Toothless to go, and Hiccup watches him fly away to the *Hiccup* theme with an atypical harmonization, seen in Figure 6.11. Toothless leaves to the *Flying B* theme and the cue ends. The final three measures of the cue are absent in the film, a sort of somber reiteration of the final gesture of the *Flying B* theme, Hiccup's sadness at having let Toothless go out into the world on his own. The entire scene plays very much like a parent allowing a child to go on an unchaperoned date, with Hiccup both excited and terrified for Toothless, afraid of losing him forever.

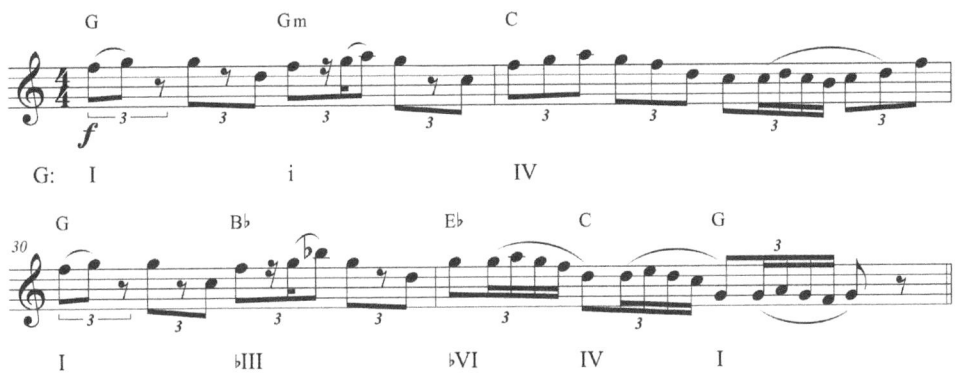

Figure 6.11. 3M11, measures 28–31, Modified *Hiccup* theme.

3M12A—Near Miss (0:47:14–0:47:56)

1–4—Furies in Love (G major)
7–14—Grimmel's Tune (G Aeolian)
14–22—Grimmel's Tune (B-flat Aeolian)

Valka flies east to ensure the Vikings haven't been followed from Berk, and the strings play a reharmonized version of the *Furies in Love* theme in A Major with a

Figure 6.12. 3M12A, measures 1–4, reharmonized *Furies in Love* theme.

lowered second scale-degree (B♭), as seen in Figure 6.12. She quickly comes across the warlords' armada at Berk, followed by Grimmel's flying machine in the distance, with *Grimmel's Tune* heard to announce his presence. She and Cloudjumper are attacked from behind, but they fight back and flee to New Berk, with Grimmel whistling his dragons back to him, in effect, ending the cue. The music contains lots of eighth-note triplets for action and texture, and mostly minor triads and half-diminished seventh chords for darker harmonies.

3M12B—Romance in the Clouds (0:48:03–0:51:00)
1–9—Light Fury Motif (F major)
2–9—Furies in Love (F Dorian)
16–19—Furies in Love (F Dorian)
28–36—Furies in Love (G Dorian)
46–66—Furies in Love (D Dorian)
67–70—The Hidden World (C Aeolian)

Toothless flies, calling out for the Light Fury. The *Light Fury Motif* initiates the cue, played by three woodwinds, with a solo cello line playing a melodic variation on the opening of the *Furies in Love* theme. The orchestration presents the two ideas separately, offset by timbres and ranges, as well as literal space on the score, as the woodwinds appear near the top of the page and the strings at the bottom. The music sounds like "his and hers" versions of the music. Toothless thinks he sees her, but it's only his shadow, and is dismayed until he hears her calling to him. The music primarily shifts back and forth between G major and D♭ major triads in measures 10–15, chords whose roots are a tritone apart, contextualizing the uniqueness of their relationship. In the second film, the tritone-related chords were used to represent earth and sky. In this film, the opposites are the Night and Light Furies. Although passing chords appear between the two, these are the structural harmonies that lead into the Light Fury's appearance, soaring alongside Toothless.

As they see each other, the *Furies in Love* theme begins in F Dorian, and Toothless makes "sexy eyes" towards her. Following the opening gesture and its repeat, the theme is paused after measure 19 as the pair go playing in the air. They enter a storm cloud, where the Light Fury shoots a fireball into the sky, flies into it, and disappears. The *Furies in Love* theme returns at this point from its beginning in G Dorian, a whole step higher than where the cue began. Toothless tries to copy the Light Fury, but he doesn't disappear. He tries again, but still fails. The *Furies in Love* theme almost is used in its entirety, but not triumphantly. Toothless hangs his head in shame, but she doesn't give up on him. He summons his lightning powers and vanishes, the music momentarily stopping in measure 43. Toothless figures out the way to make himself disappear.

The effort takes a bit out of Toothless, and he falls slightly through the air, but the Light Fury is there to catch him and support him. The *Furies in Love* theme returns in D Dorian, and in its fullest and most triumphant version in the film thus far. The pair soar above the clouds, against the backdrop of a full moon, where Toothless kisses the Light Fury and they fall and fly back down to the surface of the world, the Aurora borealis lighting the way, seen in Figure 6.13. The visual nod to Tim Burton's *Batman* (1989), where the Batwing flies high above the clouds and has the moon as its backdrop, is obvious here. The addition of the choir and horn countermelody when Toothless kisses her

6. How to Train Your Dragon: The Hidden World *Cue Analysis*

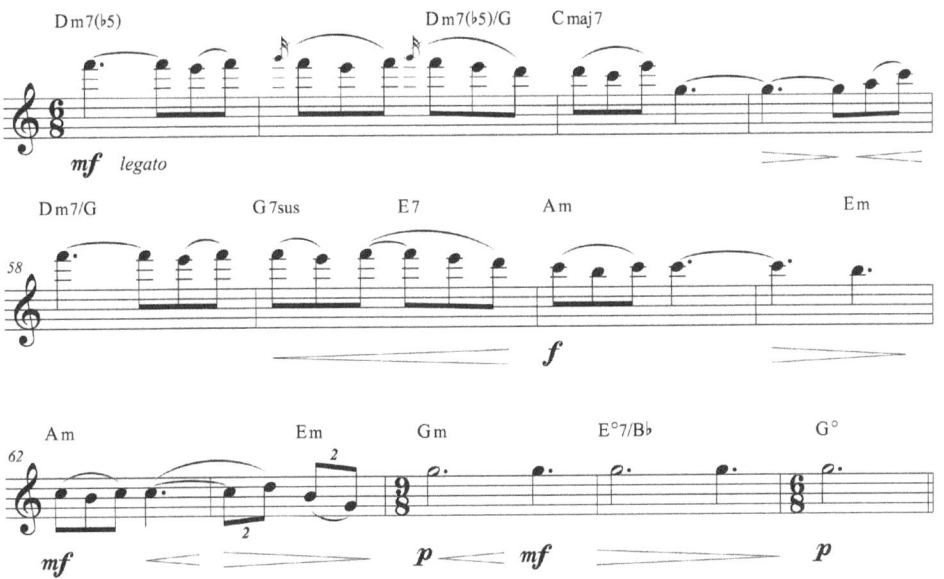

Figure 6.13. 3M12B, measures 54–66, end of *Furies in Love* theme with Ravel influences.

is another reference to Ravel's writing, and another way to make this style of music specific to the Furies. They fly side-by-side, touching their wings as though they were holding hands, and she leads him to the waterfall marking the entrance to The Hidden World.

The remainder of the cue continues to foreground Ravel's style through the orchestration, use of choir, and use of chordal sevenths and ninths. The opening of *The Hidden World* theme is used here, but not the full statement since they have not yet reached it. The final harmonies in the cue, G minor and G♭ major, represent a Neo-Riemannian **SLIDE**. It represents Toothless going into the unknown, perhaps an eerie gesture. The Light Fury senses this hesitation and grabs him, flying him down with her into The Hidden World, which remains unseen, and the action dissolves into a God's Eye View of a feast in New Berk. The **SLIDE** was first used in the second film when Hiccup tells Toothless they may encounter a female Night Fury one day in the "Map the World" cue.

3M13S—New Berk Feast (0:51:00–0:52:16)

This cue serves as source music for the celebratory feast, as the entire New Berk community comes together to celebrate their new location and thank Hiccup for his leadership. Unfortunately, Hiccup can only think about Toothless while Gobber tries to calm his anxiety. The style of the music is Celtic, based on the rhythms and the presence of pennywhistle, bodhran, Celtic harp, and sopilka. The tune itself is eight measures with a two-measure codetta. It is first in C Dorian, played twice in its entirety, then in F Dorian for the contrasting section, with a return to C Dorian for the familiar tune. Essentially, the cue is composed in a rounded binary form: ‖: 8 (+2) :‖: 8 (+2) + 8 (+2) :‖.

3M14A-B—Ambush / Cage Fight (0:52:36–0:57:38)

2–5—Grimmel's Tune B
8–10—Grimmel's Tune B
11–17—Flying A (D major)
26–34—Heroes B (C minor)
39–46—Fighting riff (A doubly harmonic minor)
47–55—Heroes B (A minor)
56–63—Flying Ostinato (A Phrygian)
56–63—Hiccup the Chief (A major)
58–64—Fighting riff (D doubly harmonic minor)
65–69—Grimmel's Tune A (A Aeolian)
70–87—Grimmel's Tune A (E Aeolian) *not in film*
88–94—Grimmel's Tune A (D Aeolian)
96–99—Grimmel's Tune A (D Aeolian)
100–122—Grimmel's Tune (A-flat Aeolian)
123–128—Flying B/Warring Vikings variation
133–145—Heroic Dragons (B-flat major)
145–149—Flying A (D-flat major)

"Ambush" begins with the B section of *Grimmel's Tune*, as Valka returns to New Berk with information. Hiccup decides to use the element of surprise and attack Grimmel before Grimmel can reach New Berk. As he says this, a very soft statement of the beginning of *Grimmel's Tune B* is sounded in the cellos and contrabasses in measures 7–9, as well as the reharmonized *Flying A* theme in measures 10–16. Hiccup's plan will likely not go as he intends.

The action cuts to Grimmel's ships, where Grimmel is concocting a dragon serum; we learn later that the drug makes the dragons obedient to him, rendering him as the Alpha. The Avengers of Berk silently approach the ships, accompanied by the *Heroes B* theme, but in C minor, another indication that their actions will not go as planned. Hiccup flies down to the ships, Grimmel's dragons hear him land, and Grimmel sends them out to investigate. As he snaps his fingers, an (0125679) septachord sounds in the full orchestra in measure 34, a dissonant sonority that "resolves" to a pulsing A in the following measure. This pulsing is similar to that from the cue 2M7A-B, "Grimmel Visits/First Fight," but this music is in ¾ as opposed to the 4/4 meter of the previously heard cue. As the Avengers survey the ships, Snotlout suggests they split up in order to be "harder to catch." The *Fighting* riff is played by a solo clarinet at a dynamic of *piano*, not the most ferocious or intense of timbres, followed by the *Heroes B* theme, now in A minor as the team, still lacking confidence, tries to distract Grimmel's dragons.

The most intricate portion of music in the entire trilogy comes next, as three themes are layered on top of each other, seen in Figure 6.14. Hiccup begins climbing a circular stairwell to the minor-mode version of the *Flying Ostinato*, a theme from the first film, beginning in D Aeolian. Adding to that, the violas play the *Hiccup the Chief* theme from the second film, but in a melodically modified version to contrapuntally fit the same tonality as the *Flying Ostinato*. Two measures later, the *Fighting* riff, also in D minor, first heard in the opening cue of this film, is layered on top in violin I and clarinet. Three themes, one from each film, come together at this point. The minor-mode

6. How to Train Your Dragon: The Hidden World *Cue Analysis* 155

Figure 6.14. 3M14A-B, measures 56–65, three simultaneous themes.

Flying Ostinato enhances tension. The modified *Hiccup the Chief* theme is unsteady and unsure, but Hiccup is trying to be a leader. The *Fighting* riff shows Hiccup is prepared to fight Grimmel, but the timbre is all wrong. As Hiccup reaches the top, opens the door, and pulls on a chain, he triggers a trap, enclosing them all inside the tower, and *Grimmel's Tune* sounds in A, the dominant of D. Grimmel is the dominant one in this battle!

The music drops out while Grimmel monologues about hunting, measures 68–85, and returns when he tells Hiccup that people and dragons living together is nonsense, with *Grimmel's Tune* presented in the horns. He gives a dose of the serum to his dragons, whistles, and they attack, the music growing in dynamic and texture, all of it leading to a forceful and cruel statement of *Grimmel's Tune* in A♭ minor in the horns. When the strings begin to play in unison, in measures 103–107, the action writing beneath the theme uses all of the chromatic notes except for C, E♭, and A♭, the notes that comprise the A♭ major triad, nearly the tonic of the previous statement of *Grimmel's Tune*. Meanwhile, the trumpets and trombones play chords containing sevenths, broken between the two groups of instruments. This section of the cue is an excellent example of stratification, multiple layers of music occurring simultaneously without any interaction. The lack of interaction is what differentiates stratification from counterpoint. Stratification can add to the implied chaos of the music, as a great deal is happening, but nothing seems to fit together, a technique perfect for this situation.

Valka signals to Hiccup to come to her, and the music has a momentary reprieve as the choir alone sings a C minor triad in measure 114 before the action resumes, dragons chasing Hiccup, spitting acid and fire. Finally, Cloudjumper joins the battle, and a variation on two themes—the *Flying B* theme and the *Warring Vikings* theme—melodic, harmonic, and rhythmic, is played by the full orchestra, shown in Figure 6.15. The team may yet escape.

The opening gesture in Figure 6.15 rhythmically and melodically resembles the *Warring Vikings* theme. After the triplets, the melodic contour begins to more closely resemble that of the end of the *Flying B* theme, although the intervals are not consistently maintained. As a result, the music is not quite a variation on the *Warring Vikings* theme, but not really a variation on the *Flying B* theme. The music synthesizes both themes, along with a new harmonization, to create a moment of uniqueness within the score. Narratively, Valka, on Cloudjumper, accounts for the *Flying B* theme. The theme is highly modified because the music is not specifically for Hiccup and Toothless. The fight to escape from Grimmel and his dragons accounts for the use of the *Warring Vikings*

Figure 6.15. 3M14A-B, measures 123–128, *Warring Vikings* + *Flying B* **variation.**

theme, but because Grimmel has the drop on them, they are only trying to escape, fighting for safety rather than against their foe, making the *Warring Vikings* theme also highly modified.

Hiccup reaches a wooden crossbeam and prepares to jump. As he does, the orchestra sustains an open fifth of A♭-E♭-A♭, with the treble instruments trilling on the high A♭. A run from D4 to A♭5, through the Octatonic (1,2) scale occurs, but Hiccup does not yet jump. The run arrives on a D°/F triad, followed by more dissonance and trills. A second run, now a D Phrygian scale, helps Hiccup across the void, narrowly avoiding Grimmel's dragon and the raging inferno below.

Valka catches him, and the *Heroic Dragon* variation sounds in the trumpets, accompanied by the *Flying Ostinato* in the violins. The team makes their escape, Grimmel's dragons presumably end up as the victims of their own carnage, the tower crumbles, and Ruffnut is somehow left behind, standing next to Grimmel as the opening of the *Flying A* theme is played in the low strings, but in D Phrygian. The team may have escaped, but at what cost?

4M15A—Stronger Together (0:58:19–0:59:18)

32–41—Hiccup/Vikings (B-flat Aeolian)
34–50—Village Hymn (B-flat Dorian)

The Vikings don't think Toothless is coming back, so when Hiccup references, "Toothless and I," he is interrupted. The cue begins with a four-measure melody that is stated seven times in a row, harmonized by G♯m and D♯m triads, and seen in Figure 6.16. These will turn out to be the harmonies used for the statement of *The Hidden World* theme in the next cue.

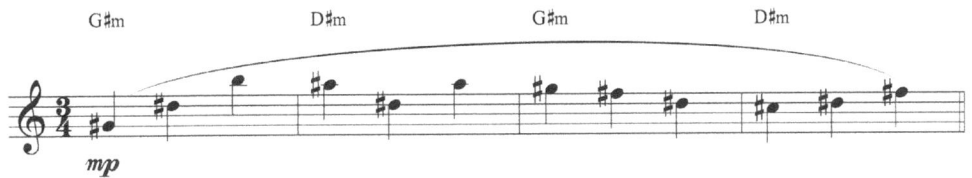

Figure 6.16. 4M15A, measures 1–4, *The Hidden World* opening harmonies.

Hiccup feels lost without Toothless, but Valka encourages Astrid to work with Hiccup to lead the village together rather than Hiccup trying to lead alone. Astrid comes over to Hiccup with her dragon, tells him to get on and they fly together, accompanied by both the *Hiccup* theme and the *Village Hymn*, both in B♭ Dorian. The Village Hymn becomes the dominant theme, reaches its conclusion, and the cue suddenly ends, the action immediately switching to the imprisoned Ruffnut.

4M15B-16A—New Island / Into the Hole (1:00:34–1:02:24)

6–11—Grimmel's Tune (B-flat Aeolian) *not in film*
17–25—Fate riff (F Aeolian)
26–34—The Hidden World (G-sharp Aeolian)

Ruffnut talks … and talks, and talks, and talks, and mentions the "new island," piquing Grimmel's interest. The cue begins at this moment, mickey-mousing Grimmel's look of surprise. As his eyebrows lift, so too do the violins, playing a broken B°7 chord. Grimmel finally becomes so annoyed with Ruffnut's talking that he throws a compass into a wooden beam. At the highest moment of his anger, a (0123678) septachord is sounded in measure 5, two different chromatic clusters, an extremely dissonant sonority. This represents the one moment where Grimmel is out of control, but he quickly recovers, and permits Ruffnut to fly away in order to follow her to New Berk. The cue then drops out; measures 6–15 are unused in the cue.

The percussion lead into the second part of the cue in measure 16, with the *Fate* riff in F Aeolian sounding in the strings as Astrid and Hiccup, riding Stormfly, search for the

Figure 6.17. 4M15B-C, measures 26–34, conclusion of *The Hidden World* theme.

Furies. Stormfly latches onto the scent of one of them and takes them to the "waterfall at the end of the world," the entrance to the Hidden World. The music modulates up a minor third to G♯ Aeolian as they circle above the hole. The oboes and female voices state *The Hidden World* theme, seen in Figure 6.17, while the horns play a countermelody. Fragments of other themes, such as the end of the *Hiccup* theme, are heard in the melodic material at the end of the cue, and the full orchestra, with dotted-quarter-eighth rhythms, imbue the music a sense of nobility. Without warning, Stormfly descends into the hole, the orchestra arrives on an EMM7/G♯ chord, and the cue ends.

Figure 6.18. 4M15B-C, measures 32–34, arpeggiating harmonies in violins.

The harmonies at the conclusion of the cue are fascinating. The music is clearly in G♯ minor, however, the final chord is an EMM^7, with the E major triad sounded in the oboes and horns and choir, and the D♯ only present in the trumpet and instruments playing the triplet-sixteenth notes. These triplet figures, illustrated in Figure 6.18, descend in thirds in the first violin part, from F♯6 to B3 over two measures, arpeggiating interlocking B major, E major, and F♯ major triads, the tonic, subdominant, and dominant harmonies in B major, not the prevailing key. On its surface, the music does not sound particularly dissonant or complex; it is flying (or falling) down into the hole. Yet, the different parts of the orchestra each try to subvert the other for tonal supremacy. The three characters, Hiccup, Astrid, and Stormfly, are represented through the three different musical threads, through the triplet figures, and through the arpeggiations of the three triads. Since we see the film through Hiccup's point-of-view, none of the musical threads exert their will, and instead, the characters enter a world of wonder.

4M16B—The Hidden World (1:02:28–1:07:36)

40–50—The Hidden World (C Dorian)
64–74—The Hidden World (C Aeolian)
75–82—The Hidden World (C Aeolian)
79–82—Flying Ostinato (C Aeolian)
83–90—The Hidden World (C Aeolian)
91–92—Furies in Love (C Aeolian)
93–96—The Hidden World (E-flat Aeolian)
96–100—Flying Ostinato (A-flat Aeolian)
102–106—Dragon Tune (A doubly harmonic minor)
131–143—Fate Tune (F Aeolian)

John Powell needed to find a way to make the musical style of The Hidden World distinct from the rest of the geography across the trilogy. Regarding that challenge, he said the following:

> In conversations as you start a movie, you look at various sections—spotting as it were—and that was the word, alien, that came from Dean. He asked, "How do we make this a [physical] space in the series we've never been to before?" We've been in caves before. There are sections in the first film that are like that and other unusual places, but the thing that we'd never done was to make it sound alien. [The Hidden World] is ultimately where the dragons all going. We have to make it feel like something we've never heard before in the series, or even anything like before. And that's when I thought, "Well, maybe we can do it with a very unusual vocalist, and then we both looked at each other and said, 'I'm sure Jónsi can do something!'"

The opening 20 measures of the cue are not clearly notated in the score because they are a result of Jónsi singing several different tracks, then overlaying them to create an alien sound, as Powell put it. As Hiccup, Astrid, and Stormfly enter the Hidden World, the score begins with Hammer Dulcimer, Ghost Dulcimer, and continued vocals from Jónsi, a new timbral environment. The Hidden World is clearly a magical and mystical place, the origin of all dragons, and not a place where people belong. As additional pre-recorded tracks enter in a different key, the geography changes along with it, shifting from largely gray to wondrously illuminated in blues and greens. The lighting is similar to a black light, allowing primarily hidden spots on Stormfly to become highly visible. The colors continue, and crotales and glockenspiel play triads that are derived from the C Dorian scale. The entrance of female voices corresponds with the visual appearance of translucent dragon eggs, further enhancing the magical sense and wonder of the Hidden World. So far, the music almost feels without pulse or meter, yet another way that the Hidden World is musically imbued with its mystical location.

The melody heard at the end of the previous cue returns in measure 40 in the strings as they pass dragons the size of seahorses. Finally, they reach an opening that looks somewhat similar to Valka's Sanctuary, but even more colorful. As they do, Jónsi's vocals return in measure 50. The accompaniment becomes block chords in eighth notes, changing every measure. The horns play the opening ascending fifth gesture of *The Hidden World* theme, first in A, then C, and finally F. As Stormfly lands and Astrid and Hiccup jump off, Hiccup exclaims, "It does exist," leading to the full thematic statement of *The Hidden World* theme.

The location is immense, full of dragons, and the two Furies in the center of it all. The Furies dive down from a ledge, dozens of dragons following, and eventually land on a crystal throne in the middle of everything. Toothless roars and all the dragons roar with him, including Drago's Bewilderbeast, missing part of its tusk. Toothless is the Alpha of *all* dragons. Even Astrid and Hiccup realize it, although for Hiccup, his realization is much sadder. The two furies nuzzle and chirp to one another, and a two-measure fragment of the *Furies in Love* theme sounds before *The Hidden World* theme is used in full as the dragons bow to their king and queen.

The afterglow of the moment features a lovely oboe solo in measures 98–101, and Hiccup suggests they leave, but they have been spotted by another dragon. Scalar runs in A minor sound in the upper woodwinds and strings as an alarm, while the opening notes of the *Dragon Tune*, slightly modified, sound in the low brass, low woodwinds, and contrabass. The presence of the *Dragon Tune* here is to indicate the hostility toward the human intruders. The dragons aren't "bad," but they will defend their territory. Action music once again is heard; eighth-note triplets abound as Hiccup and Astrid slide down the wet rocks. In measures 114–115, eight minor triads are heard, one on every beat in the two measures. Each of the chords is different, and the roots all belong to the same scale: Octatonic (2,3). This allows for non-functional harmony but with compositional parameters to avoid a clear tonal center while still using triadic harmony. Additionally, the roots all ascend, from F♯ up to F♮. Hiccup and Astrid land, and the violins play a three-beat repeating pattern over the 4/4 measures, causing metric dissonance and supporting the chaotic on-screen action. As they run, Toothless is in pursuit, trying to reach them before any other dragon does, in order to help them escape.

Toothless reaches them in time, and as he plucks them from the ground, the music shifts from sixteenth notes to eighth-note triplets in the upper woodwinds and violins in measure 130, sounding like a whirlwind, and the lower timbres of the orchestra arrive on a C major triad. In the middle, the horns and violas and cellos play the *Fate Tune*, as we finally know what it means—Toothless and the other dragons are fated to leave Berk and live in the Hidden World. The violins sustain a high G6, and the cue fades out as the action shifts to a flashback to Hiccup's childhood.

The influence of Ravel is strongly heard in this cue through the harmonic relationships, the use of vocals, the contrast in dynamics, and the orchestration. This cue represents the pinnacle of Ravel's influence on this particular theme and geographic location, making the Hidden World even more specific to dragons, and allowing Hiccup to realize that his plan of moving all of Berk to the Hidden World will not work. Hiccup begins to come to terms that he is losing his best friend, here an analogy for a parent sending a child out into the world, and why the style of music is so specific to this location and example.

4M17—With Love Comes Loss (1:08:00–1:09:00)
    4–24—Lost and Found (F Aeolian)
    24–29—Flying A (C major)

In the flashback, young Hiccup awakens because he hears Stoick crying by the fire. Stoick, acting "manly," quickly wipes his tears and is embarrassed that Hiccup has heard him. He tries to deflect, but relents and brings Hiccup over to tend to the fire. The female choir initiates the cue, singing an F minor triad, followed by the *Lost and Found* theme in the solo alto flute. Hiccup asks about a new mom, and Stoick says no. Stoick tells Hiccup, "With love comes loss. It's part of the deal." The second part of the *Lost and Found* theme plays, and ends on its concluding chord, a C major triad, the dominant in F, creating a half cadence. The loss leaves their family open, and although the family is briefly reunited much later, it will always remain open.

The action returns to present day, as Hiccup rides Toothless back to New Berk, both of them sad, but for different reasons. The reharmonized *Flying A* theme sounds anything but joyful; both make forlorn faces. The melody should begin on solfège *Mi*, but here the violin melody begins on solfège *Sol*, a third higher, the wrong starting point for the theme. The reharmonized *Flying A* theme is present but revoiced to sound incorrect. Even the planing, all voices moving in parallel motion, is strange. Figure 6.19 demonstrates the reharmonized *Flying A* theme. Hiccup and Toothless are both confused and sad, unsure of what to do next.

4M18—Grim Surprise (1:09:07–1:12:43)
    5–11—The Hidden World (A Aeolian)
    18–21—Sex riff (C Aeolian)
    23–26—Furies in Love (C Dorian)
    29–33—Fate riff (F-sharp Aeolian)
    34–35—Fate riff (E-flat Aeolian)
    38–40—Fate riff (F-sharp Aeolian)
    55–57—Warring Vikings (heroic)
    58–65—Good Alpha (A Phrygian)
    66–71—Good Alpha (A Phrygian)
    87–92—Fate Tune (A-flat Aeolian)

After a momentary break from the previous cue, "Grim Surprise" begins with an E minor triad, which has its fifth move down from B♮ to B♭, creating an E diminished triad. Hiccup realizes that Toothless belongs in The Hidden World, and the horn plays

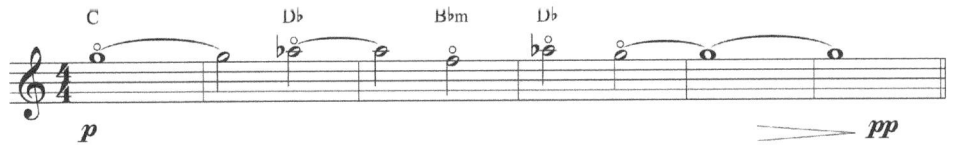

Figure 6.19. 4M17, measures 23–28, planing and reharmonized *Flying A* theme.

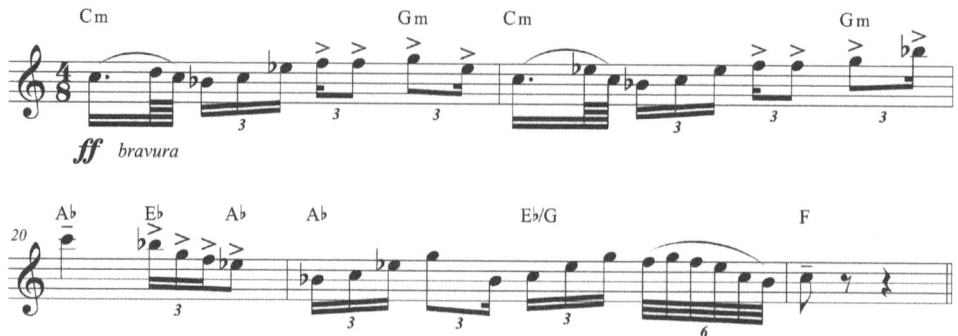

Figure 6.20. 4M18, measures 18–22, rhythmically and harmonically varied *Sex* riff.

The Hidden World theme while strings and flutes play a Ravel-like countermelody to the horn. The theme ends on an E minor triad, followed by a **SLIDE** to E♭ major as Hiccup tells Toothless they'll find a way to stay in touch. However, Toothless is distracted by something in the grass, and an E♭ Lydian scalar run in the flute in measure 12 highlights the presence of the Light Fury who has followed him back to New Berk, accounting for the use of the **SLIDE** gesture. Toothless excitedly runs to her, tongue out, to a rhythmically varied version of the *Sex* riff, seen in Figure 6.20. As he tries to get her to follow him to Hiccup, she stays put, a modified opening of the *Furies in Love* theme played only by the first violins.

Ruffnut returns "triumphantly" and the music drops out entirely, as Hiccup and Astrid immediately recognize that something is wrong because Grimmel simply allowed her to leave. The strings begin pulsing on F♯ on all three beats, beginning in measure 28, as the music is clearly leading to a reveal of Grimmel's armada. By now it should be clear that Powell is using the string pulsing to act as a precursor to an attack from Grimmel, as this is the third instance in the film when it has occurred. While the pulsing is not a melodic theme, it is certainly a recurring indicator of impending action. When the pulsing stops, the strings arrive on a C♯Mmm$^{9/7}$ chord, the dominant of F♯. Hiccup runs to Toothless, and the music resolves to an E♭ minor triad, an incorrect resolution of the previous chord. The *Fate* riff sounds and the Light Fury is spooked by something she smells. She growls and flies away, but is immediately hit by a tranquilizer dart. Toothless chases after her, as the music jumps up to F♯ minor and the *Fate* riff restarts. He growls at Grimmel, who casually hits Toothless in the wing with a second dart. Hiccup continues chasing after Toothless, who, with the Light Fury, is captured and hauled away by Grimmel. The countermelody from *The Hidden World* theme is played in the horns is played over expected harmonic pattern, but the theme's melody is absent. The score

Figure 6.21. 4M18, measures 41–44, *The Hidden World* countermelody.

indicates "ALL GONE WRONG" at measure 41 to highlight the incorrect thematic statement, seen in Figure 6.21.

As Grimmel flies away, the dragons rally to protect Toothless, their wings represented by the eighth-note and sixteenth-note triplets in the upper woodwinds and upper brass. Grimmel tells Toothless to call them off or he'll shoot the Light Fury. As Toothless makes his choice, the heroic version of the end of the *Warring Vikings* theme sounds, spurring Toothless to make the decision to spare his love and call off the swarming dragons.

A whirlwind of A minor arpeggios sound, leading into consecutive statements of the *Good Alpha* theme in A Phrygian, first in the horns, then in the woodwinds, further emphasizing the situation of the Furies. The use of the A Phrygian scale relates back to the first film, 2M9, "Dragon Training," when the Avengers are training with Gobber to learn to kill dragons. Grimmel's goal is to kill all dragons, particularly the Furies, and the use of the *Good Alpha* theme in Phrygian mode is a corruption of the theme and a call back to Drago's approach to dragons, subjugating them and building a dragon army.

Grimmel taunts Hiccup, saying "You tried your best," and letting him know that he, Grimmel, is the only true alpha, reminding Hiccup that he is "nothing without [his] dragon," as Hiccup failed to stop Grimmel in their previous encounter. Hiccup's worst fear has come to fruition. Hiccup is unable to prevent Grimmel's flight, and the opening notes of the *Fate Tune*, the theme for the leaving of the dragons, is sounded over an E♭ minor triad as Grimmel takes the dragons to his armada, the cue ending.

5M19–20A—The Hiccup I Know / Intro Into Battle (1:12:52–1:15:36)

    1–9—Warring Vikings (E Aeolian)
    9–15—Flying Ostinato (E Aeolian)
    17–38—Fate Tune (E Aeolian)
    39–43—Warring Vikings (E Aeolian)
    44–56—Grimmel's Tune (G-sharp Aeolian)
    57–61—Flying Ostinato (B Aeolian)
    62–65—Flying Ostinato (D-sharp Aeolian)
    62–64—Fate Tune (D-sharp Aeolian)
    66–72—Lost and Found (A Aeolian)
    71–84—Furies in Love (G-sharp Aeolian)

Valka sends Astrid to talk to Hiccup, since he will listen to her. This scene is parallel to the first film when Stoick has kidnapped Toothless to unwillingly lead the Vikings to the Dragons' Nest. The cue begins with a rhythmically augmented statement of the *Warring Vikings* theme in the solo horn, but only a single statement rather than the expected repeat. The minor-mode *Flying Ostinato* statement in the strings emphasizes Hiccup's sadness, and Astrid even says, "You're right. You're back to where you started," making the parallel between the first film and this film clear. But then, she begins telling him of all the positive things he's done, and a solo alto flute plays the beginning of the *Fate Tune*, and as Hiccup's confidence grows, so does the orchestration and volume of the orchestra, completing the theme.

The *Warring Vikings* theme then enters loudly in the brass; they will take action to get their dragons back safely, but the second half of the theme is played by solo clarinet, with Fishlegs asking, "How will we get our dragons back without … dragons?" The timbres reflect the excitement and heroism juxtaposed with the challenge of the task.

The action cuts to Grimmel and the armada, the sky an ominous shade of red, and *Grimmel's Tune* in the horns and trombones over a lengthy G♯ minor triad. Toothless watches as the dragons are put into cargo cages, the threat of the death of his queen if he acts. We then see the Avengers at the edge of the cliff of New Berk, as the *Flying Ostinato*, in B minor, is played in canon at the distance of a measure, cascading down through the strings. Hiccup has fashioned "wings" for everyone on the team, and they will glide down to the ships and free Toothless and the rest of the dragons, the opening notes of the *Fate Tune* played in the horns. This group of canonic entries is similar to the Avengers leaping at different times but taking the same path to reach the destination. As they soar down, the *Lost and Found* theme is played by the trombones and low strings in A minor, the loved ones they want to release far below. The themes continue one after another, with the *Furies in Love* theme in G♯ minor in the strings and flutes. Unlike the typical *Furies in Love* theme, this statement features very little harmonic motion away from the G♯ minor tonic triad; the two are trapped and cannot really do anything. Grimmel has double-crossed the warlords by keeping the Furies and plans on killing them both. The cue ends and segues into the main part of the battle.

5M20B—Armada Battle Part 1 (1:15:36–1:19:34)

5–21—Heroic Dragon (G major)
21–36—Heroic Dragon (D major)
54–57—Hiccup/Vikings (G Aeolian)
62–73—Grimmel's Tune (D Aeolian)
77–85—Fighting riff (F Aeolian)
85–94—Love theme (A major)
109–112—Dragon Tune (C doubly harmonic minor)
114–117—Flying Ostinato (G-sharp Aeolian)
126–129—Sex riff (C-sharp Aeolian)
130–140—Vikings B/C/D (starts on D♯)
141–142—Village Hymn (C-sharp Aeolian)
148–154—Lost and Found (B-flat Aeolian)
155–158—Lost and Found (C Aeolian)

The cue begins as Hiccup and the team soar down to the ships, with a short introduction leading into the *Heroic Dragon* theme. Hiccup knocks Grimmel off his perch, while Cloudjumper escapes from his cell on the ship and begins breathing fire everywhere. The freed dragons take instructions from Toothless, who is still confined, and the Avengers land on the command ship. The next portion of the cue, following a lead-up to the *Hiccup* theme, finds the team battling the warlords' army. This use of the theme is harmonized as i-III-VI-IV in G minor, so although the theme is not featured in unison or over a pedal, the harmonies all retain tonic function throughout the progression, which circles back to the G minor triad. Meanwhile, Toothless has broken free from his muzzle, underscored with scalar runs, first in E♭ Lydian-Mixolydian, then A Mixolydian, the two tonics a tritone apart. Grimmel rallies and tries to kill Toothless, but Toothless shoots a fireball, destroying Grimmel's cannon, and removing Grimmel's main weapon. Although it is somewhat buried in the mix, *Grimmel's Tune* is played in the brass while his flying craft begins to burn and fall from the sky. The action writing, with descending arpeggiating lines, polyrhythms, syncopation, and an authentic cadence at the conclusion of the first section of the battle make this cue as exciting as it should be.

The cadential progression in measures 82–83 features Fm-BMm⁷-Em, or ♭ii-V7-i in E minor. The only thing atypical from common-practice harmony is that the Neapolitan chord is a minor triad rather than the much more common major triad, most regularly in first inversion. The cadence corresponds with the action where Astrid throws a mace at a bad guy behind Hiccup, knocking him out and giving them a clear path to continue fighting. The cadence provides a moment of rest in the action, both musically and visually.

The E minor triad that served as the cadence chord becomes EMm⁷, the dominant of A major, the key where the *Love* theme is heard, as Astrid throws a smoke bomb onto the deck, and Hiccup throws his fire sword, igniting it, causing a massive explosion on the deck of the ship. This moment parallels the first film, when Astrid is idealized by a teenaged Hiccup, walking away from an explosion. It takes the traditional trope from action films and turns it into something very humorous, a momentary break from the seriousness of the battle, and another chance for Powell to shift and pivot the music. Astrid calls for Stormfly, who grabs Hiccup by the talons, and flies him up to Toothless. The harmonies in measures 97–98—A♭M-DM-BM-FM—are paired as tritones, but each is a minor third away from the next (B-D-F-A♭-B). The harmonies are presented as ascending and descending arpeggios, swirling around, defying a tonal center. Finally, a woodwind run based on the Octatonic (0,1) scale in measure 101 leads into Hiccup reaching Grimmel's faltering craft, the tonal center still unclear.

Grimmel, ever the villain, keeps hitting at Hiccup's psyche, telling him that Toothless no longer cares about him. Grimmel's flying craft is crashing, so he flies away on the Light Fury's back. The opening of the *Dragon Tune* is played by the horns, implying that Grimmel has turned Toothless against Hiccup. Hiccup is undeterred and as he prepares to jump to help Toothless escape, an ascending G Octatonic (1,2) scale helps him "wind up" and find the energy to make the leap, one additional note in the scale as compared to a typical diatonic scale. A variation on the *Flying Ostinato* sounds, Hiccup begins releasing Toothless, and as he apologizes for holding him back, the **SLIDE** motion is heard between the C♯ minor and C major triads. However, the craft fully goes down, crashing into the water, with a flurry of triads that finally settles on an B♭m triad when the splash occurs, then an FMmm⁹ᐟ⁷ chord, building anticipation for the reemergence of Toothless and Hiccup. They fly out of the water, not to a B♭m chord, but to a C♯m chord. The *Sex* riff begins as they emerge in measure 126, with the power of love causing the music to overshoot its appropriate resolution. The resolution can also be seen as a CMCR due

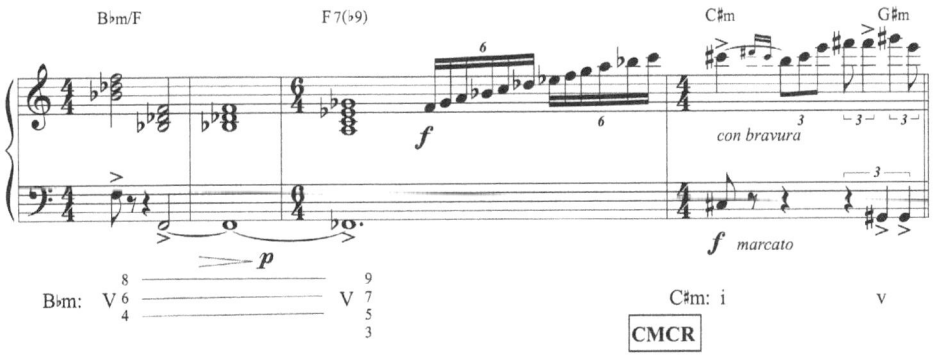

Figure 6.22. 5M20B, measures 123–126, spiraling into a CMCR

to its unexpected resolution and continuation in a different direction. With Hiccup and Toothless together one final time, there is no doubt that they'll defeat Grimmel. This brief passage is shown in Figure 6.22.

Meanwhile, the Avengers continues to fight the warlords' army. The *Vikings B-D* themes are heard as they manage to work together as a team, even without dragons, to win the day. Fishlegs even mutters, "It's almost like we're a team," while a brief variation on the *Village Hymn* sounds. Fishlegs' little baby dragon falls out of his pouch, and the BM-FM tritone-related chords, heard in the opening cue of the first film, sound. One of the bad guys provokes the baby, but the Crimson Goregutter sees him and flies in to attack, set to the *Lost and Found* theme. He will not let the baby be harmed, and smashes parts of the ships. Eventually Gobber, Eret, and Valka appear, ready to fight, with the *Lost and Found* theme ending on a half cadence in C Aeolian, concluding the cue, and segueing into the second part of the battle.

The first part of the Battle cue uses all of the devices Powell has at his disposal, as Figure 6.23 illustrates.

Measures	1	13	17	21	27	37	41	45	49	54
Marking										
Tempo	q = 210							q = 126	q = 128	
Meter	3/4							6/4	4/4	
Tonal Center	D minor	B minor	C major	D major	C major	D major	"F"	"A"	"D"	G minor

58	63	69	71	76	82	85	86	96	100
q = 132	q = 136			q = 145			q = 141		q = 120
				3/4				4/4	
D OCT (2,3)	D minor	F♯ minor	Unclear	F minor	E minor	A major	A major	Tritones	C OCT (0,1)

102	105	107	109	114	120	126	134	141	143
								q = 124	q = 119
		3/4		4/4					
C minor	Unclear	G minor	C minor	E major	B♭ minor	C♯ minor	E minor	E minor	Tritones

148	154	155	159
			End Cue
		q = 128	
	6/4	4/4	
B♭ minor	D Mixolydian	C minor	HC in C minor

Figure 6.23. Breakdown of 5M20B by measure, marking, tempo, meter, and tonal center.

Throughout this cue, the meter tends to alternate between 3/4 and 4/4, with the occasional single measure of 2/4, or a short section of 6/4. Switching between triple and quadruple meter prevents the music from becoming stale. Switching meters too often would sound somewhat chaotic, but the way in which Powell uses the meter changes allows the battle to make (unexpected) changes without sounding too messy. The tempo at the start of the cue is very similar to the tempo at the start of the battle cue from the first film, with q = 203 there. When the tempo slows in measure 49, the meter and tonal centers also change, a perfect example of how Powell describes the "turning" of the music up the stairway, as all of the parameters shift at the same time. From there, the music slowly accelerates until a significant slowdown in measure 100, with slight changes in tempo in the rest of the cue.

Once again, the most prominent device is the changing of tonal centers. As in previous films, tonal centers shifting by steps and thirds most commonly occurs, but here, Powell adds moments of octatonic scale, tritone relationships, and even tonal ambiguity. These changes are relentless, and the longest that the music remains in a single key is at the start of the cue, to ensure a clear starting point. Because so many characters are involved in this battle, constant shifts are necessary, and the tonal centers do much of the heavy lifting in the cue.

5M20C—Armada Battle Part 2 (1:19:34–1:22:09)

2–9—Fate Tune (C Aeolian)
2–8—Fate riff (C Aeolian)
12–13—Flying Ostinato (G Aeolian)
16–19—Action Motif (beginning on A)
20–24—Heroes A (C Aeolian)
26–32—Heroic Dragon (F major)
36–39—Love theme (B major)
48–53—Heroes A (B-flat Aeolian)
58–67—Grimmel's Tune (G-sharp Aeolian)
72–75—Heroes A (C-sharp Aeolian)
78–83—Dragon Tune (B doubly harmonic minor)
86–92—The Hidden World (A Aeolian)

The battle is not over! Hiccup chases Grimmel, underscored by both the *Fate riff* and the *Fate Tune*, the first time they've been played together. Toothless shoots a fireball at Grimmel, who steers the Light Fury into it, hitting her wing. An A♭M/DM polychord highlights the challenge of getting Grimmel off of the Light Fury without hurting her. This tritone-related polychord draws on the challenge Hiccup had at the start of the first film in bringing down the Night Fury, used in the cue "Anybody See That?" Back on the ships, Tuffnut's "full beard" finally gets its payoff as it is "cut in half," revealing the two braids of hair. Tuffnut becomes furious with rage, and the *Action Motif* from the first film is heard as he wildly attacks. The *Heroes A* theme is played by the full orchestra as Gobber works out of a tight spot. The Hobgoblins, now numbering nearly fifty, swarm the army, and the *Heroic Dragon* variation sounds. Astrid knocks out the man steering the ship and sets the wheel to crash it into the rest of the armada. The opening of the *Love* theme sounds, here simply as an aural identifier of Astrid, since the action is leaping between so many locations at this point, but there's still fire in the background while the theme is heard! As the ships crash

Figure 6.24. 5M20C, measures 48–53, *Heroes A* theme as brass fanfare.

into each other and explosions occur, the *Heroes A* theme is played as a brass fanfare with full choral accompaniment, seen in Figure 6.24; the team has worked together to defeat the warlords, largely without their dragons. They and their dragons begin the flight back to New Berk, having stopped the attack. This portion of the battle feels even more intense than anything in the Part 1 cue.

The action returns to the skies, where Hiccup continues to chase Grimmel. An intricate trumpet part in measures 55–58 leads into a statement of *Grimmel's Tune* as his Death Grippers attack Toothless. However, Grimmel has led them over New Berk, and as he does, his theme is immediately halted. The Berk dragons chase down the Death Grippers, and a wonderful contrary motion wedge sounds in the strings—the violins ascend while the cellos and contrabasses descend. The *Heroes A* theme, in rhythmic augmentation, sounds as a Death Gripper catches Toothless and tries to stab him with its tail. A second Death Gripper catches him as well, and Toothless and Hiccup are in trouble. Toothless summons his electrified powers to eliminate the Death Grippers, and the opening of the *Dragon Tune* sounds in the first violins. Figure 6.25 shows that instead of using triadic harmony, the harmonies in measures 78–81 are all tetrachords, pentachords, hexachords, and septachords combined in various levels of dissonance. As Toothless combusts, a G^{Mm7}-A^{Mm7} polychord is used in measure 84, seven discrete notes sounding, as we wait to see who emerges from the explosion. We see all of Grimmel's dragons fall to the ground and hear a reharmonized opening of *The Hidden World* theme, prominently featuring

Figure 6.25. 5M20C, measures 78–81, highly dissonant *Dragon Tune*.

major triads, bringing an end to the cue. The music tells us Toothless and Hiccup are safe, for now.

5M21—Ultimate Sacrifice (1:22:09–1:24:49)

2–5—Fate riff (C Aeolian)
6–9—Fate riff (E-flat Aeolian)
7–12—Fate Tune (E-flat Aeolian)
13–16—Fate riff (E-flat Aeolian)
16–26—Lost and Found (F-sharp Aeolian)
26–27—Fate riff (B-flat Aeolian)
28–29—Fate riff (A major)
30–33—Flying Ostinato (A major)
34–41—Flying A (A major)
42–51—Flying B (A major)
52–66—Furies in Love (C-sharp Aeolian)

The armada has been destroyed and Grimmel's dragons have been defeated. All that is left is to get Grimmel away from the Light Fury and defeat him. The cue opens with the *Fate* riff in C Aeolian. Hiccup and Toothless prepare to attack, but Grimmel shoots a tranquilizer dart and hits Toothless. During Grimmel's action, Hiccup is able to knock Grimmel off the Light Fury, Hiccup holding onto her muzzle, Grimmel holding onto Hiccup's prosthetic leg. The *Fate* riff moves up a minor third to E♭ Aeolian, and the opening of the *Fate Tune* sounds, Toothless falling, unconscious, to the ground. Hiccup unbuckles the muzzle from the Light Fury, instructs her to save Toothless. The *Fate* riff pauses while Hiccup releases the Light Fury, but resumes as the men begin their free fall, still in E♭ Aeolian. As the music slows, the Light Fury catches Toothless, and they land on the cliffs of New Berk, the music modulating up another minor third to F♯ Aeolian. As the two continue falling, Hiccup sees that Toothless is safe, and the choir begins singing the *Lost and Found* theme in augmentation, but with a new harmonization. Hiccup is reconciled to losing his best friend, but Toothless will never really be gone. Instead, he has found the Light Fury, who, after rescuing Toothless, has come to rescue Hiccup, similarly to how Toothless came around to Astrid in the first film. The reharmonization and reworking of the theme is this context is extraordinary. The B♭ minor triad uses a **SLIDE** motion to an A major triad in measures 26–29 as Hiccup releases his prosthetic. Grimmel falls into the ocean, and the Light Fury catches Hiccup just before he gets wet, a visual motive throughout the trilogy, now signaling acceptance of Hiccup by the Light Fury. As she does, the *Flying Ostinato*, in E major no less, sounds, followed by the complete *Flying* theme, also in E major, and she returns Hiccup to New Berk. Everyone returns, and it is a cause for celebration.

Hiccup rouses Toothless, and the introduction to the *Furies in Love* theme sounds, initially played by the celeste much earlier in the film, now played by the piccolo. She walks over, and their complete *Furies in Love* theme is played. The two nuzzle, watched by the entire village, Vikings and dragons, as the theme ends on a half cadence, which is the perfect way to conclude this cue, as Toothless and Hiccup need to part and close this chapter of their relationship. Both need to get married and have their own lives, but one final farewell scene is necessary.

5M22—Freedom (1:24:49–1:28:26)

 3–17—Fate Tune (G-sharp Aeolian)
 19–25—Fate Tune (G-sharp Aeolian)
 27–45—Lost and Found (A Aeolian)
 49–61—Lost and Found (A Aeolian)
 70–95—The Hidden World (A Aeolian)

The "last" scene between Hiccup and Toothless features the themes that would be expected: the *Fate Tune*, the *Lost and Found* theme, and *The Hidden World* theme. Segueing from the previous cue, "Freedom" begins with female voices leading into a complete statement of the *Fate Tune*, starting in the Celtic Harp before traveling through the orchestra. Hiccup takes the lead, and we see Astrid and Gobber removing the harnesses from their dragons, saying goodbye. As the thematic statement ends, it begins again, the melody remaining the same, but the harmonization changing. The second statement remains incomplete, as Hiccup speaks to Toothless, telling him to lead the dragons to The Hidden World, but before he does, we get one last moment with the friends.

As Hiccup and Toothless say their goodbyes to each other, the *Lost and Found* theme is played by the solo clarinet, then solo flute, with only harp as the initial accompaniment. The second half of the theme is played by solo piano, paralleling the ending of the first film, where the solo piano played the *Flying* theme as Hiccup awoke with his new prosthetic leg. Instead of beginning a friendship, this scene concludes their friendship, but the solo piano connects the two scenes. Their relationship will always be special and intimate. Hiccup backs away, and Toothless lets out a mighty roar, joined by all the dragons. The *Lost and Found* theme is restated by the full orchestra, and the dragons leave New Berk, led by the Light Fury. We see the Vikings crying, showing an emotion other than anger, proving the depth of the connection between people and dragons. A final statement of *The Hidden World* theme is played by the full orchestra, its rhythmic uniqueness normalized, as this event is sad but necessary. Toothless is the last to leave, looking at Hiccup one last time as tears stream down Hiccup's face. The cue concludes by alternating D minor and A minor triads several times, i-v in D Aeolian. The music sounds regal and majestic, not unlike "The Throne Room" cue at the conclusion of *Star Wars: A New Hope*, also in minor and for a celebration. This cue concludes on an A minor triad, which allows the music to shift nicely into the following cue, as A minor functions as the minor dominant in D minor, the tonality of the beginning of "Viking Wedding."

5M23—Viking Wedding (1:28:26–1:30:13)

 3–12—Village Hymn (D Aeolian)
 13–22—Village Hymn (D Aeolian)
 24–31—Village Hymn (G Aeolian)
 32–40—Village Hymn (A Aeolian)

Now that the Furies are together, it's time for Hiccup and Astrid to get married. Some time has passed since the dragons left as New Berk is covered in snow and homes have clearly been built. Connecting to the end of the previous cue, the dominant triad, A minor, resolves to the tonic, D minor, as the Celtic harp and dulcimer arpeggiate D minor triads. The full choir enters with the definitive thematic statement of the *Village Hymn*. The four-part vocal writing is very much in line with the common-practice style, even if the harmonic progression is not exclusively in that style. The harmonization uses both versions of scale degrees 6 and 7, allowing for natural and melodic minor, and cadences happen exactly how and when they should. This four-part statement gives the camera the opportunity to show off a bit of New Berk in the winter before zooming in on the entire village attending the wedding ceremony.

The second statement of the *Village Hymn* accompanies the actual ceremony, and only the soprano voices sing the melody, accompanied by Celtic and standard harps. Remaining consistent through the trilogy, the village elder does not speak. As a result, neither do Hiccup nor Astrid. Head nods, eye glances, and actions speak in this ceremony, but we know it is leading somewhere because the strings join the accompaniment in the second phrase. The couple kiss at the moment of cadence at the end of the *Village Hymn*, and celebration begins. This is yet another opportunity for the music to be given the space to work in place of dialogue.

The meter changes from 4/4 to 6/8, the music modulates up a fourth to G minor, and the full orchestra plays the *Village Hymn* and accompaniment. It remains a stately hymn in the minor mode and is the last opportunity to see the Vikings we have grown to love over the course of the three films. The fourth and final statement of the *Village Hymn* moves up yet another whole step, to A minor, and features significant percussion and the addition of bagpipes; each statement features an increase in texture than the previous one, a typical approach to classical theme-and-variations. We see Hiccup and Astrid from behind, essentially with their point-of-view as they survey New Berk. The codetta, also a typical feature of the final variation in a theme-and-variations, allows the hymn to end on a major triad through the use of a Picardy third, yet another standard technique for minor-mode chorales since the late Baroque era. The major triad sounds as Hiccup looks off into the horizon, knowing that somewhere out there, Toothless is happy.

5M24A—Boat Epilogue (1:30:13–1:32:26)

   1–9—Vikings A (D major)
   10–18—The Hidden World (E Aeolian)
   19–22—The Hidden World (E Aeolian)
   23–28—Flying A (E major)
   39–50—Flying Ostinato (C major)
   51–65—Vikings (B-flat major)

The narrative is complete, a tale as old as time: boy meets dragon, boy loves dragon, dragon loves boy, town loves dragons, dragon loves another dragon, boy loves girl, dragons leave town, boy and girl get married. But what happened with Hiccup and Astrid now that they don't have to fight against dragons or against those who would attack with dragons?

To keep with the parallel endings of the previous films, Hiccup has a voice-over narration, here accompanied by a solo piano. However, the piano plays the *Vikings A* theme rather than the *Flying* theme because Hiccup's narration is not just for us, it's for his children, a new generation of Vikings. In this flash forward, we see Hiccup and Astrid on a boat with their two children, Hiccup with a full, manly beard, looking every bit the chief of Berk. At the end of the *Vikings A* theme, the music shifts to *The Hidden World* theme, as the boat has arrived at its destination—the waterfall at the end of the world, with a score marking of "Mythological." As Hiccup continues his narration, he speaks about dragons, that they've been gone long enough to be thought of as legends, that they were never real, just an imaginary tale that parents tell their children. But Hiccup sees Toothless, the Light Fury, and their babies on a rock in the mist.

Toothless sees the boat and flies over, his pupils constricted, acting aggressively to protect the dragons from humans. Female voices sing the first four measures of *The Hidden World* theme as Hiccup starts talking to Toothless, putting his hand out. Male voices sing the first four measures of the *Flying A* theme, with a different harmonization, as Toothless doesn't quite recognize Hiccup. Toothless approaches, and for a moment we think he might not remember, but Hiccup puts his head down, turns away, and lets the dragon come to him. As soon as Toothless remembers Hiccup's scent, his pupils dilate, and everything will be fine. Hiccup becomes covered in dragon kisses and hugs to the *Flying Ostinato* in C major. The score indicates "Forbidden Scent," and the instrumentation from the "Forbidden Friendship" cue returns, most significantly, the glass and slate marimbas. Even the somewhat magical ending from that cue is reproduced here, as Hiccup brings his children over the Toothless and gets them to touch his nose. The magical ending chord here is a B♭ major triad, which is sustained for nearly the rest of the cue, as a synthetic female voice sings a highly rhythmically augmented statement of the opening of the *Vikings A* theme. In "Forbidden Friendship," the *Vikings A* theme was in B major. The difference in half step represents the generational difference, as the children are half Hiccup and half Astrid. The children are initially fearful, but Toothless looks at them with his big eyes, knows they are Hiccup's children, and nuzzles into their hands. The children get a look of great joy on their faces, and the music segues into the final cue of the film. Powell made a significant effort to connect the cues from the first and third films, saying:

> I brought the solo vox back because I realized nobody recognized the *Vikings* tune [in the first film] because it was so slow at the end of "Forbidden Friendship." In the third film, it's about twice as fast, so it makes sense. I've always liked the idea of development of melodies, expansion and contraction, so when you expand things to giant lengths, you can hide things but they still have the overall feelings of it being connected to something, even if it's not explicit. So that was one thing I did there I liked but realized nobody really got.
>
> It was also useful because I had to get through things snappier in Number 3. It's a transference of the same idea that we are all changed, but generations are changed by connection. I was trying to bring the focus down to the most intimate way of connecting because of the action of transference. I guess there was no other moment that warranted it until the end.

5M24B—Finale (1:32:26–1:34:00)

3–6—Flying Ostinato (D-flat major)
7–14—Flying A (D-flat Major)
15–24—Flying B (D-flat major)
24–32—Furies in Love (B-flat Aeolian)
36–39—Flying Ostinato (F major)
40–49—Flying B (F major)
50–52—Flying Ostinato (F major)

The excitement and joy at touching a dragon leads to final scene of the full family flying on Toothless and Stormfly as the action shifts from the boat to the air. The *Flying Ostinato* begins in D♭ major as Hiccup and his son are on Toothless, with the *Flying A* theme beginning a few seconds later. Toothless makes the ride as fun as possible with

6. How to Train Your Dragon: The Hidden World *Cue Analysis*

barrel rolls and sharp turns, and Hiccup tosses his laughing son in the air. When the *Flying B* theme begins, the Light Fury flies alongside Toothless, the babies in tow.

The three babies join Toothless, and the *Furies in Love* theme begins in the brass and strings. Hiccup's son and the white baby dragon touch "paws" as Astrid zooms by on Stormfly with her daughter. Hiccup's narration begins, again speaking of the legends of dragons. At the conclusion of the *Furies in Love* theme, a short transition shifts the music back to the *Flying Ostinato*, now in F major, followed by the *Flying B* theme, as Hiccup says they will protect the secret of the dragons. One final statement of the *Flying Ostinato* sounds as the title card appears on-screen, bagpipes added, and the film ends.

The key of the final statement of the *Flying Ostinato* and *Flying* theme is significant. At the end of the first two films, this material was in E major, the key of adventure. There was more for Hiccup and Toothless to do together. In this film, the music is in F major, the pastoral key. Both Hiccup and Toothless have paired off with their female love interests and started families. Both Hiccup and Toothless are leaders, with Toothless as the Alpha Dragon and Hiccup as the chief of Berk. They will always have a friendship, but their adventures together are complete, as they are settled into new lives and will not have much interaction in the future. It is the perfect ending to the series of films.

5M25S "Together from Afar" (1:34:00–1:37:04)

Once again, Jónsi contributes a song to the film. Like the first film, this song is wholly original and only appears in the End Credits. The lyrics speak of parting but remaining friends forever, based on the lyrics in the first verse as well as the falsetto timbre of Jónsi's singing, the opening verse can be heard as giving voice to Toothless, making the lyrics akin to Toothless speaking to Hiccup. The refrain as well as the second verse is more applicable to Hiccup's viewpoint, since Hiccup feels as though he is nothing without Toothless. The shifting perspectives of the lyrics make it impossible to be from a single viewpoint. Instead, it feels more like a conversation, with the final stanza sounding like both friends saying the lines together.

While the song doesn't use any musical material from the films, it is an appropriate tempo and style for the conclusion of the trilogy, as it accompanies images from all three films, rather than just the third film. The retrospective nature of the images and lyrics works to ensure the film series is complete, and not just an ending for this specific film.

End Credits Suite (1:37:04–1:44:00)

The End Credits feature a newly arranged suite, largely derived from four cues and locations:

3M10—Toothless Goes a-Courtin'—measures 18–24, 37–57, 130–155
2M8B—Exodus—measures 20–39, and 46–49, with new music
3M12B—Romance in the Clouds—measures 18–70
4M16B—The Hidden World—measures 67–84, with new music

7

Themes Across the Trilogy

One of the primary ways film series provide musical consistency across films is by using Leitmotifs and theme in multiple films. Once a theme is introduced in a film it can return in its original form or altered to provide a new narrative meaning. One need not look further than John Williams's music for the *Star Wars* films or Howard Shore's music for the *Lord of the Rings* trilogy for examples. However, my favorite example comes from the Indiana Jones films, also scored by Williams. In the third film, *Indiana Jones and the Last Crusade*, Indy and Elsa are in a catacomb beneath a library in Venice, Italy. Elsa sees markings and drawings on the wall and asks, "What's this one?" The cue is interrupted by the opening measures of the *Ark* theme from the first film. Indy replies with, "The Ark of the Covenant." She asks, "Are you sure?" to which he responds, deadpanning, "Pretty sure." As soon as the pair walk past, the theme is gone, and the cue resumes. The Ark is locked away in a warehouse at the end of the first film, so the callback to that theme is both unexpected and humorous in this case. The following tables provide a list of themes within each cue.

How to Train Your Dragon

	1M2	1M6	1M7A	1M7B-C	2M8	2M9	2M10	2M11	2M12	2M13	2M14
Flying A	X			X			X	X		X	X
Flying B	X										X
Flying Ostinato				X					X		X
Hiccup	X	X									
Vikings!	X	X	X	X							X
Warring Vikings	X	X	X	X		X		X	X		
Love Theme	X										
Dragon Tune	X				X	X		X	X		
Fate Theme				X							
Action Motif									X		
Calming Motif											

	2M15	3M16	3M17	3M18	3M20	3M21	3M22	3M23	3M24	3M25	3M26B
Flying A				X	X						X
Flying B					X	X					
Flying Ostinato			X		X				X	X	
Hiccup	X						X		X		
Vikings!											
Warring Vikings				X			X				
Love Theme										X	
Dragon Tune											X
Fate Theme	X		X								
Action Motif		X									
Calming Motif	X		X								

	3M26C	4M27-28	4M30	4M31	4M33-34	4M35-37	4M38	5M39	5M40	5M41
Flying A	X					X			X	X
Flying B		X		X		X			X	X
Flying Ostinato		X	X			X		X	X	X
Hiccup										
Vikings!		X		X		X		X		
Warring Vikings			X	X	X	X	X			
Love Theme	X									X
Dragon Tune		X	X	X		X	X	X		
Fate Theme				X		X				
Action Motif						X				
Calming Motif				X	X					

Figure 7.1. Breakdown of themes/motifs by cue in *HTTYD*.

Since this is the first film, no conclusions can be drawn regarding the connection of themes from one film to another. However, some conclusions can be made concerning the use of themes within this film. The *Love* theme only occurs when Hiccup and Astrid are together. It appears in the opening cue as Hiccup describes her, and then not again until they fly together on Toothless. It occurs when she tells Hiccup to tell Stoick about the dragon den, and then is only heard in the final cue when she punches Hiccup, followed by kissing him. The *Fate* theme typically occurs when Hiccup and Toothless interact, particularly early in their relationship. The *Warring Vikings* occurs with a high level of frequency, as the primary conflict is between the Vikings fighting the dragons. Of course, the *Flying* theme and *Flying Ostinato* are the film's main themes, and they occur in moments where Hiccup and Toothless are connecting. Prior to cue 3M20, "Test Drive," the *Flying B* theme only occurs in the opening cue and in 2M14, "Forbidden Friendship." In 2M14, the timbre is much more delicate than in 3M20, where the cue presents a triumphant version of both the *Flying A* and *B* themes. The markings for the *Dragon Tune* include the *Heroic Dragon* variation of the theme, so not every appearance of the theme is antagonistic. Through its absence in the second half of the film, Powell reveals that the *Hiccup* theme is not significant, as the film is not about him but rather the connection he has made with Toothless and wants to share with the entirety of Berk.

How to Train Your Dragon 2

	1M1	1M2S	1M3–4	1M5	1M6	2M7	2M8	2M9	2M10	2M11
Flying A	X									
Flying B	X	X								
Flying Ostinato	X	X	X	X	X				X	
Hiccup	X		X			X				
Vikings!	X						X	X		
Warring Vikings	X						X		X	X
Love Theme	X		X	X					X	
Dragon Tune			X							
Fate Theme										
Action Motif										
Calming Motif										
Hiccup the Chief			X			X	X	X	X	
Drago's Tune									X	
Drago Riff									X	
Valka's Tune				X						
Map the World			X			X	X	X		
Lost and Found										X
Good Alpha										X
Courting Song										

	2M12	2M13	2M14	2M15–16	3M17–18	3M19	3M20	3M21	3M22	3M25–26
Flying A				X				X	X	
Flying B		X						X		

7. Themes Across the Trilogy

	2M12	2M13	2M14	2M15–16	3M17–18	3M19	3M20	3M21	3M22	3M25–26
Flying Ostinato										
Hiccup		X								
Vikings!									X	
Warring Vikings		X		X					X	X
Love Theme						X				
Dragon Tune					X	X			X	
Fate Theme										
Action Motif										
Calming Motif	X									
Hiccup the Chief										
Drago's Tune				X					X	
Drago Riff									X	
Valka's Tune		X	X					X		
Map the World				X			X			
Lost and Found					X		X	X		X
Good Alpha	X				X					
Courting Song										

	3M27	3M28S	4M29	4M30	4M31	4M32	4M33	4M35	4M36–37	5M38
Flying A				X					X	X
Flying B				X			X		X	
Flying Ostinato				X	X		X			X
Hiccup									X	
Vikings!				X				X		
Warring Vikings	X			X	X					
Love Theme				X						

	3M27	3M28S	4M29	4M30	4M31	4M32	4M33	4M35	4M36–37	5M38
Dragon Tune	X			X	X				X	
Fate Theme										
Action Motif				X						
Calming Motif										
Hiccup the Chief										
Drago's Tune				X	X					
Drago Riff				X						
Valka's Tune										
Map the World	X						X			
Lost and Found						X				X
Good Alpha				X	X	X				X
Courting Song		X	X		X		X			

	5M39A	5M39B	5M40S
Flying A		X	
Flying B			X
Flying Ostinato		X	X
Hiccup			
Vikings!		X	
Warring Vikings			
Love Theme		X	
Dragon Tune	X		
Fate Theme			
Action Motif			
Calming Motif			
Hiccup the Chief		X	
Drago's Tune	X		
Drago Riff			
Valka's Tune			

7. Themes Across the Trilogy 179

	5M39A	5M39B	5M40S
Map the World			
Lost and Found	X		
Good Alpha		X	
Courting Song			

Figure 7.2. Breakdown of themes/motifs by cue in *HTTYD2*.

The second film begins by recapitulating most of the themes from the first film, closely musically paralleling the opening cue "This is Berk." The first two new themes introduced are *Hiccup the Chief* and *Map the World*. From this information, the conflicts are clear. First, at some point, Hiccup will need to take on the responsibilities of the chief. Second, as Hiccup's world expands, drastic changes will occur, both positive and negative, and every action will be faced with a consequence. The *Warring Vikings* theme is used until Stoick's death. This is not a coincidence. Stoick has a history with Drago, and once the villain is introduced, Stoick takes measures to defend Berk from potential invasion. Once Hiccup assumes the role of chief of Berk, the *Warring Vikings* theme is not used again. Hiccup is a different type of leader than Stoick, more cerebral and less physically intimidating, resulting in the absence of that particular theme. The *Dragon Tune* returns as Drago has both a dragon army and his own Alpha, the Bewilderbeast, all of which are used for antagonistic purposes. This also includes the uses of the *Heroic Dragon* variation, so not every use in the table is going to be for an antagonistic purpose. The *Love* theme is used sparingly in this film but expands its use beyond the Hiccup/Astrid pair as it is used humorously for Ruffnut's infatuation with Eret. Once again, the theme returns at the film's conclusion with Hiccup and Astrid kissing before the ceremony where Hiccup is appointed as the new chief of Berk. Also used sparingly are the *Hiccup* theme and the *Vikings* theme. Rather than the *Hiccup* theme, the music that typically is associated with Hiccup in this film is the *Hiccup the Chief* theme, so when the *Hiccup* theme is used, the scene is more about him in a childlike role rather than in a leadership role, particularly when he first meets his mother and when he is avoiding his father and talk of becoming the chief. When the Vikings are doing Viking things, such as flying dragons, working in Berk, or intimidating Eret and the dragon trappers, is when Powell uses the *Vikings* theme. They are not actively fighting, just doing the regular activities that Vikings do. The *Fate* theme is entirely absent from this film, as it is not necessary at all. Hiccup has learned how to tame dragons and has taught everyone in Berk how to do it as well. That was his fate, and since it has been realized, there's no need for that theme to appear in this film. The *Flying* music returns in times of joy, safety, and in times where Drago must be defeated. It both opens and closes this film, asserting its position as main theme across the trilogy.

Although *Lost and Found* is not used more often than any theme written specifically for this film, it appears in the most prominent scenes and situations—when Hiccup is taken from Toothless, when Valka gives her recollection of being taken by the dragon 20 years earlier, when Hiccup and Valka spend time together, when Stoick encounters Valka, at Stoick's funeral, and when Hiccup has to get Toothless back from the Bewilderbeast's control. The use of *Lost and Found* in these locations gives enough prominence to the theme to call it the primary theme for this film. The *Good Alpha* theme occurs in as many cues as *Lost and Found*, but the *Good Alpha* theme is often transformed and corrupted into the antagonistic version representing Drago's Bewilderbeast, and not Valka's or, eventually, Toothless. The *Courting Song*, *Drago's Tune*, and the *Drago* riff are all introduced in this film, but none appear in the final installment of the trilogy. Drago is presumed dead at the end of the second film, so there's no real reason to hear his music in the next film, and because Stoick sacrifices his life for Hiccup's, there is no reason to hear the *Courting Song*, a song for Valka and Stoick, in the third film, either.

How to Train Your Dragon: The Hidden World

	1M1	1M2A-B	1M2C-1M3	1M4	2M5	2M6A-B	2M7A-B	2M8A-B	2M9A-B	3M10
Flying A				X					X	
Flying B		X								
Flying Ostinato		X	X							
Hiccup										
Vikings!									X	
Warring Vikings		X	X						X	
Love Theme				X						
Dragon Tune		X								
Fate Theme									X	
Action Motif										
Calming Motif										
Hiccup the Chief										
Drago's Tune										
Drago Riff										
Valka's Tune										
Map the World				X						
Lost and Found		X								
Good Alpha										
Courting Song										
Grimmel's Tune				X			X	X	X	
Heroes	X	X							X	

7. Themes Across the Trilogy

	1M1	1M2A-B	1M2C-1M3	1M4	2M5	2M6A-B	2M7A-B	2M8A-B	2M9A-B	3M10
March of the Warlords	X		X							
Furies in Love				X	X	X		X		X
Light Fury Motif	X			X						X
Village Hymn				X	X		X	X		
Fate Tune				X				X	X	
Fate Riff								X		
Sex Riff							X			X
Courting Riff										
Fighting Riff	X							X		
The Hidden World				X						

	3M11	3M12A	3M12B	3M13S	3M14A-B	4M15A	4M15B-4M16	4M16B	4M17
Flying A					X				X
Flying B	X				X				
Flying Ostinato	X				X			X	
Hiccup	X					X			
Vikings!									
Warring Vikings					X				
Love Theme									
Dragon Tune					X			X	
Fate Theme									
Action Motif									
Calming Motif									
Hiccup the Chief					X				
Drago's Tune									
Drago Riff									

	3M11	3M12A	3M12B	3M13S	3M14A-B	4M15A	4M15B-4M16	4M16B	4M17
Valka's Tune									
Map the World									
Lost and Found									X
Good Alpha									
Courting Song									
Grimmel's Tune		X					X		
Heroes					X				
March of the Warlords									
Furies in Love	X	X	X					X	
Light Fury Motif			X						
Village Hymn						X			
Fate Tune								X	
Fate Riff							X		
Sex Riff	X								
Courting Riff									
Fighting Riff					X				
The Hidden World	X			X			X	X	

	4M18	5M19–20A	5M20B	5M20C	5M21	5M22	5M23	5M24A	5M24B
Flying A					X			X	X
Flying B					X				X
Flying Ostinato		X	X	X	X			X	X
Hiccup			X						
Vikings!			X					X	
Warring Vikings	X	X							
Love Theme			X	X					
Dragon Tune			X	X					
Fate Theme									
Action Motif				X					

7. Themes Across the Trilogy

	4M18	5M19–20A	5M20B	5M20C	5M21	5M22	5M23	5M24A	5M24B
Calming Motif									
Hiccup the Chief									
Drago's Tune									
Drago Riff									
Valka's Tune									
Map the World									
Lost and Found		X	X		X	X			
Good Alpha	X								
Courting Song									
Grimmel's Tune		X	X	X					
Heroes				X					
March of the Warlords									
Furies in Love	X	X			X				X
Light Fury Motif									
Village Hymn			X				X		
Fate Tune	X	X			X	X	X		
Fate Riff	X			X	X				
Sex Riff			X						
Courting Riff									
Fighting Riff									
The Hidden World	X			X		X		X	

Figure 7.3. Breakdown of themes/motifs by cue in *HTTYD: THW*.

As the protagonist of the three films, it might be expected to hear the *Hiccup* theme or even *Hiccup the Chief* throughout the third film. However, neither one is used often. The *Hiccup* theme is only used three times in the film, while *Hiccup the Chief* is only used once. Because Hiccup has grown into the role of the chief of Berk, the *Hiccup the Chief* theme, a theme used to contrast his childlike nature, is rendered unnecessary. The *Hiccup* theme is used in the "Armada Battle" cue, along with the scene where he allows Toothless to fly on his own and the cue "Stronger Together," where he implores the inhabitants of Berk to work as a collective rather than as several fragments. Instead of Hiccup's childlike nature and avoidance of responsibility, the uses of the *Hiccup* theme in this film represent his ability to find ways to believe in and support others, quite a maturation for Hiccup, even if he doesn't always believe in himself.

Several themes from the first film appear sparingly in this third film of the trilogy. The *Love* theme also only occurs three times in the film, two of which are in the two parts of the "Armada Battle," with the third occurring when Gobber tells them they should get married toward the start of the film. When the *Love* theme is first used in the first film, it accompanies Astrid walking away from an explosion. In one of its uses in the Armada Battle sequence, Hiccup and Astrid work in tandem to create an explosion that they walk away from together, the *Love* theme again accompanying an image of an explosion, flipping the trope visually and musically. The *Vikings* theme is used in three cues, initially in this film when New Berk is being set up, then later in the Armada Battle, and finally when Hiccup and Astrid's children meet Toothless and the other dragons in the film's epilogue. That final instance adds something to the narrative, as Vikings engage in dragon taming activities, not dragon fighting. The *Dragon Tune* occurs five times, with two landing in the "Armada Battle" cues. Aside from the clear use of the *Heroic Dragon* variation, the *Dragon Tune* is used when Grimmel has his drugged dragons that he controls on display. The *Warring Vikings* theme is also used five times, most commonly when the Avengers are battling Grimmel and his army. Very little changes across the three films in the use of this theme, as it is strong, noble, and righteous.

The main themes of the trilogy, the *Flying* theme and the *Flying Ostinato*, occur more often than any other theme from the first film, as should be expected. Although the *Flying* music doesn't appear in the opening cue, it does appear in the second cue, when the Avengers return to Berk. Like the previous two films, this film ends with the *Flying* music again, with both each film and the entire trilogy bookended with this familiar and wonderful music.

The only theme from the second film that is used more than once in the third film is the *Lost and Found* theme, the second film's primary theme. This is not a surprise, as the thrust of the film deals with Hiccup needing to allow Toothless to be with the Light Fury and have a life of his own outside of Berk. Perhaps the most significant scene where the *Lost and Found* theme is heard is when Hiccup has a flashback to when he was a boy and Stoick tells him, "With love comes loss." Hiccup knows he has to allow Toothless to be on his own in the Hidden World. Four of the six uses of this theme occur within the final portion of the film once Grimmel abducts both Toothless and the Light Fury. Hiccup and the Avengers defeat Grimmel and release all the dragons in New Berk, the emotional impact felt by all the inhabitants, along with the audience.

As I pointed out in the Hidden World film chapter, my favorite thematic connection across the films is the use of the solo vox in "Forbidden Friendship" in the first film, and then in "Boat Epilogue" in the third film. In both instances, the music uses the *Vikings A* theme. In "Forbidden Friendship," the use of the theme tells the audience that perhaps Vikings don't harm dragons. In "Boat Epilogue," the children have never seen dragons before, with Hiccup's voice-over narration implying that dragons may have just been a myth. However, the children get the opportunity to touch and fly Toothless just as Hiccup did, Hiccup passing along his secrets to the next generation. It allows for both generations of Vikings and dragons to interact, bringing a finality to the trilogy that is appropriate, fulfilling, and satisfying.

Conclusion

With nearly four hours of music across three films, John Powell created a sonic world of Vikings and dragons, of love and loss, of joy and exhilaration, of villains, of redemption, and ultimately, of growth and lasting relationships. The musical themes created for the films are memorable, and the *Flying* theme will be forever associated with the trilogy, and with the joy, excitement, and freedom of flying and friendship. Though the course of this book, the music for all three films has been analyzed, so what kinds of trends emerge in the music of the world of Vikings and Dragons?

Regarding themes, Powell tends to write themes longer than eight measures, and those most commonly have two parts rather than two halves, with each part somewhat closed. The sentence structure is used in the opening part of his themes more than any other structure, largely because it can end with either a half cadence or authentic cadence, as opposed to other structures such as periods, which require authentic cadential closure. The presence of two parts to themes has multiple implications for the way they can be used in the score. Powell can use just the first part, just the second part, can insert additional material between the parts, and use the complete theme, depending on the narrative context. Additional techniques such as reharmonizing the melodies of themes and creating specific thematic variations demonstrate how melodic themes are the primary driver of musical recognition, rather than harmony. Themes also take on different characters and can fit into both duple and triple meter, but themes do not cross from simple to compound meter. Harmonies derived from the octatonic scale and from non-tertian means occur when situations become dangerous or potentially harmful, but those typically resolve back to functional means once the danger has passed.

The theme most closely associated with the film trilogy is clearly the *Flying* theme as it is heard across all three films, notably at the ends. If a main theme exists for the second film, it is the *Lost and Found* theme, as it speaks to the finding of Hiccup's mother and the death/loss of his father, among several other ideas. It is heard the most of any of the newly created themes for the second film and is also the most adapted in various ways and styles. Finding a main theme for the third film is a bit trickier. Would it be *The Hidden World*, since that's where the dragons are ultimately headed? Would it be the *Village Hymn*, used for Hiccup and Astrid's wedding near the end of the film? Would it be the *Fate Tune*, as the destiny of the dragons is to leave Berk? Or would it be the *Furies in Love* theme, introduced incrementally until it is fully realized in the clouds? None of those choices seem to have primacy based on the number of times they are heard. *Furies in Love* returns in the final cue of the film, sandwiched between statements of the *Flying* theme, so that gives the theme significance. Perhaps a "main theme" doesn't need to be as important as the way in which the themes interact across the films. Powell has a clear method of organizing his music:

> When I do sequels, I do a crib sheet of what the tunes were. Actually, I do it on every movie. Once I'm up and running, I then go back and say, "I'm going to make a single sheet of paper with all of my tunes on it so that when I sit here, I can look at them" and ask, "Can that one go slow enough that it will work really well for this," or, "Can this one go faster?" Rather than keeping them all in my head, because I don't remember anything, I use this crib sheet, and sometimes that is still around. Even if the tunes aren't right, it's a starting place. Sometimes I'll look at the crib sheet and think, "Well, that's clearly wrong," and I'll just ignore the bits that are wrong. I'll look at the crib sheet and the first four bars are correct, but then bars 5 and 6 aren't. But once I've played the first four bars, I'll remember the better version of 5 and 6, so I won't bother to fix the crib sheet because the only place it goes correctly is into Logic.

The stark contrast between consonant and dissonant sounds, between tertian harmonies and pitch-class set collections, further highlights how Powell is able to create a sound world that not only supports the narrative, but enhances it when danger and doubt strike. He's also able to integrate several different styles of music into a coherent whole, almost making us forget that Vikings are from the Nordic countries, not Scotland, Ireland, or England. This is not a real world. Our belief in reality is suspended, and one of the ways is through the music that combines so many different elements. Only in the hands of a true master composer could all those different styles, scales, and sounds be used so intelligently and so well.

Powell's view on action sequences, and more generally, longer cues, is quite logical. The music cannot continue to get higher and faster; the musicians have a breaking point, and so does the audience. Making the shifts, turning, changing tonal centers and tempos at the same time, changing meters, keeps the music moving forward while still potentially slowing down or moving somewhere unexpected. Through all of this, some trends do emerge. Modulations typically occur as ascending minor thirds. Ascending major thirds are not uncommon. Tempos over the course of a longer cue often start quickly, pull back, and then accelerate in the second half of the cue. Modes are more significant than functional keys.

Authentic cadences happen with little frequency; half cadences occur more often. The film where cadences conclude the greatest number of cues is the third film. As the film progresses to its inexorable conclusion, full stops via cadence become more necessary for narrative punctuation and pause. When authentic cadences are heard in the first two films, they stand out quite prominently because they occur so infrequently. The finality of the cadence brings a complete stop to the action, often accompanied by a moment of reflection for a character.

Harmonic progressions rarely conform to strict common-practice ideals, due partially to the fact that so many of the themes are modal, and partially because that is not what is narratively useful. Chromatic mediants are used, both major-mode and minor-mode pairs, to illustrate ideas such as heroism, magic, and evil. Triads with roots a tritone apart are also used commonly, often to signal distance between land and sky, but also to indicate the difference between opposite sides of a conflict.

Neo-Riemannian Theory can rarely be applied consistently, except one operation, due to how rarely it is used. The **SLIDE** function is not used at all in the first film. It is used once in the second film, in the cue "Together We Map the World." When Hiccup says to Toothless, "Maybe we'll track down another Night Fury," the harmonies

Em-E♭M are used. The **SLIDE** function is used four times in the final film. In "Romance in the Clouds," the Gm-G♭M motion represents the two furies and The Hidden World. In "Grim Surprise," the motion between Em-E♭M narratively supports that Hiccup and Toothless will always be friends, no matter if they are apart. The "Armada Battle Part 1" finds Hiccup apologizing to Toothless for being selfish and holding him back, as the music slides from C♯m to CM. Finally, in "Ultimate Sacrifice," Hiccup releases his prosthesis, dooming Grimmel in the process. As he falls, he is saved by the Light Fury with a motion of B♭m-AM. The **SLIDE** motion is specific to the relationship between the Night Fury, the Light Fury, and Hiccup, a special bond between special characters using a special harmonic relationship.

The magic number in a film series seems to be three. The trilogy is somewhat divine, so naturally trilogies can be found across genres. Some of the most famous include the *Star Wars* trilogy (the originals), the Indiana Jones trilogy (the 1980s films), the *Matrix* trilogy (the most recent film not withstanding), and the *Lord of the Rings* trilogy. In all of those instances, the same composer wrote the music for the complete series. Where does the music of the *How to Train Your Dragon* trilogy rank among the top trilogies? I have to say that John Williams's music for *Star Wars* and the Indiana Jones films would be 1 and 2, but I feel that John Powell's *Dragon* music is better than everything else, including Howard Shore's *Lord of the Rings* music. His ability to write memorable themes, to adapt them, to combine them, to reimagine them, to juxtapose them with dissonance, to connect them across films, gives the music a level of sophistication beyond anyone not named John Williams. It's no accident that Powell scored the standalone *Solo* film, receiving universal acclaim for easily finding his way in that sound world.

With Hiccup's final narration the film trilogy is closed. The story of a boy and his dragon, growing together, and needing to go their separate ways, is a wonderful metaphor for life, and John Powell's music transformed good films into great films. His music for the trilogy is some of the best of the 2010s, an outstanding accomplishment among film trilogies, and music that will continue to be loved for generations. Even though no more new music will come from Powell for this series, we don't have to be sad. Like Hiccup visiting Toothless, we can revisit this music any time, and remember the joy and wonder it brought to us.

Appendix

Cue list for *How to Train Your Dragon*

Cue	Title	In	Out	Elapsed Time
1M2alt	This is Berk	0:00:01	0:06:05	6:04
1M6	Anybody See That?	0:06:08	0:07:22	1:14
1M7A	War Room	0:09:17	0:09:55	0:38
1M7B-C	Training Out There	0:11:16	0:14:45	3:29
2M8	Hiccup Comes Home	0:15:11	0:15:29	0:18
2M9	Dragon Training	0:16:52	0:19:58	3:06
2M10	Wounded	0:20:41	0:22:03	1:22
2M11	The Dragon Book	0:23:16	0:25:33	2:15
2M12	Hiccup Focus	0:25:43	0:27:42	1:59
2M13	Offering	0:27:43	0:28:29	0:46
2M14	Forbidden Friendship	0:29:03	0:33:11	4:08
2M15	New Tail	0:34:17	0:37:00	2:43
3M16	Teamwork	0:37:09	0:37:47	0:38
3M17	Charming the Pziiffelback	0:38:31	0:38:53	0:22
3M18	See You Tomorrow	0:39:03	0:42:55	3:52
3M20	Test Drive	0:43:27	0:45:55	2:28
3M21	Not So Fireproof	0:46:39	0:47:10	0:31
3M22	This Time for Sure	0:49:39	0:50:17	0:38
3M23	Astrid Finds Toothless	0:51:57	0:52:30	0:33
3M24	Astrid Goes for a Spin	0:53:30	0:54:13	0:43
3M25	Romantic Flight	0:54:14	0:56:06	1:52
3M26B	Dragon's Den	0:57:07	0:58:42	1:35
3M26C	Let's Find Dad	0:58:51	0:59:54	1:03
4M27-28	Kill Ring/Stop the Fight	1:00:31	1:04:55	4:24
4M30	Not a Viking	1:05:33	1:06:28	0:55
4M31	Ready/Confront	1:06:28	1:07:49	1:21
4M31	Ready/Confront (continued)	1:08:48	1:11:00	2:12
4M33-34	Relax/Stroke/Hell	1:11:48	1:12:54	1:06

Cue	Title	In	Out	Elapsed Time
4M35–37	Over/Less Okay	1:14:11	1:20:27	6:16
4M38	Wings	1:20:27	1:21:39	1:12
5M39	Counter Attack	1:21:43	1:23:29	1:46
5M40	Where's Hiccup	1:24:13	1:26:56	2:43
5M41	Coming Back Around	1:26:57	1:29:01	2:04
5M42S	Sticks and Stones	1:29:01	1:31:02	2:01
	End Titles	1:31:03	1:37:39	6:36
	End of Film		**1:37:50**	**1:14:53**

The London Orchestra and Metro Voices, conducted by Gavin Greenaway, recorded at Air Studios, London, January 23–28, 2010.

Orchestrators: John Aston Thomas and Dave Metzger

Additional Orchestration: Gavin Greenaway, Jessica Wells, Daniel Baker, James K. Lee, Angus O'Sullivan, Stefan Schneider, Germaine Franco, and Dominic Lewis

Music Editor: Adam Smalley

Soloists:

Violin—Perry Montague-Mason

Hardanger Fiddle—Dermot Crehan

Pennywhistle—Helen Keen

Vocals—Dee Lewis-Clay

Guitar and Dulcimer—Vivian Milanova

Warpipes—Richard Baughman, Eric Bernard, Alastair Boase, Bobby Burke, Chris Carson, Paul Cathers, Nick Coseboom, Harry Farrar, Jennifer Febre, Alex MacGillivray, George MacGillivray, John McDonald, Karen McIlvena, Trevor Takahashi

Cue list for *How to Train Your Dragon 2*

Cue	Title	In	Out	Elapsed Time
1M1	Dragon Racing	0:00:29	0:05:00	4:31
1M2S	Where No One Goes	0:05:17	0:07:39	2:22
1M3–4	Together We Map the World	0:07:55	0:10:29	2:34
1M5	Hiccup's Gonna Be Chief	0:11:33	0:14:34	3:01
1M6	Eret Educates Hiccup	0:15:23	0:17:02	1:39
2M7	Drago's Coming	0:19:42	0:21:29	1:47
2M8	Eret Has Visitors	0:21:41	0:22:38	0:57
2M9	Me Likey	0:23:38	0:24:36	0:58
2M10	War is What He Wants	0:25:25	0:27:06	1:31
2M11	Hiccup and Toothless Attacked	0:27:37	0:30:03	2:26
2M12	Dragons' Lair	---	---	Unused
2M13	Should I Know You?	0:31:52	0:33:42	1:50
2M14	Valka's Dragon Sanctuary	0:34:10	0:35:00	0:50
2M15–16	Hiccup and Valka Bond	0:35:02	0:37:29	2:27

Cue	Title	In	Out	Elapsed Time
3M17–18	Valka's Flash(back) / Good Alpha	0:37:38	0:40:57	3:19
3M19	I Grew Facial Hair for You	0:41:01	0:42:16	1:15
3M20	Flying with Mother	0:42:18	0:45:01	2:43
3M21	Can We Start Over?	0:45:08	0:46:57	1:49
3M22	Meet Drago	0:47:33	0:51:54	4:21
3M25–26	Stoick Finds Beauty	0:52:14	0:54:36	2:22
3M27	Get 'Em You Son of an Eret	0:55:02	0:56:17	1:15
3M28S	Courting Song	0:57:20	0:59:48	2:28
4M29	Courting Song Instrumental	0:59:52	1:00:34	0:42
4M30	Battle	1:00:46	1:06:57	6:11
4M31	Hiccup Confronts Drago	1:07:32	1:11:35	4:03
4M32	Stoick Saves Hiccup	1:11:40	1:13:53	2:13
4M33	Off to Valhalla	1:14:00	1:17:41	3:41
4M35	Riding to Drago's	1:17:42	1:18:34	0:52
4M36alt-37	Alpha Comes to Berk	1:18:43	1:20:52	2:09
5M38	Toothless Comes Back	1:21:10	1:24:44	3:34
5M39A	Challenging the Alpha	1:24:45	1:27:30	2:45
5M39B	The Chief Has Come Home	1:27:44	1:30:59	3:15
5M40S	Where No One Goes Reprise	1:30:59	1:34:38	3:39
	End Titles	1:34:39	1:41:45	7:06
			1:41:54	**1:26:35**

The London Orchestra and Metro Voices, conducted by Gavin Greenaway, recorded at Air Studios, London, January 27–28 and January 30–February 5, 2014.

Additional Music: Anthony Willis and Paul Mounsey

Supervising Orchestrator: John Ashton Thomas

Orchestrators: Andrew Kinney, Randy Kerber, Dave Metzger, and Tommy Laurence

Additional Orchestration: Pete Anthony, Germaine Franco, and Jeff Atmajian

Music Editor: Tom Carlson

Soloists:

Violin—Perry Montague-Mason

Bodhrán—Kieran Leonard

Pennywhistle—Andy Findon

Vocals—Dee Lewis-Clay

Guitar and Dulcimer—Vivian Milanova

Uilleann Pipes—Calum Stewart

Bagpipes—The Red Hot Chili Pipers (Lorne MacDougall, Craig Munro, Kyle Stuart Howie, Dougie McCance, Cameron Barnes)

Cue list for *How to Train Your Dragon: The Hidden World*

Cue	Title	In	Out	Elapsed Time
1M1	Rescue Mission	0:00:59	0:05:00	4:01
1M2A-B	Busy Busy Berk	0:05:01	0:06:25	1:24
1M2A-B	Busy Busy Berk (continued)	0:07:20	0:08:19	0:59
1M2C-3	Marry Her / Grimmel Terms	0:09:42	0:11:18	1:36
1M2C-3	Grimmel Terms (continued)	0:12:32	0:13:32	1:00
1M4	Legend Has It	0:13:33	0:17:59	4:26
2M5	Mysterious Creature	0:18:26	0:20:53	1:27
2M6A-B	In Love / Dart Trap	0:21:02	0:24:44	3:42
2M7A-B	Grimmel's Visit / First Fight	0:25:17	0:28:45	3:28
2M8A-B	Townhall / Exodus	0:30:08	0:34:37	4:29
2M9A-B	Setting Up Camp / Valka Warning	0:36:42	0:37:39	0:57
3M10	Toothless Goes a-Courtin'	0:37:52	0:44:34	6:42
3M11	Toothless Flies Alone	0:45:49	0:47:06	1:17
3M12A	Near Miss	0:47:14	0:47:56	0:42
3M12B	Romance in the Clouds	0:48:03	0:51:00	2:57
3M13S	New Berk Feast	0:51:00	0:52:16	1:16
3M14A-B	Ambush / Cage Fight	0:52:36	0:57:38	5:02
4M15A	Stronger Together	0:58:19	0:59:18	0:59
4M15B-16	New Island / Into the Hole	1:00:34	1:02:24	1:50
4M16B	The Hidden World	1:02:28	1:07:36	5:08
4M17	With Love Comes Loss	1:08:00	1:09:00	1:00
4M18	Grim Surprise	1:09:07	1:12:43	3:36
5M19-20A	The Hiccup I Know / Intro Into Battle	1:12:52	1:15:36	2:44
5M20B	Armada Battle Part A	1:15:36	1:19:34	3:58
5M20C	Armada Battle Part B	1:19:34	1:22:09	2:35
5M21	Ultimate Sacrifice	1:22:09	1:24:49	2:40
5M22	Freedom	1:24:49	1:28:26	3:37
5M23	Viking Wedding	1:28:26	1:30:13	1:47
5M24A	Boat Epilogue	1:30:13	1:32:26	2:13
5M24B	Finale	1:32:26	1:34:00	1:34
5M25S	Together from Afar	1:34:00	1:37:04	3:04
	End Credits Suite	1:37:04	1:44:00	6:56
			1:44:06	**1:29:06**

London Orchestra, conducted by Gavin Greenaway, and the Eric Whitacre Singers, conducted by Eric Whitacre, recorded at Abbey Road Studios, London, October 15–23, 2018.
Additional Music: Batu Sener, Anthony Willis, and Paul Mounsey
Supervising Orchestrator: John Ashton Thomas

Orchestrators: Tommy Laurence, Jeff Lawson, Andrew Kinney, Randy Kerber, Jon Kull, and Rick Giovinazzo
Music Editor: Jack Dolman
Soloists:
Celtic Harp—Maeve Gilchrist
Ethnic Woodwinds—Jan Hendrickse
Bodhrán—Kieran Leonard
Vocals—Dee Lewis-Clay and Jónsi
Uilleann Pipes—Calum Stewart
Bagpipes—The Red Hot Chili Pipers (Lorne MacDougall, Craig Munro, Craig Muirhead, and Kyle Stuart Howie)

Chapter Notes

Introduction

1. Sara Ross, "Invitation to the Voyage: The Flight Sequence in Contemporary 3D Cinema," *Film History: An International Journal* 24/2 (2012): 211.
2. Ross, 211.
3. Scott C. Richmond, "On Learning to Fly at the Movies: *Avatar* and *How to Train Your Dragon*," *Journal of Narrative Theory* 46/2 (Summer 2016): 256.
4. Ross, 211.
5. Richmond, 270.
6. Isabella van Elferen, "Fantasy Music: Epic Soundtrack, Magical Instruments, Musical Metaphysics," *Journal of the Fantastic in the Arts* 24/1 (2013): 6.
7. Elferen, 6–7.
8. Elferen, 14–15.
9. Erin Hawley, *Environmental Communication for Children: Media, Young Audiences, and the More-Than-Human World* (Cham, Switzerland: Palgrave Macmillan, 2022), 162.
10. Hawley, 161.
11. Hawley, 162.
12. Hawley, 161.

Chapter 1

1. Steve Pond and John Powell, "John Powell Goes Epic to Score 'Dragon,'" *The Wrap*. https://www.thewrap.com/john-powell-goes-epic-score-dragon-24619/ (accessed November 4, 2021).
2. Pond and Powell.
3. Mina Miller, "Interlude 3: Tonality, Tempo Relations and Performance," in *The Nielsen Companion*, ed. Mina Miller (Portland, OR: Amadeus Press, 1994), 289.
4. Daniel M. Grimley, *Carl Nielsen and the Idea of Modernism* (Rochester, NY: Boydell & Brewer, 2010), 103–104.
5. Harald Krebs, "Tonal Structure in Nielsen's Symphonies: Some Addenda to Robert Simpson's Analyses," in *The Nielsen Companion*, ed. Mina Miller (Portland, OR: Amadeus Press, 1994), 214.
6. Robert Rival, "Flatwards Bound: Defining Harmonic Flavour in Late Nielsen," *Carl Nielsen Studies* 5 (2012): 258–279. https://doi.org/10.7146/cns.v5i0.27772.
7. Krebs, 247.
8. Matti Huttunen, "The National Composer and the Idea of Finnishness," in *The Cambridge Companion to Sibelius*, ed. Daniel M. Grimley (Cambridge: Cambridge University Press, 2004), 19.
9. Jean Sibelius, quoted on http://www.sibelius.fi/english/musiikki/js_saveltajana_04.html (accessed November 4, 2021).
10. Author unknown, quoted from http://www.sibelius.fi/english/musiikki/js_saveltajana_02.html (accessed November 4, 2021).
11. Alain Frogley, "Constructing Englishness in Music: National Character and the Reception of Ralph Vaughan Williams," in *Vaughan Williams Studies*, ed. Alain Frogley (Cambridge: Cambridge University Press, 1996), 1.
12. James Day, *Vaughan Williams*, 3rd ed. (Oxford University Press, 1998), 259.
13. Day, 263.
14. Barbara L. Kelly, "Maurice Ravel," *Grove Music Online* (accessed November 8, 2021). https://doi-org.ezproxy.okcu.edu/10.1093/gmo/9781561592630.article.52145
15. Ibid.
16. Tim Greiving, How to Train Your Dragon *Deluxe Edition*, VCL 1020 1205, 2020.
17. A video of this performance can be accessed here: https://www.youtube.com/watch?v=Lk3D5431SPs
18. Kenneth Elliott, Francis Collinson, and Peggy Duesenberry, "Scotland," *Grove Music Online* (accessed November 8, 2021). https://doi-org.ezproxy.okcu.edu/10.1093/gmo/9781561592630.article.40113.
19. Ibid.
20. Nicholas Carolan, "Ireland," *Grove Music Online* (accessed November 8, 2021). https://doi-org.ezproxy.okcu.edu/10.1093/gmo/9781561592630.article.13901.
21. Ibid.
22. Ibid.
23. Philip Glass, "Ira Glass Interviews His Cousin, Philip Glass," *Fresh Air on NPR*, January 31, 2012 (Accessed July 21, 2023). https://www.npr.org/2012/01/31/146092923/ira-glass-interviews-his-cousin-composer-philip-glass.

Chapter 3

1. Frank Lehman, "Hollywood Cadences: Music and the Structure of Cinematic Expectation," *Music Theory Online* 19/4 (December 2013): [4.2]. https://www.mtosmt.org/issues/mto.13.19.4/mto.13.19.4.lehman.html.
2. Erik Heine, "Chromatic Mediants and Narrative Context in Film," *Music Analysis* 37/1 (2018): 108. doi:10.1111/musa.12106.
3. David Johnson, "Scotch Snap," *Grove Music Online* (accessed November 5, 2021). https://doi-org.ezproxy.okcu.edu/10.1093/gmo/9781561592630.article.25244.
4. Richard Hudson and Meredith Ellis Little, "Sarabande," *Grove Music Online* (accessed November 5, 2021). https://doi-org.ezproxy.okcu.edu/10.1093/gmo/9781561592630.article.24574.
5. Tim Rodier, How to Train Your Dragon *in Full Score by John Powell* (Los Angeles: Omni Music Publishing, 2020), iii.
6. Author's note: The Bach piece has this attribution because it was played by Dr. Jekyll in the 1931 film adaptation of *Dr. Jekyll and Mr. Hyde*, as well as being used in the opening credits.
7. Murphy first raised this idea in a YouTube video: https://www.youtube.com/watch?v=YSKAt3pmYBs (accessed July 23, 2023).
8. Heine, 108.
9. I am thankful for Frank Lehman, who brought this connection to my attention.

Chapter 4

1. Dan Obluda, "Using Topic Theory to Expand on Recent Neo-Riemannian Analyses of Film Music," 2021 AMS Annual Meeting, https://www.youtube.com/watch?v=cX3y5d0CJxM (Accessed January 8, 2022).
2. Michael Spitzer, *Music as Philosophy: Adorno and Beethoven's Late Style* (Bloomington: Indiana University Press, 2006), 21.
3. Sara Ross, "Invitation to the Voyage: The Flight Sequence in Contemporary 3D Cinema," *Film History: An International Journal* 24/2 (2012): 218.
4. Tim Rodier, How to Train Your Dragon *in Full Score by John Powell* (Los Angeles: Omni Music Publishing, 2020), xvi.

Chapter 5

1. I owe a debt of gratitude to Frank Lehman and Zachary Cairns for helping me work out this portion of the analysis.

Bibliography

Carolan, Nicholas. "Ireland." *Grove Music Online* (accessed November 8, 2021). https://doi-org.ezproxy.okcu.edu/10.1093/gmo/9781561592630.article.13901.

Day, James. *Vaughan Williams*, 3rd ed. Oxford: Oxford University Press, 1998.

Elliott, Kenneth, Francis Collinson, and Peggy Duesenberry. "Scotland." *Grove Music Online* (accessed November 8, 2021). https://doi-org.ezproxy.okcu.edu/10.1093/gmo/9781561592630.article.40113.

Frogley, Alain. *Vaughan Williams Studies*. Cambridge and New York: Cambridge University Press, 1996.

Glass, Ira, and Philip Glass. "Ira Glass Interviews His Cousin, Philip Glass." *Fresh Air on NPR*. January 31, 2012 (accessed July 21, 2023). https://www.npr.org/2012/01/31/146092923/ira-glass-interviews-his-cousin-composer-philip-glass.

Greiving, Tim. How to Train Your Dragon *Deluxe Edition*. VCL 1020 1205, 2020.

Grimley, Daniel M., ed. *The Cambridge Companion to Sibelius*. Cambridge: Cambridge University Press, 2004.

Grimley, Daniel M. *Carl Nielsen and the Idea of Modernism*. Rochester, NY: Boydell & Brewer, 2010.

Hawley, Erin. *Environmental Communication for Children: Media, Young Audiences, and the More-Than-Human World*. Cham, Switzerland: Palgrave Macmillan, 2022.

Heine, Erik. "Chromatic Mediants and Narrative Context in Film." *Music Analysis* 37/1 (2018): 103–132. doi:10.1111/musa.12106.

Hudson, Richard, and Meredith Ellis Little. "Sarabande." *Grove Music Online* (accessed November 5, 2021). https://doi-org.ezproxy.okcu.edu/10.1093/gmo/9781561592630.article.24574.

Jean Sibelius—The Website. https://www.sibelius.info/English/.

Johnson, David. "Scotch Snap." *Grove Music Online* (accessed November 5, 2021). https://doi-org.ezproxy.okcu.edu/10.1093/gmo/9781561592630.article.25244.

Kelly, Barbara L. "Maurice Ravel," *Grove Music Online* (accessed November 8, 2021). https://doi-org.ezproxy.okcu.edu/10.1093/gmo/9781561592630.article.52145.

Lehman, Frank. "Hollywood Cadences: Music and the Structure of Cinematic Expectation." *Music Theory Online* 19/4 (December 2013) (accessed October 21, 2021). https://www.mtosmt.org/issues/mto.13.19.4/mto.13.19.4.lehman.html.

Miller, Mina, ed. *The Nielsen Companion*. Portland, OR: Amadeus Press, 1994.

Murphy, Scott. "How to Imitate a Whole Lot of Hollywood Film Music in Four Easy Steps." (accessed 23 July 2023). https://www.youtube.com/watch?v=YSKAt3pmYBs

Obluda, Dan. "Using Topic Theory to Expand on Recent Neo-Riemannian Analyses of Film Music." 2021 AMS Annual Meeting (accessed January 8, 2022). https://www.youtube.com/watch?v=cX3y5d0CJxM.

Pond, Steve, and John Powell. "John Powell Goes Epic to Score 'Dragon.'" *The Wrap* (accessed November 4, 2021). https://www.thewrap.com/john-powell-goes-epic-score-dragon-24619/.

Powell, John. How to Train Your Dragon *in Full Score*. Los Angeles: Omni Music Publishing, 2020.

Richmond, Scott C. "On Learning to Fly at the Movies: *Avatar* and *How to Train Your Dragon*." *Journal of Narrative Theory* 46/2 (Summer 2016): 254–283.

Rival, Robert. "Flatwards Bound: Defining Harmonic Flavour in Late Nielsen." *Carl Nielsen Studies* 5 (2012): 258–279. https://doi.org/10.7146/cns.v5i0.27772.

Ross, Sara. "Invitation to the Voyage: The Flight Sequence in Contemporary 3D Cinema." *Film History: An International Journal* 24/2 (2012): 210–220.

Spitzer, Michael. *Music as Philosophy: Adorno and Beethoven's Late Style*. Bloomington: Indiana University Press, 2006.

van Elferen, Isabella. "Fantasy Music: Epic Soundtrack, Magical Instruments, Musical Metaphysics." *Journal of the Fantastic in the Arts* 24/1 (2013): 4–24.

Index

Aeolian *see* scales
action motif *see* themes
Astrid *see* characters
atonal 16–18, 23

bagpipes 9–10, 21–22, 66, 83, 94, 115, 125, 127, 171, 173, 191, 193
bewilderbeast *see* characters

calming motif *see* themes
characters: Astrid Hofferson 5–6, 8–9, 35–37, 48, 50, 60–62, 66, 68–69, 74–75, 78–80, 83–84, 87–88, 93–94, 98, 101–103, 105–107, 114, 117–118, 120, 122, 133, 135–141, 143–145, 157–160, 162–167, 169–173, 175, 179, 183–185, 189; bewilderbeast 6, 45, 103, 113, 115, 121–123, 129–130, 133, 160, 179–180; Drago Bludvist 6, 12, 40–43, 45, 47, 105–108, 112–113, 117–133, 134, 136, 138, 160, 163, 176–183, 190–191; Eret, Son of Eret 8, 37, 104–109, 114, 117–118, 120, 122, 130, 133, 138, 141, 166, 179, 190–191; Fishlegs Ingerman 48, 86, 98, 114, 122, 135, 137–138, 163, 166; Gobber the Belch 11–12, 61, 66–68, 72, 80, 84, 86, 93, 98, 108, 111, 118–120, 122–123, 127, 130, 133, 138, 141, 143–144, 153, 163, 166–167, 170, 183; Grimmel the Grisly 6, 10, 47–50, 53, 138–139, 141–144, 151–152, 154–158, 162–169, 180–184, 187, 192; Hiccup Horrendous Haddock III 1, 5–12, 17, 19–20, 30–33, 35–37, 39–41, 43–45, 47–48, 50, 54–55, 59–89, 91–94, 96–116, 118–120, 122–133, 134–145, 147–151, 153–173, 175–176, 179–180, 183–187; Light Fury 6, 50–52, 55, 101, 134, 137, 139–141, 144–150, 152–153, 162–163, 165, 167, 169–170, 172–3, 181–184, 187; The Red Death 5, 80, 86–89, 91–92, 131, 136; Ruffnut Thorston 8, 35, 37, 48, 68, 98, 107–108, 122, 136, 157–158, 162, 179; Snotlout Jorgenson 48, 85, 87–88, 98, 114, 122, 135–136, 144, 154; Stoick the Vast 5, 6, 11, 33, 40, 44–46, 60, 63, 65, 67, 74–75, 77, 80–89, 97, 99, 101–102, 105–106, 108, 111, 113, 118–127, 129, 133, 139, 142, 150, 161, 163, 176, 179–180, 184, 191; Toothless 5–11, 17, 20, 30–31, 41–45, 47, 50, 55–56, 62, 65–67, 69–89, 91–94, 99–103, 105, 109–110, 112–113, 115–116, 123, 125–127, 129–133, 137–153, 156–157, 160–173, 176, 179–180, 183–184, 186–187; Tuffnut Thorston 48, 68, 74, 138, 141, 167; Valka 6, 35, 43–46, 49, 99, 103–104, 110–123, 125–127, 131, 133, 136–137, 144–145, 151, 154, 156–157, 160, 163, 166, 176–183, 190–192
courting riff *see* themes
courting song *see* themes

DeBlois, Dean 8, 20
Dorian *see* scales
doubly-harmonic minor *see* scales
Drago Bludvist *see* characters
Drago Riff *see* themes
Drago's Tune *see* themes
Dragon Tune *see* themes
dulcimer 67, 94, 159, 170, 190–191

Eret *see* characters
fate riff *see* themes
fate theme *see* themes
fate tune *see* themes
fighting riff *see* themes
fishlegs *see* characters
flying *see* themes
flying ostinato *see* themes
Furies in love *see* themes

glass marimba 9, 20, 63, 70, 147, 149
Gobber *see* characters
good alpha *see* themes
Grimmel *see* characters
Grimmel's Tune *see* themes

Hardanger fiddle 9, 66–67, 190
harmonic minor *see* scales
harmonium 80, 120, 126
heroes *see* themes

Hiccup *see* characters
Hiccup/Vikings *see* themes
Hiccup the Chief *see* themes
the hidden world *see* themes
hurdy-gurdy 9, 65, 72

Ionian *see* scales
Irish flute 148–149

Jónsi 8–9, 15, 18, 20, 69, 94, 99, 133, 159–160, 173, 193

Light Fury *see* characters
Light Fury motif *see* themes
lost and found *see* themes
love theme *see* themes
Lydian *see* scales

map the world *see* themes
March of the Warlords *see* themes
Mixolydian *see* scales

Nielsen, Carl 15–18

octatonic *see* scales

pennywhistle 59, 72, 121, 153, 190–191
Phrygian *see* scales

Ravel, Maurice 16, 19–20, 149, 152–153, 160–162
Red Death *see* characters
Ruffnut *see* characters

scales: Aeolian 22, 25–27, 37, 39, 43–45, 47–48, 53–57, 58, 60, 62–64, 66–68, 71, 73–74, 77–78, 80, 82–85, 91, 96–98, 100–101, 104–118, 120–121, 125–132, 137–146, 150–154, 157–161, 163–167, 169–172; Dorian 19, 22, 25, 33, 35, 39, 41, 43, 48, 50, 53, 58, 60, 64–65, 71–72, 85, 91, 96, 105, 110–112, 121, 125, 134–138, 141–144, 146, 150, 152–153, 157, 159, 161 ; doubly harmonic minor 26–27, 37, 42, 58, 66–69, 79–80, 82–83, 85, 91, 105–106, 108, 113, 117, 121, 125, 134–136, 154, 159, 164, 167; harmonic

minor 26, 37, 53, 67; Ionian 22, 27, 33, 35, 44, 48; Lydian 27, 91, 162; Mixolydian 22, 27–28, 41, 58, 85, 100, 106, 113, 121, 132–133, 164, 166; octatonic 22, 28–29, 39, 65–66, 69, 72–75, 88, 98, 106, 114, 117, 136, 143, 157, 160, 165, 167, 185; Phrygian 26, 52, 64–67, 83, 87, 91, 96, 101, 108–109, 121, 129–130, 154, 157, 161–163; whole-tone 24–25, 29, 68, 91, 111, 123, 125, 138
Scotch snap 21, 33–35, 39, 103
sex riff *see* themes
Sibelius, Jean 15–18, 20–21
Sigur rós 8, 10, 15, 18, 20, 69, 99
slate marimba 10, 20, 69, 72, 112, 117, 149–150
Snotlout *see* characters
sopilka 9–10, 70, 72–74, 95, 139–140, 147–149, 153
Stoick *see* characters

themes: action motif 39–40, 55, 67–68, 72, 85–87, 121–122, 167, 174–182; calming motif 40, 62, 71–73, 83–85, 102, 110, 174–183; courting riff 56, 181–183; courting song 46, 99, 120–121, 123, 125, 127, 176–183, 191; Drago riff 42–43, 108, 117–118, 121, 123, 176–183; Dragon tune 37–38, 42, 47, 58, 61–62, 66–68, 77, 79–87, 91–92, 98, 106, 113–114, 125, 135, 137, 159–160, 164–165, 167–168, 174–184; Drago's tune 41–42, 47, 108, 112–113, 117, 121, 123, 125, 132, 138, 176–183; fate riff 55, 143–144, 157–158, 161–162, 167, 169, 181–183; fate theme 39, 54, 62, 64–65, 71–74, 83, 85, 96, 98, 139, 145, 174–182; fate tune 54, 139, 143–145, 159–161, 163–164, 167, 169–170, 181–183, 185; fighting riff 134–136, 141, 143, 154–155, 164, 181–183; flying 7–9, 30–35, 58–59, 62–65, 67, 69–70, 73–77, 79–88, 92–94, 96, 99, 110–113, 116–118, 121–123, 127–133, 137, 140, 145, 150–151, 154–157, 161, 169–173, 174–185; flying Ostinato 7, 32, 55, 62, 64–65, 67, 69–71, 73–76, 78–82, 85–88, 91–94, 96, 98–105, 108, 121–22, 125–133, 137–139, 150–151, 154–155, 157, 159, 163–165, 167, 169, 171–173, 176–184; Furies in love 50–51, 139–141, 143–144, 146–148, 150–153, 159–164, 169, 172–173, 181–183, 185; good alpha 45–46, 101–103, 108–110, 112–113, 121–123, 125–127, 130–133, 161–163, 176–183, 191; Grimmel's tune 47–48, 138–139, 141–144, 151–152, 154–158, 163–164, 167–168, 180–183; heroes 48–49, 134–137, 143–144, 154, 167–168, 180–183; Hiccup the Chief 40–41, 101–102, 105–108, 132–133, 154–155, 176–183; Hiccup/Vikings 20, 32–33, 35, 37, 39, 41, 58–61, 63–64, 71, 77–78, 96–98, 101–102, 105–106, 110–111, 129–130, 137, 150–151, 157–158, 164, 174–183; the hidden world 20, 56–57, 139–140, 150, 152–153, 157–162, 167–168, 170–173, 181–183, 185, 192; light Fury motif 52, 134, 137, 139–140, 145–146, 152, 181–183; lost and found 44–45, 108–109, 113–116, 118–119, 126, 130–132, 137, 160, 163–164, 166, 169–170, 176–185; love theme 8, 35–37, 47, 50, 58, 60–62, 79–80, 93, 96, 98, 100–102, 107, 114, 121–122, 126, 132–133, 135, 139–140, 164–167, 169, 173, 174–185; map the world 43–44, 100–102, 104–106, 112, 114–115, 120, 126, 138, 153, 176–183; march of the warlords 49–50, 134, 138, 181–183; sex riff 55–56, 140–141, 145–150, 161–162, 164–165, 181–183; Valka's tune 43, 104, 110–112, 116, 136, 176–183; Vikings! 22, 33–35, 39, 58–60, 63–65, 69–71, 83, 86–87, 91–92, 94–95, 96–97, 107, 121–122, 129, 132–133, 164–166, 171–172, 174–184; village hymn 53–54, 138–141, 143–144, 157, 164–166, 170–171, 181–183, 185; warring Vikings 19, 35, 39, 58–69, 73–74, 77–78, 82–87, 91, 96–99, 105–108, 110–113, 117–118, 120–125, 137–138, 144, 154–157, 161–163, 174–184
Toothless *see* characters
Tuffnut *see* characters

Uilleann pipes 9, 22, 60, 72, 115, 121, 125, 127, 147, 149, 191, 193

Valka *see* characters
Valka's tune *see* themes
Vaughan Williams, Ralph 18–19, 54, 64, 127–128, 143
Vikings! *see* themes
village hymn *see* themes

warpipes 9, 61, 190
warring Vikings *see* themes
whole-tone *see* scales

www.ingramcontent.com/pod-product-compliance
Ingram Content Group UK Ltd.
Pitfield, Milton Keynes, MK11 3LW, UK
UKHW051850210426
5322IPUK00025B/637